THE MODERNS

THE MODERNS

A TREASURY OF PAINTING
THROUGHOUT THE WORLD

BY

GASTON DIEHL

CROWN PUBLISHERS, INC. ~ NEW YORK

Translated from the French by
EDWARD LUCIE-SMITH

Library of Congress Cataloging-in-Publication Data
Diehl, Gaston.
    The moderns : a treasury of painting throughout the world.

    Translation of: la peinture moderne dans le monde.
    Bibliography: p. 218.
    1. Painting, Modern—20th century—History.
I. Title.

ISBN 0-517-01331-2

PRINTED IN ITALY – © 1978 BY BONFINI PRESS CORPORATION, NAEFELS, SWITZERLAND
ALL RIGHTS OF REPRODUCTION OF ILLUSTRATIONS BY S.P.A.D.E.M. AND A.D.A.G.P., PARIS
ALL RIGHTS IN THE U.S.A. RESERVED BY CROWN PUBLISHERS, INC., NEW YORK, N.Y.

EDGAR DEGAS *France* Woman Washing Herself 1892
Museum of Art, Basel

I

THE TRUE FACE OF THE 20TH CENTURY

Despite our advantages, if only those of contact with its beginnings, we still know little about the art of our own century. No doubt this is due to the changes of fortune it has gone through. First it was treated as an outcast; then barely tolerated as an intruder. Now, under the names of « independent art » or « living art », it has almost entered the domain of history, to the point where critics no longer find the way blocked by the imposing presence of an academism in which they no longer believe.

Official acceptance came late in France — with the famous retrospective exhibition at the Petit Palais in 1937.

5

Elsewhere, at that moment, its situation was hardly enviable. It was proscribed and persecuted in Germany, disdained and vilified in Italy, banned almost from its beginnings in the U.S.S.R. Only America, from 1929, provided it with the welcoming haven of The Museum of Modern Art in New York.

I remember — not without shame — the state of the Musée du Luxembourg at this period, where an unimportant picture by Braque was banished to the darkest corner — the only specimen of this kind of art admitted to this wretched sanctuary of contemporary art in Paris.

No one who did not live through these years of struggle, or who does not keep constantly in mind what they were like, can appreciate at their true value the wonderful changes which have come about in the course of these last twenty years, as much in official attitudes as in the taste of the general public.

Success has also brought with it excesses caused by fear of being behind the fashion. All over the world we have seen, in the past few years, the most astonishing bidding for future primacy; and the bitterest competition for the roles of martyrs and pioneers exhumed from oblivion.

These massive conversions, these rivalries fed by a blind chauvinism, these too-hasty rehabilitations, lead one to suppose that many prejudices and misjudgements continue to be current under other forms.

Our age was betrayed once by its incomprehension. Is it now in danger of being reduced to sectarianism and partisanship? We must try and bring back its true appearance, and to do this we must begin by getting rid of falsely restrictive conventions.

NECESSARY REVISIONS

Two of these conventions are commonly accepted, but no longer have any foundation. The first comes from the practice which we accept as valid for our own age, though no longer for previous ones, of delimiting art-history by countries, and imprisoning art within frontiers. The second rests on the double postulate that the modern artist is in conflict with society, and that his work owes its existence to some lucky chance. How can we allow so many artificial barriers to encumber the artistic scene, merely for the sake of foolish national pride, at the very moment the means of communication grow more and more numerous?

Repeated wars and political crises have accentuated these divisions by providing excuses for an aggressive patriotism. And, in turn, the force of nationalism has been felt in the arts. From their point of view, critics and artists tried to protect themselves and to single themselves out by new and arbitrary divisions.

Nevertheless, a general account can pay no heed to these niggling divisions, sprung from vain rivalries and often reduced to the status of storms-in-a-teacup.

In order to put the future in its true perspective, the historian, who now thinks on a global scale, must reject the traditional vertical arrangement, whereby each country and each individual is dealt with separately. For this he substitutes the much truer conception of a simultaneous unrolling of time-space. This horizontal method allows him to interpret correctly the rapidity of the synchronised developments of different tendencies in art, and the intensity of international interchange.

And why should we any longer put up with the perpetuation of false ideas about the place and the role of the artist in current society? It would be all too easy, by basing our argument on certain tragic destinies, to extend the legend of the *artiste maudit* to every other profession.

The myth of a divorce, of perpetual misunderstanding between modern art and its publics, has been only too thoroughly exploited. So have all the accusations of isolationism, of eccentricity, of desire to create a scandal, which are made against the creators. It is no longer possible to give credit to all this.

When we gaze into the upturned hour-glass of the past half century, the image which we see is now completely reversed. The massive battalions of the members of the official academies are now more than a pale shadow, manifestly unfit for life in the high-speed machine-age. Their works are eclipsed in the museums, and have faded from men's memories without leaving a trace.

On the other hand, many other figures have returned from oblivion. In every country they are being added to the roll of those responsible for the birth of modern art, and they show by their very numbers the common

PAUL GAUGUIN *France* Maternity at the Seashore (Tahiti) Detail 1899
Hermitage, Leningrad

purpose behind very different explorations. These explorations resemble each other, however widely separated. Pictorial inventions which were once thought to have been produced by rebellion, by madness, by genius or by chance, and which were conceived of as being solitary and dispersed, are seen to fall into a pattern, and to form part of a concerted human effort, intellectual, technical and social at the same time. We can follow the plain links from work to work, which lead from one artist, to another, which lead us, by many echoes, across whole continents. We discover the formation of a common plastic language which is in harmony with a civilization whose exterior forms clothe everywhere the same identity.

IN HARMONY WITH THE AGE

The setting up of an innovatory art does not merely depend, as first Baudelaire, then the Realists, and the Impressionists supposed, on the transcription of the appearances of modern life as the camera does. The profound changes of orientation which happened in painting, especially in the last ten years of the

19th century, correspond to the sudden enlargement of man's horizons which happened at this very time, everywhere following the similar expansion of space and time.

Space became as wide as the world: the political and economic expansion of Europe — into Asia, Africa and Oceania— revealed the richness of the cultures which were then met with. Ethnographers, sociologists and archeologists followed to find an extension, or sometimes a new foundation, for their respective disciplines. History, followed by the museums, began to pay attention to primitive art. The interest thus awakened was general. Gauguin was not the only one to turn towards primitive cultures; Tylor and Frazer had done so well before him, followed later by Lévy-Brühl.

Music did not remain indifferent. Themes taken from a negro spiritual appear in Dvorak's *Fifth Symphony* of 1894, and then in Debussy's *Gollywogs* of 1908.

Nor was the exploration of time neglected. Prehistory, its authority increased, explored the milleniums methodically, and after 1900, though not without a struggle, achieved recognition for the art of the cavemen. These explorations converged on each other from their different starting points and ended in a new breakthrough, on the subject of mankind.

Psychology became very active, and undertook explorations in depth, examining both pathological cases and the normal reactions of the individual. Certain publications, such as Bergson's *Essay* of 1888, and Ribot's *Psychology of the Feelings* of 1896, seem concerned with the same preoccupations as those expressed by Cézanne or by Van Gogh in their canvasses.

Shortly afterwards, Freud proposed an explanation of dreams, and Piaget an infantine psychology, thus preceeding by several years the artistic exploration of these problems.

Folklore showed how local variants appear on the same common basis of humanity, thus reawakening the old dream of the fraternity of mankind. Its appeal aroused enthusiasm in literary, musical and artistic circles. While Gauguin and his friends at Pont Aven were taking an intense interest in the Breton calvaries, Rémy de Gourmont's and Alfred Jarry's review *L'Imagier* was revealing the riches of popular imagery.

The scope of art history had to broaden continually in order to accommodate, willy-nilly, a multitude of cultures and forms of expression till then unknown or despised. These, by their presence, soon broke the established order, and required the setting up of a new scale of values.

Absolutely simultaneously, there came profound technical and industrial changes, thanks to multiplying new inventions which offered unlimited possibilities. Science, too, broke its traditional bounds. In 1896, Hannequin formulated the atomic hypothesis; and soon Henri Poincaré, Langevin, and above all Einstein and Minkowski, destroyed traditional assumptions with their theories, and postulated new dimensions for the universe. Our epoch has been fated to be bewildered by the revelation of immensities of time and space which reason can no longer grasp.

But for the moment, mankind, becoming aware of the powers put at its disposal, felt the intoxication of freedom and a need for the total revision of all values with which a secret *angst* was sometimes mingled.

A comparison with literature, though not as conclusive as one might suppose, because of the confusions brought by a later symbolism, would show how both in science and in art the same enthusiastic aspirations for the exploration of the new horizons which were opening made themselves felt, and the same rejection of the yoke of a conformism definitively outgrown took place. But there is no space for it here. Larbaud and Cendrars, before the war started a literary Cosmopolitism where they paid homage to the poetry of speed and to the poetry of the machine.

A VOCATION FOR UNIVERSALITY

Many arguments have arisen about the date when this profound change in aesthetic and intellectual values began. Difficult as it is to give a positive answer, 1900, which used to be commonly accepted, is no longer held correct by those who, like Bernard Dorival, Jean Cassou and, above all Pierre Francastel, have recently given most thought to this problem in all its complexity.

VINCENT VAN GOGH *Holland, France* Head of a Woman 1887
Coll. Rudolf Staechlin, Museum of Art, Basel

ODILON REDON *France* The Birth of Venus 1912
Petit Palais Museum, Paris

GEORGES SEURAT *France* The Model 1887 ▷
Louvre Museum, Paris

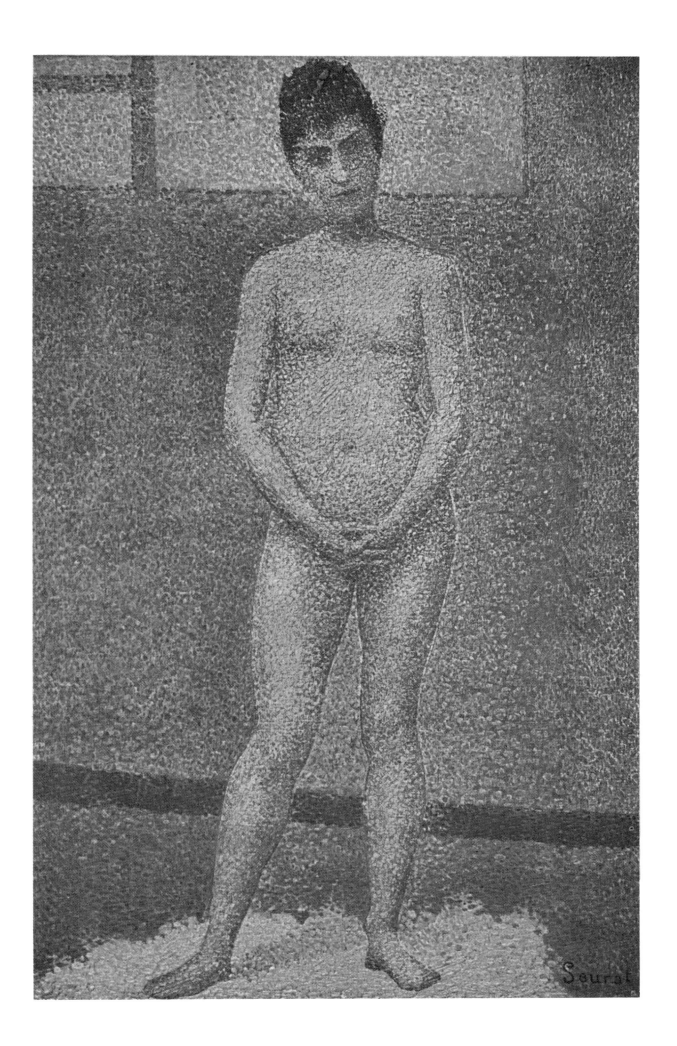

PAUL CÉZANNE *France* Mardi Gras 1888
Pushkin Museum, Moscow

In fact, as we have already noted, the change from one age to another began somewhere around 1889. The *Exposition Universelle* is the living symbol of this exceptional conjuncture of events, of hopes and fulfilments. Favourable political and economic circumstances permitted an assembly of endeavours from every corner of the world. The confrontation proved how much they had in common.

Technology and engineering, the centres of the exhibition, had given birth to a new and universal culture, whose first appearance was in Paris, and was again manifested at the Chicago Exhibition four years later. In addition to this searching intensification of exchanges between peoples, made possible by the rapid development of communications by land and sea, the human spirit was delivering itself from age-old conditions, and preparing with pride to make use of the different powers which it had progressively succeeded in bringing in control and which were now about to transform everyday living: electricity, hydroelectric power, the bicycle, the automobile, the cinema, etc.

The machine was put at the service of that power of the will evoked by Nietzsche and of that sense of movement extolled by Bergson. But it brought with it the formation of those urban and industrial concentrations which would, in most countries, determine what the age would look like.

Revolutionary innovations were quickly introduced in the most collective and utilitarian forms of art: in architecture, in furnishings, in objects, in posters— and all this in just those places where the change from craft to industry was most marked: Glasgow, Nancy, Brussells, Lyons, Vienna, Berlin, Amsterdam, etc.

This sudden creative outburst was not a decadent *fin de siècle*, the product of scattered inspirations. It was a huge movement which ignored frontiers and made nonsense of arguments about priority.

Its simultaneity and its unity were fully proved by the recent exhibition *Sources of the 20th Century*, with furnishings by Mackintosh, Voysey or Macknurdo, by Horta, by Van de Velde, by Majorelle, by Riemerschmid or by Endell. But these qualities have been concealed by the many names given to it in different countries: Art Nouveau in Belgium, the old label of Arts and Crafts in England, Le Modern-Style in France, Jugendstil in Germany, Secession in Austria, Liberty style in Italy.

Such an abundance of names is proof of the fact that we are here dealing with the imperious necessity of a spontaneous phenomenon, lacking a true doctrinal base, but swiftly propagated, especially by The Studio despite the fact that the number of its effectives was everywhere limited, and despite the inability of observers to understand the general nature of a movement which had come, not before time, to do away with the antagonisms and the traditional imbalances among nations.

These observers have made too much of certain superficial aspects, outworn, and pushed to excess by fashion, such as the absurd employment of linear arabesque, and the too evident borrowings from the art of the Far East in the effort to escape from reminiscences of past styles.

But the essential thing was search for new forms. The creators' deepest intention, which is the exact beginning of the artistic ambitions of our own century, was to regulate and unify the many aspects of the settings for private or public life.

These creators had, for the most part, the desire to link architecture and decoration intimately together. They wanted everything to be the work of one mind — to provide designs for typography, for posters, for metalwork, for jewellery and ceramics, as well as for everything to do with furnishing, including the wallpaper, the furnishing fabrics, the lamps and light-fittings.

We must allow, as part of established history, that these enormous ambitions were abandoned on the way, and with them the domination of a decorative stylisation which vanished around 1905.

But we must recognise that, as Pierre Francastel has demonstrated, the principal gains remained. Many pioneers continued to work and formed schools. The different branches of artistic activity profited from this unanimous force which entirely changed them, and which brought them closer together.

From this common purpose, from this progressive international unification, sprang a new aesthetic conception which shows itself most clearly in architecture, which is directly subject to the progress of technology.

At the Exhibition of 1889, the Eiffel Tower proved spectacularly what could be done with a material which was far from unknown: iron. Iron, too, provided the basis for another triumph which came about thanks to the closely associated endeavours of an engineer and an architect— the *Gallery of Machines*, where the rational plan of the huge hall conformed to new collective needs which were also expressed in such near-contemporary constructions as the railway stations and, above all, the great department stores: the *Bon Marché* and the *Printemps* in Paris, the Marshall-Field building designed by H. Richardson in Chicago and, later but more suitable to their purpose, the Wertheim store built by Alfred Messel in Berlin, and the *Maison du Peuple* built by Horta in Brussels in 1898. Across the Atlantic, similar experiments were made in response to the industrial effort and to the staggering increase of population.

The solutions used by this school of architects in their skyscrapers — by Daniel Hudson Burnham, William Lebaron-Jenney and Louis Sullivan — were prompted by these immediate needs. But pride of place, in the Home Insurance Building, in the ten-storey Chicago Auditorium, in the second Leiter Building, and above all in the sixteen-storey Monatock Block, was given to the double principle of a metallic armature and of a carefully planned functionalism, and this, surely, was due to the influence of Viollet-le-Duc's *Conversations on Architecture*, and, at least in the cases of Lebarron-Jenney and Sullivan, to a Parisian training.

In fact, circumstances favoured the establishment of mutual artistic exchanges between the two continents — in painting thanks to the opening of the Durand-Ruel Gallery in New York; in the decorative arts thanks to the Chicago Exhibition and the activity of Tiffany; and in architecture simply thanks to similarity of experience. No doubt the time spent in the United States by Adolphe Loos, Horta, and later on Berlage, helped the new orientation towards a more sparing use of ornament and towards rational simplification.

This evolution was little hindered by the regrettable adaptation of metal to exterior decoration, more visible in Paris in the entrances to the Metro designed by Guimard, whose work seems to harden into a formula, than in Vienna with Otto Wagner, who taught the purity of structural form.

Soon enough, his pupils publicised the position he had taken up. Olbrich, at Vienna and then at Darmstadt; and Joseph Hoffman, especially in his work on the Palais Stoclet at Brussels. This building, completed in 1911, is, with uninterrupted verticals and horizontals, its decorative unity between interior and exterior, the best and most typical example of the new international style, rigidly constructivist, which Loos had been preaching with vigour since 1898.

Then, too, the work done at Glasgow by Mackintosh, who was a faithful exponent of the regular geometrisation of facades, was much admired when it was shown at Vienna in 1900, and later at Darmstadt; and Frank Lloyd Wright's first exhibition in Europe received a triumphal reception at Berlin in 1910.

The so-called « historic » styles opposed these developments, and mounted a counter-attack which led to the bastardised compromises made by the United States and France for the Exhibition of 1900.

It is unimportant that the stark masses of romanesque architecture very probably supplied Berlage with a model in his Amsterdam Bourse built in 1903, when this, in its turn, inspired the flowering of a magnificent local school of architecture. It is unimportant, too, that Gaudi, at Barcelona, pushing his search for expressive forms and for the plastic value of materials to extremes, remained necessarily an isolated figure.

New recruits rapidly joined the movement. An example was the young winner of the *Prix de Rome*, Tony Garnier. Garnier's project for an *Industrial City*, founded in 1901, which was followed in Italy a decade later by the plan for an *Ideal City* envisioned by Antonio Sant' Elia, provided a prophetic vision of the urbanism of our own day. But, through ill-luck, neither plan came to fruition.

The *Garden Cities of To-morrow*, proposed in 1899 by Ebenezer Howard, had better luck, and bore fruit soon enough in both England and Germany. In this latter country, Peter Behrens, who became in 1907 technical adviser to a Berlin firm manufacturing electrical equipment, was able to apply his sense of functionalism and organisation to street-lamps and shop-fronts as well as to factory-buildings. At the same time Olbrich was working on coachwork for Opel cars and on a railway station.

However, it was the systematic use of a relatively new material — concrete — which set architecture free from the past, and gave it its cosmopolitan character. This was the economic and social answer for the future.

14

JAMES ENSOR *Belgium* Carnival 1890
Stedelijk Museum, Amsterdam

The Perret brothers, in their block of flats in the Rue Franklin, and still more in their Ponthieu garage of 1905, followed by François Le Coeur with his telephone exchange of 1910 and by Duchamp Villon with his project for a Cubist house exhibited in the *Salon d'Automne* of the same year, and followed in Switzerland by the technical work of Maillart, in Germany by Walter Gropius in his Fagus factory-building — all these established the same principles for construction in concrete. These principles presupposed a rigorous adaptation to function, bare geometric forms, and a visible structure. Supports were freed in order to make the most of the space available, walls were transformed at will into glass screens.

SYMBIOSIS OF EAST AND WEST

There is, in this century, another phenomenom whose importance has hardly been recognised. This is the mutual *rapprochement* of East and West.

It was not by pure chance that, at the beginning of the century, Strzygowski chose for the title of his book *The Orient or Rome* — words which simultaneously implied a choice and a programme.

Though it confined itself to the influence of the Orient on the formation of Christian Art in the West, and though it took up again arguments formulated before by Courajod and by Dieulafoy, this work aroused innumerable polemics. The violence of these bore witness to the fact that the public had now become aware of problems vaster than the quarrels of nationalism.

We know, as well, of the profound influence exercised on Kandinsky by the similar work by Worringer published in 1907, *Abstraktion und Einfühlung*. This also sort to dethrone classicism in favour of the Orient. Having passed the traditional stage of easy exoticism, orientalism penetrated by many routes and awoke an interest which has continued to grow right up to our own time.

Sometimes direct relations were established after Europe had gained, through the use of force, access to Japan, to China, and later to Tunisia and Morocco. Other ways were more circuitous, and went by the ancient routes across Byzantium and the Near East, in use since the Middle Ages and of such interest to archaeologists.

If Japan was eager to borrow from the West, the West itself was yet more enamoured of things Japanese.

The speed which the vogue came in can be measured by the difference between the modest showing of prints at the *Porte Océane* shop which opened in 1860, and the big exhibition of Japanese Art put on in 1890 in the sacred precincts of the *École National Supérieure des Beaux Arts*.

From the chance and superficial liking which had however been enough to awaken misgiving and the idea of doing likewise in the breasts of the Impressionists or Van Gogh, things changed to the more informed interest which can be seen in Bing's review *Le Japon Artistique*, which was published at this period.

There were still other forces at this period, such as the frequent exhibitions of Islamic Art which drew artists to Paris and to Munich, where these showings alternated with those devoted to Chinese or Japanese Art. The aura of Vienna, which became a preferred centre of Byzantine studies, seems to be reflected in the painting of Klimt, and, less directly, in that of Kokoschka.

Indeed, Russia began gradually to occupy an important place in the European scene, first with Dostoevsky and Tolstoy, then with Rimsky Korsakov and Borodine, later still with the ballets of Diaghilev, Stravinsky and Bakst, and the innumerable Russians, who played a part in all the French and German *avant garde* movements, and who by their very presence swayed the balance, and reduced the distance between East and West.

The conquering influence of the Orient was at the bottom of the desire which European artists felt to be free of their own past. They wanted to familiarise themselves with the ideas of space, expression and style which they were gradually discovering, and to adapt these to their own needs.

In these ideas the generation of Gauguin, Toulouse Lautrec and the Nabis found the first elements for a complete recasting of pictorial plasticity, and at the same time the Art Nouveau movement incontestably drew from there its principal sources of floral and rhythmic inspiration.

It must be remembered that Bing, before he brought together many European artists in the first Art Nouveau exhibition of 1895, and opened in the following year his famous gallery of the same name, had, since 1871, devoted himself to the study of the art of the Far East, and had even travelled there himself.

Many others, such as Gaillard and de Feure, Gallé and Grasset, shared with him, though he did not set the direction of their taste, a common passion for China, Japan and Islam.

From the beginning of the century, Strzygowski's audacious theory was proved more thoroughly than he had foreseen — the division from Rome was no longer possible, the choice was now ineluctable.

As in the age of the earliest Christian Art, Matisse recognised, and all his generation with him, that illumination had always come to him from the East.

Picasso profited from Andalusia, Kandinsky, Macke and Klée from North Africa (and also, as Pierre Francastel has suggested, the architect Loos), and Nolde, Pechstein and many others from their travels outside Europe. The last distinguishing frontier between the art of Europe and that of the Orient was crossed when abstraction, abandoning all reference to physical realities, claimed for itself the sole power of expressing spirituality, and took complete freedom of choice in the realm of the plastic arts.

Georges Duthuit, surveying the age a little later in his *Chinese Mysticism and Modern Painting*, discovered many

HENRI ROUSSEAU (LE DOUANIER) *France* The Cart of Père Juniet 1908
Coll. P. Guillaume, Paris

PIERRE BONNARD
France
Woman with Fruit 1920
Baltimore Museum of Art
Cone Collection
◁

▷
MARIE LAURENCIN
France
The Girls 1921
Coll. LeRay Berdeau,
Palm Beach, Florida

MAURICE UTRILLO *France* Montmartre 1906 Coll. Philippe Bemberg, Paris.

formal analogies beween these works, divided by the narrowest of margins despite their distance from each other in time.

And literature, as Paul Claudel has said, also showed sometimes, as with Victor Ségalen, Blaise Cendrars, the desire to become part of this deeper understanding of the East.

But music had to await the possibilities of direct registration, before attempting, in the person of Olivier Messiaen, to bridge the huge gap which had for so long existed between the two forms of civilization.

The Europe of between the wars, distracted by politics, which drove some into exile and some to silence, did not bother to keep up this extraordinary current of artistic interchange, or even turned determinedly away from it. But in America things were very different.

From 1921, Katherine Dreier lived for a period in China before undertaking her campaign across the United States in the cause of Abstract Art.

Frank Lloyd Wright had long borrowed from Japanese architecture its love of nature and its sense of organic unity. Macdonald-Wright travelled to Japan, and Mark Tobey studied Chinese calligraphy on the spot. Many American writers, as eager for experience as Malraux or Michaux, went to live in Asia.

« The second vogue for Japan », as Michel Ragon called it, and the School of the Pacific, came into being before the American occupation of Japan, which played a part only in the calligraphic formation of Appleby. The United States have contributed a great deal to the spread throughout the world of the exclusive taste for the use of the Sign in the plastic arts, and for tachisme. This latter currently epitomises the deep impregnation of Western Art by the spirit and the traditions of the Orient. However, Hartung has since achieved, without the need to go elsewhere, a more demanding symbiosis, in which each side plays its part.

The culture of Japan, though not alone in its influence, has preserved a privileged position in art as it is today, as much through the Japanese expatriates in the United States, Brazil and Europe, who play an active part in the artistic life of these places, by its eagerness for contacts abroad, and through travelling exhibitions of calligraphy, as by its manifold spiritual riches. Its influence in Germany has even led to the formation of a group of Zen painters.

In default of competition from other cultures, such as that of China, Japan has become in the eyes of the young everywhere a new Rome. They, like Alechinsky, dream of travelling there, and of making a fruitful pilgrimage to the source of things.

THE NEW HUMANISM

It may seem paradoxical to claim the label « humanist » for 20th century painting, when humanism is what it is so often accused of lacking, at every moment of its history, by detractors anxious to deny it any right to this adjective, in order that they themselves may the more conveniently shelter behind the curtain of humanism, a word deprived of all meaning, by reducing it to the representation of man's outward semblance.

But contemporary artists have not failed in the essentials of their task. They have tried to be true interpreters of their times, and to give society a means of expression which responds to its needs.

Unluckily, because their work has ceaselessly modified itself in response to the very transformation of conditions of living, their audience has usually had the feeling that it was struggling along behind, and that here was a ceaselessly changing image in which it no longer recognised itself.

The supposed divorce between the public and modern art was born of this misunderstanding, widespread in a Europe which set value upon references to the past, but usually almost unknown in the United States and South America, so eager to adapt themselves without reserve to rapid changes.

Despite many false assertions, modern art continues to centre itself upon man, who remains, and rightly, its point of departure, and still more than formerly, as we shall see, its unique finality.

The public began to believe itself defrauded from the moment when, forced to abandon little by little the accustomed representation of beings and things, which for several centuries had served it as a means of expression, art found itself with no other recourse but to concentrate on the study of the creator's own essence.

In the face of this, the outlines of reality melted away just the degree that the artist was tempted to explore in the new world opening before him, with its limitless horizons where the overturning of canons of proportion left only the smallest of places for the human shadow, now summoned to dissolve itself in the anonymity of the multitude.

This dislocation of appearances came to the help of the artist, enabling him to hammer out his own salvation, and to concentrate all his attention upon himself. The liberty of creative intuition was grafted naturally to the idea of human liberty. In the elation which drew a whole civilization towards the possibilities of the future, this took on a lyrical consciousness of the present and the future.

Upon the wish to exteriorise sensation and its emotive content, was soon superposed the ambition to bring order into being, to create a language, through the exercise of the intelligence. As a faithful interpreter of his environment, the artist aspired also to profit, with astonishing lucidity, and in his own domain, from the creative power unfolding all around him; dominating nature so that he could reinvent it in all its parts, arranging it to suit himself, and restoring to it its expressive power.

As the judicious definition of Pierre Francastel has it: « *Avant-garde* art is not just the tilting-ground for the aesthetic debates of the contemporary world; it is also an instrument in all the experiments in adaptation made in new societies with economic and technical conditions sprung from the science of the West. »

We may note, with regard to this, that it will be more difficult for the East, accustomed as it is to conform to the mould of age-old traditions, to carry out speedily the necessary joining together of all its endeavours. On the contrary, European art will find its complete independence without too much difficulty, by putting itself in harmony with the researches of the moment.

Far from being its dangerous rivals, photography, the cinema, illustrated magazines and newspapers and television aid it by taking over its secondary and adventitious functions.

Their successive interventions precipitated its evolution and put the seal on its autonomy. They moved it, in fact, to take less and less from reality; they forced it to an interior gain in depth, to a reconsideration of what was specific in it, to an extension of its field of action in all the sectors and materials within its grasp. Expression, where by plastic means alone, takes on its full significance, and serves better every day as a refuge for a spirituality threatened by progressive mechanisation.

It gets its own back upon this latter in advance, by pursuing, within its own domain, the integration of all contemporary discoveries — simultaneity of images, rhythmic dynamism, concision of style, epitomisation through synthesis. Sometimes the fancy has moved it to take over the machine itself; equally, it has succeeded by brilliant intuition in revealing many areas hardly as yet opened to human knowledge, reaching from visions of the infinitely tiny to evocations of illimitable space.

More and more detached from the demands of reality, and having brought to a high pitch the technique of elision which at first sight makes its assemblages of marks and signs (the means of expression to which it is now often curtailed), painting preserves none the less its essential qualities.

Its colouristic organisation and formal structure, now even more manifest than they used to be, seem to be charged with astonishing expressive power, fit to transcribe the contrasting alternations of hope and despair through which our civilization is passing.

By exploring his own essence, the artist discovers, from day to day, the manifold riches and virtualities of the interior life — its complexity, the infinite possibility of its secret impulses and dreams.

He thus arrives at the true universality of the living being, by getting rid, once and for all, of the impediments raised up in the past by differences of race, creed or milieu. And thus he makes himself the interpreter of human solidarity on the world scale, and this directs it, in turn, towards the idea of a common aesthetic.

The desire so clearly expressed by Théo van Doesburg in 1921 is now on the way to becoming a reality: « The evolution of modern art towards the abstract and the universal, by eliminating what is external and individualistic, has made possible, through common effort and common understanding, the achievement of a collective style which raises itself above individual or national considerations. »

22

ÉDOUARD VUILLARD *France* The Artist in His Studio 1910
Private Collection, Paris

It is hard not to conclude, *a fortiori*, that we are now witnesses of the triumph of this social art so much longed for by the innovators of the last century.

No doubt few of those who were present at the birth of this idea and who became its advocates — not Proudhon nor the St-Simonians, not Paul Desjardins nor Roger Marx, and, certainly not William Morris, with his blind opposition to the machine — would now admit that their dream had come to realisation in the Abstract Art of today. And it has never been accepted by those politicians who have taken up the idea.

Nor is it certain, as Michel Ragon ironically notes, that they would now be pleased to see their most cherished principles applied, in one case, to window-displays, and in the other to kitchen-planning.

The public itself, in great majority, continues to reject the evidence and to oppose modern art which, in many other guises, has invaded every aspect of existence.

The war cry of the 1890's, echoed by Jean Verkade: « No more easel pictures — but let us have walls to decorate! » was to be heard throughout the world.

If men and circumstances prevented Seurat and Gauguin from fulfilling their loudly expressed desire to explore the magnificent heritage left by Puvis de Chavannes; Toulouse-Lautrec, even better than Hodler or Ensor, revealed his genius to a popular audience, and at the same time Klimt, in his ceiling paintings for the University of Vienna, exercised, according to the tenets of a rich experience, the close alliance between decoration and architecture which brought him close to abstraction in the Palais Stocklet at Brussels.

In this pre-war period, Munch crowned his career with his frescoes for the University of Oslo.

But in France, the strong hold of academism on all official bodies prevented any kind of public commission; only the Nabis, were able to show what they could do in the Théâtre des Champs Elysées. Matisse and Picasso were not given the chance, to satisfy their aspirations, and Delaunay and Dufy had to wait till 1937. However, the need was growing everywhere for a monumental art which would be more intimately associated with new architectural and social demands. In 1917 the Stijl group in Holland, and in 1919 the Bauhaus in Germany, arrived to attempt a grand synthesis. In an unforeseen way, these endeavours bore fruit indirectly and in a different form, thanks to political circumstances, in Mexico, where the talented school of Diego Rivera, Orozco, Siquieros and Tamayo, made its influence felt in the United States and neighbouring countries, and even across the Atlantic.

In a second, more recent phase, mural painting, now sometimes called mural mosaic began to make its appearance on the outsides of buildings, and competed in the streets, as Fernand Léger had wished, with posters and illuminated signs, and spread superbly across whole facades of buildings and churches.

Mexico, Brasil and Venezuela saw, often before Europe, the unfolding of this new movement, and its conversion to the ideas of neo-plasticism eased the task and opened many new possibilities for it.

Parallel was the magnificent flowering in tapestry and stained glass; and also the variety of methods which were discovered for using such materials as iron and aluminium. These, which take their inspiration from the functional necessities which rule our epoch, form so many proofs in support of the general direction of taste.

Modern art, which people have tended, from the very day of its birth, to believe was condemned to prompt disappearance and confined to *avant garde* circles and the temples of snobbism, has continually extended its conquests, and has associated itself still more closely with every kind of human enterprise. It has penetrated yet further into the domain of technology, and mingled more freely with the herd.

All man's creative activities owe something to it. It has had an influence over every detail of everyday life. The face of our time has little by little been modelled in its image, and this has spread through the world.

Moreover, why do people insist on associating it with a well-defined social category, with a political creed, or even, in a certain sense, with a religion, when it is now exclusively at the service of mankind, and when its masterpieces are within reach of all?

Not only are they available to the public in museums and galleries which more and more people visit, but reproductions and books now take them to the furthest corners of the world, disseminating their message everywhere and assuring that their influence is perrenial.

II

THE FIRST AGE OF MODERN ART
THE TIME OF CONQUESTS AND AFFIRMATIONS
1889-1917

The choice of the two dates above is not quite as arbitrary as it might seem. In fact, they correspond to what one might call the graph of the development of a pictorial movement which began to show itself in many countries between 1889 and 1917, which grew up, transformed itself and spread very widely in the following years, and achieved a feverish apotheosis between 1912 and 1914.

Henri Matisse *France* Young Sailor 1906 Coll. Hans Seligmann, Basel

ALBERT MARQUET *France* The Seashore at Fécamp 1906
Museum of Modern Art, Paris

26

HENRI MATISSE *France* The Dream 1940 Coll. Family of the Artist

Despite the growing pressure of circumstances, it lasted and continued to influence men's minds until, in 1917, the break was almost complete.

The fecundity of this period, the multiplicity of its experiments and the results they achieved, the numerous roads it opened to the future, have earned it the title « The Golden Age of Modern Art », and its promotors have preserved, or even recovered, their authority in our own day, and their work continues to draw disciples to it and to make history.

The period is unique through its vitality, its rich profusion, its daring revelations, its mutual exchanges and its aura of enthusiastic rivalry. It will probably remain forever unrivalled, because the Great War which followed destroyed, by millions of deaths, its vitality, and sapped the hopes and confidence of men.

THE END OF IMPRESSIONISM

The many movements which sprang up throughout Europe at the end of the last century, presaged a double change — of generation and of direction.

The birth of the group of *Indépendants* and of the opposing group of Neo—Impressionists in Paris in 1884, was soon followed by that of the *Cercle des XX* in Brussels. This group, between 1884 and 1893, seemed to prefigure the future by its admirable choice of guest-exhibitors: Seurat, Gauguin, Cézanne, Van Gogh, etc.

In 1886, the *Konstnärsförbundet* was founded by Ernst Josephson at Stockholm, and in London the New English Art Club by Walter Sickert and his friends. At the Hague, the *Cercle des Arts* was formed in 1890.

In 1892, after the scandal caused by the Munch exhibition, the *Sécession* made its appearance, first in Munich and then at Berlin. The *Viennese Secession* was organised in 1897 under the presidency of Klimt. At St. Petersburg, Serge Diaghilev, Alexandre Benois and Constantin Somov joined forces in 1899 to launch the review *Mir Iskustva* (The World of Art), and at Cracow Stanislavski formed the *Sztuka* group.

Though they obeyed principles which were not always precisely the same, these movements bore witness to the need felt by artists to rally to new standards, and to escape from the tutelage of academism, and to look without. France was to be the principal beneficiary of this curiosity.

Bitter battles were fought out there. Despite the public consecration brought to it by its first great restrospective showings in 1889, Impression was declining, sapped both from within and from without. From within by such apostates as Seurat, Van Gogh, Cézanne and Gauguin, who were then in the process of elaborating the whole basis of modern art; and from without by opposing trends — Symbolism and Expressionism, which gained a new vitality at this period.

Because his colleagues were for the time being out of sight due to untimely death or their solitary way of living, Gauguin became the rallying point of this battle against Impressionism and provided weapons to all the combatants. His immediate influence on the younger generation and on his times is to be explained as much by his relations with his disciples at Pont Aven and the favour he met with in literary circles, as by his work shown in the galleries or at the Hôtel Drouot.

The vicissitudes of his existence, such as the publication of *Noa-Noa*, helped to prolong, after his departure for the South Seas, an influence which also made itself felt abroad, through the Danes Willumsen and Mogens-Ballin, the Swiss Cuno Amiet, and the Swede Yvan Agueli.

THE NABIS. - In France, an enthusiastic young generation discovered Gauguin and determined to spread his name and his ideas. These were the *Nabis*, a title taken from the Hebrew word for « prophets », which they themselves assumed. Their group and their doctrinal basis sprang from the «talisman» which Sérusier brought back from Pont Aven and from the *Café Volpini* exhibition of 1889, which was organised by Gauguin together with Anguetin and Emile Bernard, and was the seal of their common admiration and of their desire to break with the past.

Are the Nabis to be classified as the spiritual heirs of Gauguin, as Maurice Denis so insistently claimed at their beginnings? Or are they to be classified as prodigal sons, who having dissipated a splendid revolutionary heritage, mostly turned away from it after 1900 and demanded a return to classicism? Even if their first impetus failed to last, we should forget the failings and lapses of their mature years in favour of their fruitful earlier boldness, and in favour of the superb legacy which Pierre Bonnard has left us.

Linked by friendship, in the last decade of the century they actively took part in numerous exhibitions and showed at the Paris and Brussels *salons*. They also undertook much else — designing posters, working in the theatre or as lithographers or designers of stained glass etc. Their dynamism, their relationships with writers and musicians, and the support they received from the *Revue Blanche*, brought them a self-assurance and a prestige which the older generation never managed to achieve.

Very cultivated and gifted, tender and ironic, full of sparkle and energy, they squandered carelessly, in these early years, a prodigal inventiveness and an unexpected freedom, which brought them, sometimes unknown even to themselves, to the very borders of what would later be fauvism, abstraction or tachism.

In particular, Vuillard and Bonnard, while conjuring up their scenes of family intimacy or of ordinary Parisian life, combined consummate address with a delicious ambiguity in the play of brush-strokes, the subtlety of arabesque dear to Maurice Denis, and the refined charm of those subdued harmonies which were so much to the taste of the period.

Nearly all the Nabis abandoned, fairly early, brilliant tonalities in favour of the finesse of half-tones and matt colouring; they mixed intelligent borrowing from the Japanese, as regards the balance of their compositions and the silhouettes, with what they had learned from Gauguin — but this was hardly more than something of the expressive possibilities of simplifications and slatterned modelling, and the need to disengage themselves from reality by plastic and poetic transpositions.

They were born lucky; everything about them pleased. When he was hardly twenty, Maurice Denis formulated in 1890 in *Art et Critique* his famous definition of what painting is which became that of the whole modern movement. At twenty-three, Vuillard had his first exhibition, and in that same year, 1891, Bonnard showed in the *Salon des Indépendants* a huge composition painted in distemper.

In 1892, and nearly every year thereafter, Vuillard received important commissions for decorative panels from Mme Desmarais, André Natanson and Thadée Natanson, Dr. Vaquez, Claude Anet or Princess Bibesco, and in these he showed an incomparable mastery.

But, after these successes, Vuillard, no doubt from fear that his work would become mannered, did not hesitate to give up an art so concerned with visual delectation, which so many of his successors, like Braque and Brianchon, were to practice in their turn. But the formula is too typically French to find much response abroad — only Rippl-Ronai succeeded to some extent in acclimatising it in Hungary, after the war.

From before 1895, the rest of the group, as if their very success and the atmosphere around them forced them to bring everything into question, had already, when hardly come to maturity, abandoned their first allegiance and the infatuations of their youth.

They were influenced by different motives. With some it was the revelation offered by Cézanne and Italy. Religious conversion and mysticism were the cause with Denis, Verkade and Sérusier; with K. X. Roussel it was the attraction to a bucolic poetry, with Valadon the taste for biting realism. Escaping the sad fate of his colleagues, Bonnard maintained, indifferent to time and fashion, the discreet grandeur of his style, in which an honest candour of eye, and ironic tenderness towards the whole of nature, were played off against an intense chromatic subtlety.

To the very end of his life, his lyricism continued to grow in sincerity and tonal richness, until the vibrant density, the inner splendour of his Mediterranean period, brought him the leadership, in company with Villon, of the young generation during the Second World War.

SYMBOLISM AND PRIMITIVISM. - The young painters of 1890 found it still more difficult to escape from literary influence when, in the pages of the new reviews *La Plume* and the *Mercure de France*, Gauguin saw himself hailed as the leader of Symbolism in art by Georges Albert Aurier. And it was under the ban-

Kees van Dongen *Holland, France* Champs Élysées 1920
Watercolour, Private Collection

SUSANNE VALADON *France* After the Bath 1911
Pencil, Museum of Modern Art, Paris

ner of Symbolism that the exhibitions at the Le Barc de Boutteville Gallery were presented.

The literary movement gradually extended its influence, to Belgium especially, and Germany, and as far as Russia and the new writers of the American continent, where its influence was long to be felt; but its sway was less marked in the field of painting. It revived the reputations, just before they died, of Puvis de Chavannes and Gustave Moreau, and, less deservedly of Hans von Marees, then already dead, and Boecklin. The revelations made by this idealistic philosophy were apt to produce dangerous confusions in painting, as can be seen, at this time, in the circle of the Rosicrucians.

Academism, veiled by allegory and mystery, often spoilt the work of those whom, this movement currently made much of in various countries — Xavier Mellery and Fernand Khnopff in Belgium, Ferdinand Hodler in Switzerland, Gustav Klimt in Austria.

Odilon Redon fortunately had other claims on the praise he received from Huysmans in 1889, and on the admiration of the Nabis when he exhibited his first pictures and pastels in 1894. His art is that of a creator and a visionary. With him, forms and colours suggest the musical poetry of the illimitable spaces of the inner life. His feeling for dreams and the irrational, his gradual expansion of unease into coloured light, seem a preparation for the passage of surrealism into abstraction.

Another current began to develop for which Gauguin, as we see in connection with the work of Serusier, shares the responsibility together with the general interest taken during the period in folklore and the archaic, and this is the taste for primitivism.

Long before Apollinaire and his cubist friends paid their tribute to him in 1908, Douanier Rousseau and Sunday Painting had taken their place in the *Salon des Indépendants*.

The craftsmanlike honesty of the old man, his astonishing gifts for harmony and composity, his confident, almost boastful candour, added to his simplicity of heart, bring his pictures near the very sources of dream and poetry. Almost without thinking about it, he clumsily and patiently makes the image of his own kind of world — one which touches us by its moving truthfulness.

Raised by fashion to the status of a new form of art, naivety was everywhere acclaimed.

Many artists, such as Marie Laurencin in France, the Swede Nils Bardel, the Belgium Edgard Tytgat, and the Dane Kai Fjell, found it a source for sophisticated effects.

All over the world, primitive artists are more and more valued and sought after. Within the bounds of the narrow world in which they move, they create a painting purely dependent on instinct, undeniably charming, with a freshness and an innocence which are far to seek in our time.

For some time now, the genre has been recognised and sought after. There is hardly a land which does not now pride itself, with a certain nationalism, on the possession of primitive artists whose reputation has sometimes become world-wide.

In France, these painters were taken up early, and there are many of them — Séraphine Louis, Bauchant, Vivin, Déchelette, Chaissac, Caillaud. In Switzerland, Adolf Dietrich, in Italy Orneore Metelli, in Belgium de Laëttre, in Hungary the visionary Csontvary, in Yugoslavia Ivan Généralic, in Poland Nikifor, in Finland Sipilä, in Germany Paps, have recently achieved deserved reputations.

The United States, and rightly, has treated primitive art as the source of its native tradition in painting. There are such figures as Pickett, who was a contemporary of Douanier Rousseau, there is the Englishman John Kane, the famous Grandma Moses, Hirshfield, Horace Pippin, and so forth.

In Haiti, there has been a whole school of primitive painters — Philomé Obin and Hector Hyppolite in the older generation, and Prefete Duffaut and Auguste Toussaint among the younger.

In Uruguay we find the attractive and expert Pedro Figari, in Canada Mary Bouchard, in Brasil José Pancetti and above all Elisa Martins de Silviera, in Venezuela Feliciano Carvallo, in Mexico Guadelupe Posada, in Chile Luis Herrera Guevara, in Peru Mario Urteaga, in Argentina Gramajo Gutierrez, in Ecuador Luis Alberto Herredia, in Nicaragua Guillon, in Cuba Acevedo, in Honduras Jose Antonio Velasquez and even in Morocco there is Moulay Ahmed Drissi, who possesses a remarkable plastic sense; there is Tamiji Kitagawa in Japan, and Jamini Roy in India.

Should not this international fashion for primitive art be referred to the old basis of common humanity, which appears, without much notice being taken of it, in all folk art and in the votive objects of all religions!

THE FINAL RESURGENCE OF IMPRESSIONISM. - Placed in international perspective, the evolution of the Nabis and of all those who were given the label « Post Impressionist », does not appear as an isolated phenomenom.

At the beginning of the century, or at least during its opening decade, Impressionism recovered some of its former prestige both in France and elsewhere, through its public dissemination by means of the many books devoted to it, and the great retrospective exhibitions which made it better understood, which took place in Berlin and London in 1905, and by the still vigorous presence of its leaders, Monet, Renoir and Degas, and of their contemporaries such as Guillaumin and Lebourg.

Working side by side with the innovatory movement which was beginning, and often acting in concert with it in bringing about the transition, were many artists who were Impressionism's heirs, and whose prestige were now increased.

In Germany, Max Slevogt and Lovis Corinth mingled an exquisite sensibility with vigorous sensuality and visionary imagination.

In Holland, even before 1900, Breitner, the friend of Van Gogh, and Isaac Israëls were passionately interested in rendering the urban scene; in England, Walter Sickert and Philip Steer produced wonderfully atmospheric painting, marked, in the work of the latter, by an emphasis on graphic qualities; the same search for luminosity was to be found in America in the work of Childe Hassam, and especially in that of Prendergast, who produced boldly composed scenes of popular entertainment. The influence of Impressionism also spread to Poland, thanks to Joseph Pankiewicz, and to Australia via John Russel, who worked with Monet and Van Gogh, and to Brasil with Eliseu Visconti.

A short period spent in Venezuela by Antonio Boggio, after the first war, turned a whole generation towards landscape painting, and helped Armando Reveron to decide that he would measure his gift — successfully — against the blinding luminosity of the Tropics.

FROM EXPRESSIONISM TO FAUVISM. - Though still scattered, other forces, already for some time in existence, were now about to carry the torch of revolt which was soon to fire the whole of Europe. Van Gogh, Ensor, Munch and Toulouse Lautrec belonged to a generation earlier than that of the Nabis,

CHARLES DUFRESNE *France* Study of « Leda »
Pen and Ink, Gallery Dufresne, Paris

but had remained out of fashion and out of the current of the time. Up to now they had only been appreciated by groups of friends, and had been exhibited rarely, without much success and without publicity.

Only at the beginning of the new century did they achieve belated, sometimes posthumous fame, when their work suddenly revealed them to the new generation.

An Ensor retrospective was organised by *La Plume* in 1899; there was a Van Gogh retrospective at the Bernheim Gallery in 1901, and two retrospective exhibitions of Lautrec's work in 1902 — at the *Salon des Indépendants* and at the *Libre Esthétique* in Brussels; and, in the same year there was the Munch exhibition at the Berlin *Sécession*.

Solitaries by temperament, and withdrawing still further into solitude because of the incomprehension with which they found themselves surrounded, they, like Gauguin with whom they had many links, were now canonised as *peintres maudit*, because their moving subjectivity often took on a confessional tinge.

However, these pioneers were not isolated. Their wild individualism, the honesty of a message drawn from instinctive sources and bearing the imprint of genuine mysticism, their proud violence, their caustic comments which were always inspired by deep compassion — these made them very much part of an age where the current of humanitarianism and social protest was growing ever stronger.

Their work is related, sometimes very closely, and, in the case of Munch perhaps too closely, to the work of Ibsen, Tolstoy, Nietzsche and D'Annunzio.

Their graphic work, sharp and satirical, in which they played rich and masterly variations in the manner of Gauguin — wood-engravings, etchings, lithography, etc., — fits in with the fashion for *Gil Blas*, and the Steinlen drawings which so much impressed the young Picasso in Barcelona, and also the *Assiette de Beurre* and *Simplicissimus*, which numbered among their contributors, Kupka, Feininger and Villon.

The foolish extremism with which they were reproached, the eloquence of their sometimes brutal foreshortenings and distortions, the startling greatness which they gave to human and trivial things, the wild lyricism for the colour and lines which they used so expertly to express their passion for living or as a means of escape from inner stress — all these have their equivalent in primitive and popular art. Henceforth their contribution would be seen at its true worth; these simplifications, the fecund humanity of their style, would awake responses all over the world. In addition, this development was aided when circumstances offered new means of disseminating their ideas.

THE ERA OF INTERNATIONAL EXCHANGES. - In various countries an unexpected phenomenom now appeared, which seems to have sprung essentially from disinterested curiosity, from the desire to keep abreast of artistic developments elsewhere.

Associations and societies, rather than private galleries, took the lead in bringing in works of art from other countries, and especially from France. This had happened quite a bit already in Brussels, but now, in 1898 there was an exhibition of French art in Stockholm which included pictures by Van Gogh; in 1899 Diaghilev organised an important international exhibition of modern art in St. Petersburg; and in Berlin, in 1903, the *Sécession* brought together works by Cézanne, Gauguin, Van Gogh, Munch, Gauguin, and Bonnard.

Interest was strong in Germany, especially in Munich, the old artistic capital where the *Sécession* had already, in 1901, found a place for Van Gogh. In 1904 the *Kunstverein* exhibited Cézanne, Van Gogh and Gauguin, and yearly the *Phalanx*, through Kandinsky, showed the Impressionists and Post Impressionists.

The presence of these precursors was everywhere a stimulant, and showed which road was to be followed. The Van Gogh exhibition at the Arnold Gallery in Dresden in 1905, and that at the Brack Gallery in Munich in 1909, served to strengthen the resolutions recently taken by the artists of the *Brücke*.

At the same time, in Paris the big retrospective exhibitions of Seurat, Gauguin and Cézanne, organised by the *Salon des Indépendants* and the *Salon d'Automne*, helped to give direction to Fauvism and Cubism.

In addition, the *Salon d'Automne* in 1907 and 1908 acted as host to an exhibition of Russian and Finnish art, and in 1910 showed an exhibition of German decorative art.

The artists of the period gained many benefits from this current of exchanges, which in the succeeding years, was to develop a size and an impetus which we find it hard to imagine to-day.

New trends and ideas spread rapidly to many countries: already, in 1908, Matisse was exhibiting in Berlin and participating, with his Fauve colleagues in the *Toison d'Or* at St. Petersburg. His manifesto was published simultaneously in Paris, Berlin and Moscow. In 1910, thanks to the new Association of Artists founded in the previous year by Kandinsky and Jawlensky, Munich received Braque, Derain, Vlaminck, Picasso, Rouault, and Van Dongen.

In New York, Alfred Steiglitz devoted three successive exhibitions, in 1908, 1910 and 1912 to Matisse, and held a Picasso exhibition in 1911. Between 1910 and 1913 Cubism made itself effectively known in London, Brussels, Barcelona, Munich and Berlin, as well as in the principal cities of Russia through a travelling exhibition. It became known in Moscow through the *Valet de Carreau*, in Amsterdam through the *Kunstkring*, and in Prague through the *Manès Society* and through Alexandre Mercereau.

In Japan, from 1913 on, the *Nika-Kai* group took on the defence of modern art.

After Marinetti's lecture-tour in 1910 to Moscow and St. Petersburg, an exhibition of Futurist painters travelled to Paris, London, Berlin, Brussels, Hamburg, Amsterdam, Dresden, Zurich, Munich, Vienna, etc.

Before the war came to put a stop to all these endeavours, things became, in later years, more and more ambitious in scope, and produced correspondingly greater results: thus the second exhibition put on by Roger Fry in 1912 at the Crafton Galleries in London, the Cologne *Sonderbund* of 1912, where more than a thousand canvasses were shown, and the *Der Sturm* exhibitions organised by Walden in Berlin and the first German *Salon D'Automne* in 1913, had the character of vast international confrontations.

Even vaster was the Armony Show, put on by Walt Kuhn, Jerome Myers and Arthur B. Davies, which brought together nearly 1800 works in a New York barracks, and which was later transferred first to Chicago, then to Boston, and which was seen by over 250,000 visitors.

In addition to this, artists everywhere acquired the habit of travel, and of meeting each other frequently; above all, they came to France, where this influx of foreigners led to the formation of the *École de Paris*.

THE EXPRESSIONIST CURRENT. - Expressionism, except at rare moments when temporary groups were formed, such as that of the Fauves in France, and that of *Die Brücke* in Germany, near in aesthetic tenets though these were never properly formulated, is to be defined less as a movement than as a current, offered to many artists in nearly all countries a pledge of individuality.

To insist on considering it essentially nordic, because the Germans were consistently most receptive is to forget the fact that both Goya and Daumier can be considered to be among its spiritual forbears.

The first artists in France to feel its influence, without knowing it themselves, were Rouault, Suzanne Valadon, Utrillo, and Picasso in his early work (if one accepts the just attitude taken up by Bernard Dorival).

Rouault, who was by the sumptuosity of his colour and his technique the heir of Gustave Moreau, has never figured as the leader of a school, though fellow pupils in the studio, Léon Bonhomme and for the moment Desvallières, followed him in his pathetic depictions of the lower depths.

Like the promotors of Expressionism, he was isolated by his own work which always, as he said himself, retained a confessional quality. His revolt expressed itself first of all on the human level, without however neglecting pictorial problems. Prostitutes, and circus performers — such as those he conjured up after 1902 — were still close enough to Toulouse Lautrec, from whom, in any case, he was separated by only a very short space of time. But they differed already in respect of violence of colouring, abruptness of colouring, and through the distortions used.

With the war, he more and more began to draw up an indictment against the whole of society, portraying caricatured judges and clowns. Soon, he began to express his religious faith in terms no less vehement and with a striking grandeur which recalls the eloquence of his friend Léon Bloy, though without a trace of literary allusion. His work for long caused offence in Catholic circles, as at the same time in Belgium did

RAOUL DUFY *France* At the Fair 1906
Coll. Emil Bührle, Zürich

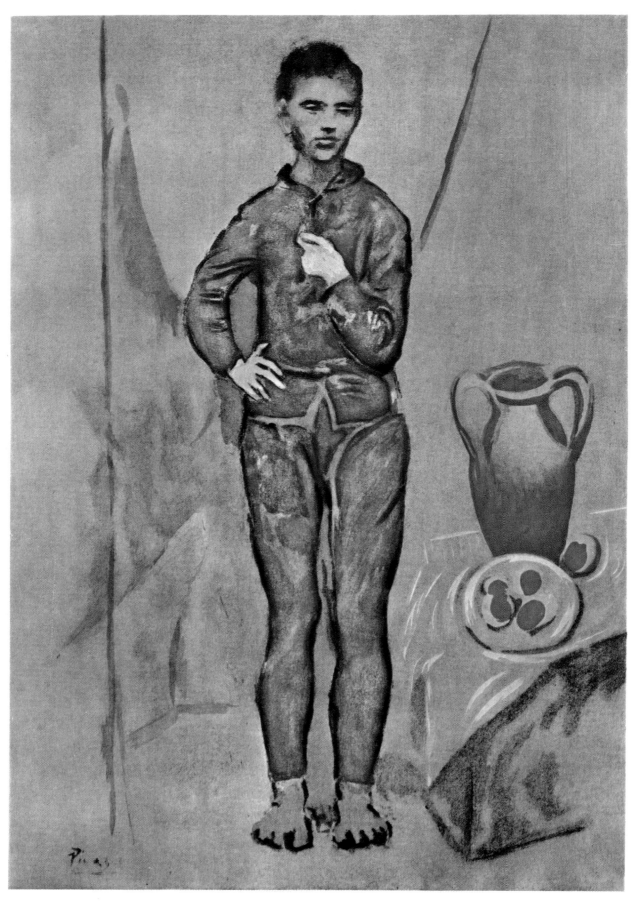

PABLO PICASSO *Spain, France* Juggler with Still Life 1905
Chester Dale Coll. National Gallery of Art, Washington D. C.

MOÏSE KISLING *Russia, France* Woman with Red Shawl 1920
Museum of Modern Art, Paris

MAURICE DE VLAMINCK *France* Still Life – Cubistic Forms 1910
Private Collection, New York

40

GEORGES ROUAULT *France* The Clown 1906
Gouache, Private Collection

that of Servaes, who resembles Rouault in his anguished and insistent linearity.

This passionate religious feeling appeared also in Holland just before the war, in a more stylised form in the work of the young Sluyters, and in that of his friend Jean Toorop, who, after his conversion in 1905, returned to his former admiration for Ensor and Van Gogh after a long period of Symbolism and Neo-Impressionism. With Rouault, painting is a cry from the heart, an anguished appeal. The colour, with its enamel-like quality, flames with purples and dark blues, contained, like the stained glass of the middle ages in heavy bandings of black, from which there spring out brutal, tortured forms. This emotive power, this visionary accent, evolved gradually after 1930 towards a more serene art, which helped win for Rouault his tardy acceptance. Suzanne Valadon, whose art was formed by natural inclination in the company of Degas and Toulouse Lautrec, for both of whom, she posed as a model, uses something of the same steely line to depict, both in her early drawings, and after 1905 in her painting, the starved face of misery. Some years later another woman artist, the Dutch Charley Toorop, joined just such brutal candour, which often attains monumentality, to an art showing interior stresses like those which appear in the work of Valadon.

Valadon's son Maurice Utrillo, under the promising auspices of his mother and those of his boyhood friend André Utter, did his best work between 1908 and 1916, beneath an apparent naivety, his painting was for Utrillo a means of escape and salvation. With an instinctive energy, he expressed in it his sorrows, his hopes. Through the picture postcards which he took as his inspiration, he found a means for quiet and honest self-revelation, without ever striking a false note. His peeling walls, sordid alleys, spires pointing to heaven, give permanent life, though more and more superficially during the last twenty years, to his memories of his miserable youth in Montmartre, and to his moments of childhood revelation.

From the moment of his arrival in Paris, and even before, the young Picasso showed his attraction to the example of Steinlen and Toulouse Lautrec, and also to the direction taken by his friend Nonell y Monturiol, whose work sometimes recalls, the unquiet humanity of Van Gogh.

Was he not predisposed towards these by his very origins? Anguish and the Baroque are part of the Spanish cast of mind, we can see them in Unamuno's *The Tragic Sense in Life*, published in 1913, and in the work of that other solitary painter, Solana. This latter, from 1904 on, was however concerned with almost the same themes as those of his friend Ramona Gomez de la Serna: the sordid and fascinating world, the strange scenes, the haunting masquerade of popular Spanish life, painted in heavy impasto, and observed with a certain bitterness. These pictures are linked, in spirit, to Expressionism with an element of the «problem picture». Picasso also shows something of these tendencies in his early work, so well described by Apollinaire as « damp and blue as the bottom of the abyss ».

His world of outcasts and starving acrobats, even when he embarks on his more cheerful Rose period, is depicted objectively, as if it were part of some fantastic play.

However, beneath this apparent detachment, beneath the kind of lofty irony which the artist affects, beneath the superb virtuosity, we can see the hidden concern of a man full of humanity, tortured and impetuous, whose impatience is shown more and more clearly in the nervous, fretful, agressive touch which we find him using, even when he has given up, after 1906, depicting these derilicts. It appears in all the rest of his work as well, and is the distinguishing work of his personality.

This interest in squalor was in the air. We find it again, almost simultaneously, on the other side of the Atlantic, as part of the first independent movement in American painting.

The Eight or Ash Can group, first formed in Philadelphia, moved to New York in 1908. Around Prendergast, with his subtle richness of colour, and Robert Henri, an able teacher, various artists gathered.

There were Arthur B. Davies, Ernest Lawson, John Sloan with his vigorous handling, William Glackens George Luks, and Everett Shinn. These, in the name of the naturalism of the past, wished to emphasise the sad bareness of everyday life.

Then revolt, though somewhat superficial, and without great feeling for the plastic, except as regards a certain expressive energy, ripened a little later with George Bellows, who showed an interest in prize-fight

42

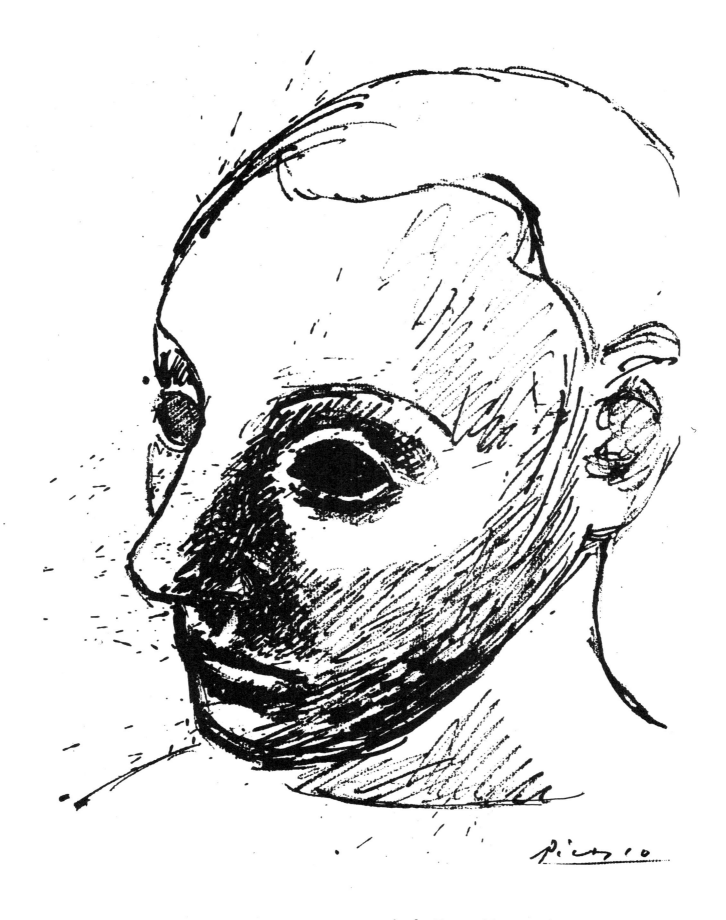

PABLO PICASSO *Spain, France* Head of a Toung Man 1906
Pen and Ink, Baltimore Museum of Art, Cone Collection

scenes paralled to that of his French contemporaries Dunoyer de Segonzac and Luc Albert Moreau. More important still, it prepared a feeling of expectancy and understanding favourable to modern art.

FAUVISM. - Even if one admits that there was a certain ambiguity in its origins, this movement, in its few recognised years of existence from 1905 to 1908, brought with it an extraordinary access of energy which benefited every branch of painting.

It owed its beginnings to chance studio friendships, just as the Nabis group did, but with this difference — from the very start those who took part in it refused to subscribe to any fixed theory or programme. When Matisse attempted to define Fauvism, this was a sign that the movement had already broken down.

In 1899 Moreau, Manguin, Marquet and Camoin followed Matisse, who was already a leader, from the studio of Gustave Moreau to the *Académie Carrière*. Here they fell in with Jean Puy, Laprade, Chabaud and Derain. This last introduced them to Vlaminck, who was his working companion at Chatou, at the time of the Van Gogh retrospective of 1901.

In the course of time the group was successively joined by Valtat, Marinot, and by three artists from Le Havre who had just escaped from the clutches of the Studio Bonnat and Impressionism — namely Friesz, Raoul Dufy, and Braque and Van Dongen in 1906.

EMIL OTHON FRIESZ *France* The Coast at Honfleur 1930
Charcoal, Coll. P. Pétrides, Paris

MAURICE DE VLAMINCK *France* The White House 1920
Private Collection, New York

45

ANDRÉ DERAIN *France* St. Paul's Cathedral, London 1906
Perls Galleries, New York

46

ERNST LUDWIG KIRCHNER *Germany, Switzerland* Landscape, Zurich 1926
Coll. Mr. and Mrs. Bruce B. Dayton, Minneapolis

47

EDWARD MUNCH *Norway* The Vampire 1906
Museum of Art, Göteborg

As early as 1899, Matisse, in his Corsican landscapes and later in his studio interiors, used pure tones and a free touch. Marquet, his faithful disciple, did the same.

But before 1904 there was a long period of abstinence, during which Matisse was perfecting his sense of compositional balance and pictorial values under the influence of his admiration for Cézanne.

Vlaminck too turned very early towards a summary style and brilliant colouring. He was influenced in this by his own instinctive lyricism and by a feeling for popular imagery which soon brought him under the spell of African sculpture. He was responsible, in turn, for the direction taken by Derain.

But what was responsible for the sudden liberation which showed itself, with a brutal vigour which caused an uproar in the 1905 *Salon D'Automne*, in the work of all these artists? What put them in the vanguard, as if all of them, till now scattered, had suddenly heard the call to arms of that which was to be named « Fauvism »? Matisse and Derain, then at Collioure, were led to raise the standard through the twin lessons of Pointillism and of Gauguin. They, in turn, sparked off the rest of the group, many of whom had come, in the same year, to study under Signac at St. Tropez. Their common denominators were a joyful spontaneity, a roughness of brushwork, and the passion for intense colour of which they were for some years the standard-bearers, and which earned them, at one period, the sobriquet of « The Incoherents » or « The Invertebrates ». The intensest possible colour, directly translating the artist's emotions, was master in the new pictorial space which they invented. They chose pure tones — reds, blues and oranges — which, as one of them said « appealed directly to man's basic sensuality »; they used forced contrasts to heighten these colours still further. They worked in broad brushstrokes and without shadings, with a kind of savage frenzy, a violent appetite for painting. Often the contours were heavily emphasised.

For two more years their unanimity continued. Newcomers fell into step with the initiators, their canvasses showed the same violent, clashing colours, the same break—up of form, the same almost barbaric robustness of handling, the same daring negligence mixed with a brutal exaltation. But under the Expressionism of the handling, the composition was frequently very deliberate.

This slightly forced grouping — even Rouault found himself classified among the Fauves — did not last long. Quite a few fell away almost from the start, as if from weariness, and preferred to return gently towards the then current semi-impressionism.

The younger artists, already feeling the call of other gods and of the great Cézanne retrospective of 1907, were given, through their impetuosity, a more honourable means of leaving the group and of giving up the exaggerated chromaticism and the formal experiments which were becoming wholly gratuitous.

Braque, discovering a new interest in structure and in constructive power, moved towards Cubism.

After several years under the discipline of Cézanne, which did his work a great deal of good, Vlaminck returned to the energetic naturalism which was thereafter to claim his allegiance, imprisonning himself in a style which often resorted to tricks and artifice despite the apparent generosity of touch and the nostalgic verve of a popular idiom.

Friesz adhered to classical methods of composition until about 1912, and was thereafter satisfied by the exercise, without undue effort, of an innate sensuality and an apparent freedom of handling.

Derain, after divagations towards primitivism and to the very borders of cubism, after the war employed his intelligence in a vain attempt to renew the classical tradition. Bravura, affected elegance and Claudian tonalities characterise his work.

Only Van Dongen, despite some exaggeration of his effects, remained faithful to an Expressionism which suited his talent and which links him closely to his friends in the *Brücke*. He retained his boisterous, eloquent style, after the war, to mirror an epoch of which he was the most observant portraitist.

But, between 1907 and 1908, a new tendency made itself felt among the Fauves. Matisse was its leader, and made it the occasion, for what amounts to a formal profession of faith. He, the first Fauve and the instigator and originator of the whole movement, now wished to introduce rules and regulations in place of instinctive excess. The influence of Cézanne's severe architecture played a part, but more powerful still was his wish to renew

PAULA MODERSOHN-BECKER *Germany* Mother and Child
Charcoal, Private Collection

his links with the magical rhythms of Seurat. Seurat had in fact always been a powerful influence of Matisse's work, especially from 1904 onwards.

Leaving his former allies to the feebler dictates of their own temperaments, which led them to fritter away, little by little, the precious gain in simplification of means which they had achieved, Matisse remained almost alone in giving purpose and continuity to Fauvism. Methodically and with foresight, he began to analyse the choice he had made, and to bring back to it its original emotive energy. He retained the principle of the brilliant, expressive picture-surface, and gave first place to colour itself. Put on with broad, vigorous brush-strokes which balance and set each other off, his colour suggests space and volume simply by the play of contrasts. This colour charms and sparkles, despite its intensity, because it is so superbly harmonious, so supplely contained within a decorative arabesque.

Matisse, far from being a painter of violent, emphemeral emotion, seeks for stability, tranquillity, and seductiveness. He succeeds in this through extreme condensation, through the harmony of his line and his tonal accords, which achieve an astonishing feeling of calmness and grandeur.

The teaching-studio which he directed between 1908 and 1911 brought Fauvism immense success abroad, even if the consequences were not always those which he might have wished.

After a long period spent in regathering his forces, which was devoted to work of a sensual intimism, and above all after his decoration painted for the Barnes Foundation in 1933, Matisse returned to his original route with admirable logic. In his illustrations and paintings, and later still in his *collages* and in the last synthesis of the work for his chapel at Vence, Matisse, overcoming the difficulties of ill-health, expressed right up to his death, in the energy of his colour, his inventive line with its wonderful dynamism, his luminous intelligence with its feeling for the human scale, a joy in life and living which has forever assured him one of the leading places in the history of modern art.

Consistently, but at some distance, Raoul Dufy followed the road taken by Matisse. Less disciplined (though at one point his pictures catch the manner of gothic engravings), Dufy still remained happy in the dextrous expression of a spring-like fancy and a lively exuberance. He painted and drew as freely as a bird sings, with the same apparent ease and freedom as Matisse. Dufy reduces appearance to a kind of graphic shorthand, scattered decoratively and inventively on broad background areas of luminous colour.

DIE BRÜCKE. – A movement was developing at this very moment in Germany which was closely linked to Fauvism by the generation to which its participants belonged, the direction they took and the spirit which inspired them. Only blind nationalism in both countries can be responsible for the fact that, despite the undeniable friendships and admirations which joined the two groups, people have so often refused to see the link between the groups. The excuse is that the artists of the *Brücke* (the Bridge), are more consciously heirs of Grunewald than of Daumier. But is not the technique of Van Gogh and Gauguin even more visible than of Munch in their graphic work?

The fact that they lacked the prestige of having a Matisse among them, should not prevent us from giving them the credit of having maintained their unity for some years. No doubt this was due to the fact that they were more isolated. But they persisted longer in their chosen road with the means at their disposal.

In 1901, student friendship in Dresden brought together Kirchner and Bleyl. Then they made the joint discovery of Japanese prints and African sculpture, as well as of the literature of the period — Strindberg, Dostoevsky and Nietzsche.

By 1905 the group was in existence, linked by work together in the country and in Kirchner's studio where were also now to be found Heckel and Schmidt-Rottluff, and also by the conscious desire of each member to join together with others in order to escape from the past and find a new means of pictorial expression. They were joined by Emil Nolde and by the Swiss Cuno Amiet, both of whom exhibited at Dresden in 1906, and in the same year by Max Pechstein and the Finn Axel Gellen. Finally, in 1910, by Otto Mueller.

Their first exhibition of 1906, which took place in modest circumstances at a lamp-maker's, was followed almost immediately by the publication of an album of engravings.

After 1907, they held an exhibition at the Richter Gallery almost every year, until 1911 when Kirchner decided, after certain departures and exclusions, to transfer the group to Berlin and then to dissolve it.

The *Blaue Reiter* also showed, in its second exhibition of graphic art, work by Kirchner, Pechstein, Mueller and Nolde. But they had all already determined to go their separate ways.

For them the struggle against poverty was made more difficult by the fact that they lived in a provincial environment, but on the other hand they showed great determination and a kind of social vocation which was unknown among the Fauves, and which sometimes weighs a bit heavily upon their work.

Though they were clumsier and more hesitant, and though they sometimes even preferred to exaggerate their own self-taught gaucheness, they achieved the same liberation, through broad, violent, brilliantly coloured brushwork, and through their use of angular distortions and heavily stressed linework. This use of line was emphasised still further by their extensive practice in wood engraving.

They felt themselves so much in tune with what was going on in Paris, which in any case most of them visited, that in 1908 they even invited Van Dongen to exhibit with them.

But even amidst their unity, which they owed to the lively leadership of Kirchner, these artists, whose work was filled with a sort of anguish in living which linked it to that of Munch, began quite soon to pursue different courses. Pechstein, who was the first to move away from the group, had already achieved, before

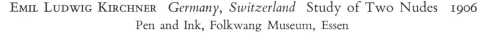

EMIL LUDWIG KIRCHNER *Germany, Switzerland* Study of Two Nudes 1906
Pen and Ink, Folkwang Museum, Essen

FRANZ MARC *Germany* Fighting Forms 1914
Bavarian State Collection, Munich

ALEXEJ DE JAWLENSKY *Russia, Germany* Self-Portrait 1912
Private Collection

OSKAR KOKOSCHKA *Austria, England* Portrait of Herwarth Walden 1910
Coll. Mr. and Mrs. Samuel Maslon, Minneapolis ▷

AUGUST MACKE *Germany* Walking on the Bridge 1913
Bernhard Koehler Collection, Berlin

he gave himself up to the attraction of exotic art which was to draw him away to the Palaos Islands, a more intimate harmony of plastic resources, which gave his work real beauty of expressive form and made him rapidly successful.

From 1908, Nolde withdrew into solitude and became more and more concerned, perhaps under the influence of Ensor, with a hallucinatory mysticism expressed in strong, acid tonalities.

Schmidt Rottluff, robust and massive, preserved a feeling for nature and for simplification. He used this to express a colourful lyricism, which drew him once more towards organising the picture space in depth.

Only Kirchner achieved a real style of his own, with rich tonalities compressed within firm design. This style had satirical elements, and with the approach of war Kirchner began to emphasise feelings of urban anguish and loneliness. Later, working in Davros, where he took refuge and finally committed suicide, he portrayed the peaceable spirituality of the mountains.

Apart from the group, Paula Modersohn worked in solitude at Worpswede. Her search was, as she herself wrote, for « poor little mankind ». She had discovered Gauguin through her visits to Paris, and she too achieved, just before her premature death, an analogous pictorial language; just as Rohlfs did in old age from the Van Goghs in the Folkwang Museum.

These manifold endeavours, though in part they came to nothing, nevertheless brought German art on to the international scene, and prepared the future, more complete flowering of modern art which was to come later in Munich and Berlin.

PROGRESS IN OTHER COUNTRIES. - The impulse given by this outbreak of feeling for pure colour soon reached nearly every European country in the years before the war. More and more artists joined in, and this led, in some places to the almost total neglect of Cubism when this, too, made its appearance. The nordic countries, who had sent many pupils to the *Académie Matisse*, were the most deeply influenced. In Sweden, the young artists who had come back home from Paris organised an exhibition in 1909; and soon a movement led by Isaac Grunewald came into being. He replaced the fiery, highly coloured Expressionism of Gösta Sandels and the simplified Romanticism based on the practice of Matisse characteristic of Leander Engström, with a lighter, more measured art. He employed the ample cadences of this style, with its rich harmonies, in numerous frescoes and designs.

A little later, Norwegian art also felt the influence of Matisse. Henrik Sörensen had in fact abandoned a style based on Matisse in order to follow the humanitarian direction taken by Munch, but now Matisse's style was again taken up, and with more vigour, by a remarkable group of artists. This formed itself around Jean Heiberg, who had a fine sense of construction by means of colour, though he tended, as this became more and more deliberate, to reduce the level of the tonality. Per Krogh and Axel Rewold, later imitated by Alf Rolfsen, applied, in their vast frescoes, painted from 1920 onwards, their dynamic colour and expressive force to the problems of wall-decoration.

In Denmark J. F. Willumsen exercised a continuing authority. And two young artists, on their return from Paris, founded the Grenningen Salon, which produced Edward Weie and Olaf Rude, both of whom worked in a brilliantly coloured lyrical style, though the latter underwent a brief flirtation with Cubism.

More slowly, Fauvism made its mark in Italy with Gino Rossi, in Czeckoslovakia with Vaclav Spala, in Yugoslavia with Peter Dobrovic and Jovan Bijelic, in Hungary with Bela Czobel who worked for a long period with Matisse. Matthew Smith, robustly sensual, brought Fauvism to England, and became a steady champion of modern art.

Post-Impressionism was introduced to Finland by Magnus Enckell on his return from Paris, while the self-taught Julio Rissanen evolved spontaneously towards Expressionism with a decorative flavour, and Tyko Sallinen, after his period in Paris, expressed a strong visionary sense in somewhat subdued tones.

From 1909 the Russian Ballet began to visit Paris. The Fauves were delighted to discover « orgies of colour » in the scenic designs by Alexandre Benois and by Bakst; while at the same time in Moscow Paul

Kunetsov and Nicholas Sapunov were introducing the plain-chant of colour into their canvasses.

In Switzerland, Maurice Barraud had placed himself from the very beginning of his artistic career under the banner of Matisse. At Geneva in 1914 he set up the Lantern Group. And Alexandre Cingria afterwards launched the Guild of St. Luke, the aim of which was to renew religious art.

Belgium had lost the promotional talent of Evenopoel. But many possibilities were summed up in the person of Rik Wouters who, having abandoned sculpture, put his time in Paris to good use in paintings which, skilfully expressed, in brilliant colour, the simple expansive happiness of which fate was so soon to deprive him. Brusselman's, schematised, strong painting developed quietly and continuously.

Though the Canadian, James Wilson Morice, another friend of Matisse, had hardly time to propagate Matisse's influence in his own country; on the other hand, in the United States, after their return from Paris, Max Weber and Maurice Sterne, who had been taught by Matisse, John Marin, Maurer, etc., gathered under the banner of Fauvism at the 291 Gallery run by Alfred Stieglitz, and played an active part in the Armory Show. Kandinsky's most faithful friend and companion, Jawlensky, before he settled in Wiesbaden at the end of the war and proceeded to give himself up to a typically Slav mysticism, was after 1909, the best representative of Fauvism in Germany. He was Gauguin's heir as well as Matisse's, as one observes from his monumental static simplifications, his areas of sensual, brilliant colour contained within deliberate boundaries. Matisse's German pupils, called « The Domiers »: Purmann, Rudolf Lévy, Oscar Moll, soon took the life out of his teaching. In Vienna, what might be called « pure Expressionism » returned to fashion. But is it altogether surprising to find Holdler, in 1904, triumphing in this capital of the Baroque? Under this influence and also, naturally, that of Klimt, Oscar Kokoschka began his career, with the encouragement of Loos, the architect, to support him. In Cuba Victor Manuel follow the movement.

He soon emancipated himself. His dramatic expressionism caused an uproar. After 1908, his anguished visionary portraits, feverishly penetrating, made their appearance. In painting these Kokoschka was followed, with a change in direction towards Japanese art, by his fellow-scholar Egon Schiele. Inspired by the *Brücke*, whose traces he found in Dresden after the war, Kokoschka later added, in his landscapes, a touch loaded with vibrant colour to a pictural construction which was still exasperated and nervous.

THE NEED FOR ORDER: FROM CUBISM TO FUTURISM

A new trend began to play a part in Europe between the years 1908 and 1912. The various national manifestations of this: Cubism, Futurism, and less directly the *Blaue Reiter*, Suprematism and Neo-Plasticism, were all moving in the same direction and remained relatively close to each other.

This tendency owed its origin to a need clearly defined by Matisse — the need to oppose the unfolding of tender intuitions and emotional impulses by some kind of intellectual control, capable of arriving at a more demanding and rigorous kind of art.

There were two main influences: that of Cézanne the effect of whose art was strongly felt after the Cézanne retrospective of 1907, indisputably so in the case of Braque, less obviously in the case of Picasso and many others; and the influence of Seurat which seems to have been even more powerful and prolonged.

Neo-Impressionism had steadily grown in influence since the publication of Signac's book in 1899, to the point where most painters, including Picasso, Matisse and Braque, had made an apprenticeship to it. After the retrospective exhibition of 1905, Seurat acquired yet greater importance in the eyes of the new generation. It was very soon after that Delaunay began re-reading the works of Chevreul.

In Italy, divisionism had already struck root with Previati and Pelizza da Volpedo; but Balla, Severini and their friends made their beginnings under the banner of Neo-Impressionism.

If the laws of simultaneous contrast awoke the interest of painters, the geometric simplifications, the powerful feeling of rhythm and the triumphant energy of Seurat's ultimate works played a still greater role in opening up the new way, and proved of the most use to the members of the *Section d'Or*.

EMIL NOLDE *Germany* Adoration of the Magi
Coll. Emil Henke, Essen-Bredeney

CUBISM. - The origins of Cubism lie yet more in the legend created around the Bateau Lavoir group, than in Braque's exhibition in 1898 with Kahnweiler (who became the well-informed advocate of the movement), and Picasso in 1909 with Vollard. Grouped about the already famous personality of Picasso, who drew Braque in his wake, were assembled those friends of Picasso who became the publicists of the work they had seen in his studio. These were Apollinaire, Raynal and Salmon, and they stated or invented the theories to which the young generation of 1909 rallied with such enthusiasim.

A group met at Mercerau's to discuss them. It included Delaunay, Metzinger, Gleizes and Le Fauconnier. They were to gather again a little later at Puteaux where Villon and Marcel Duchamp were living, together with La Fresnaye, Marcoussis and Picabia.

But by the time Cubism had received official recognition in the Salons of 1910 and 1911, where it appeared as a coherent group, its originators Braque and Picasso had already departed, and were engaged, in company with their follower Juan Gris, in a personal divergence which was rapidly to become more marked. Cubism came of age in 1912, and by that time they were already divided in all kinds of different directions which Apollinaire tried in vain, at the period, to number and catalogue. There was what might be called the « orthodox » Cubism of Picasso and Braque; there was the emphemeral but very promising Orphism of Léger, Duchamp, Picabia, Villon and their friends of the *Section d'Or*.

Constant Permeke *Belgium* The Sailor 1924
Pencil, Coll. Gustav von Geluwe, Brussels

The final flowering of his latent Expressionism and a masterly anticipation of the future was the *Demoiselles d'Avignon*, painted by Picasso in 1907 under the stimulus of Oceanian or African primitive art; this served Braque as a kind of talisman, and the two artists for several years explored together the lesson of Cézanne. They sought a more and more rigorous simplification of forms and volume, reducing these to simple geometric units, and stylising the planes of light as if they were the facets of a prism; and thus they escaped, after 1909, from the enticing geometric crystallisation which so many of their presumed followers used in far too facile a way — a technique which, sadly, often figures as Cubist in the history books.

From this period until the outbreak of war, they gave themselves up to detailed experimentation with their means of expression, to a deep examination of space and rhythm in order to make a living synthesis which, in the later years, would flower again into colour.

Gradually disengaging themselves from too strict a link with nature and from evident attachments to the world of appearances, they soon risked splitting up their subjects into fragments which they could then make into patterns as it suited them, and which they could use as expressive symbols. Turning to the study of composition, they channelled their energy into a rigorous decorum which shed all narrative elements, any easily sensuous appeal of handling of material, and any attempt to be descriptive.

But progressively they discovered, with a sort of joyful pride which is obvious in their work, that the infinite variation of possibile spaces, the multiplication of viewpoints (which they had previously used already in dealing with objects), the fragmentation of structure and the multiplication of lines of force, all helped to bring about a real increase in dynamism and in rhythm.

This entirely recreated universe, which gave scope to their inventiveness both in painting and in the *collages* they began to make in 1912, was now very often reduced to a diagram of expressive constructivism, where the idea of reality was poetically incarnated in a few letters of print or through the imitation of such substances as wood or marble.

But already, among those who had skilfully followed Picasso and Braque in making this difficult conquest of a new, somewhat austere and hermetic language, a certain weariness began to show itself. Gris soon transfixed himself on vainly logical rationalisation, Marcoussis turned back towards a new submission to nature, Serge Ferrat shut himself up in a delicately familiar intimism. Braque, too, on his return from the front, preferred quietude and the unobtrusive reintroduction of appearances, to analysis of the innerness of objects and of life itself. Between 1930 and 1935 his art showed an exquisite visual sensuality composed of envelopping arabesques and rare harmonies, and a refinement created by the play of surfaces; and ended by inclining dangerously towards elegant preciosity and virtuoso craftsmanship.

Picasso, abandonning a too lofty lyricism for a period where his colour became mannered, also moderated his trajectory after the war. His restless genius soon found a powerful language in which distortions which are Expressionist are allied to an exciting chromatism, contained within a suprising rhythmic discipline. His universe expanded continually, thanks to a search – carried on to this day – for living forms ceaselessly recreated by his imagination, and for the unknown realms which he reveals to us.

His passion for life, his obsession with death, cause an alternation in his work of elliptical, sensual line and aggressive schematisation. From the greatest severity of style, he passes to a prolix, tormented expressiveness. This passionate individual, with his excess, his eternal dissatisfaction, carries within himself his own interior drama, and suffers as well, intensely, the whole tragedy of our times.

His work has had great weight in deciding the fortunes of art to-day. But is not this ascendancy due to just this painful instability, the obsessive disquiet strangely mingled with sarcasm, to the wildness contained within it? Our age has ended by recognising in terror its own image there, and it has come to see the interest of this direct and human testimony.

Among the 30 exhibitors at the *Salon de la Section D'Or* opened in the Rue de la Boetie in 1912, that « wonderful year which, more and more, seems to have been the high point of painting in this century » as Seuphor once wrote, were at least three artists who until then had stood somewhat apart from Cubism. They now

PIET MONDRIAN *Holland* The Blue Tree 1911
Museum of Art, The Hague

showed works which strike us as being among the most complete and accomplished products of the movement, before the war blocked the way or turned them towards Dadaism.

Léger, Marcel Duchamp and Picabia put forward, in several of their large canvasses, a truly monumental synthesis possessed of an eloquent and intensive sweep, where space was at once closed and multiple, with a sufficiently rich structure of colour and with a powerful suggestion of forms and volumes (which, however, owed nothing to reality or conventional perspective), and with a secret life of its own – all of them things which those called orthodox Cubists had only partially realised.

With the boldness of youth, or through overweening ambition, they seem afterwards to have turned aside, in order to explore the idea of movement which also fascinated the Futurists. The source of this idea must be looked for in the cinema, and in the work being done at the *Institut Marey* where Noguès and Bulle were researching into chronophotography – the speeding up and slowing down of images.

On his return from the front, Léger, like his comrade Marcel Duchamp, who was fascinated by the idea of movement to the point where he ironically invented complex psychological machinery, continued, with greater maturity, to apply himself to the dynamism of forms and colours. Patiently he fashioned, just as in his film and in his designs for the theatre, a universe where the machine was triumphant, and where, in a newly created space, there seemed to move a strict and harmonious assembly of connecting-rods, gears and robots, created by vigorous, more and more colorful, strokes of the brush.

He introduced once more a whole world of real but transposed forms, of type-objects, yet never lost his rough but monumental – sometimes rather monotonous – style with its popular accent, which he put so magnificently to work in his late mural designs and which explains his preponderating influence on contemporary mural design.

Other participants in the *Section d'Or* showed astonishing promise: in particular, La Fresnaye, with his naturally elevated style which owed much to the example of Cézanne, and which condensed, made ethereal and spiritualised reality, orchestrating colour and structure in all their fullness with intuitive formal inventiveness. But the war, alas, was to reduce this power to impotence. Then, too, there were Gleizes and Lhote who both committed themselves to the dead-end of a doctrinaire system (though the latter now seems to be making his escape), and Villon, who was already preoccupied with techniques of construction through form and colour, which led him without too much struggle to the borders of abstraction.

He alone was to reach a happy conclusion, after years of retreat imposed by circumstances. In fact, Villon, though always accorded, from the very beginning, an intellectual prestige by the associates who grouped themselves about him, only achieved his place of importance after some little time, through his ascendancy of the artists of a younger generation.

He possesses a painstaking sense of construction, an acute but weighty line, a precise and personal feeling for pictorial values, a demanding need for the concise solution, which makes each of his pictures a true symphony in colour. He composes a world which is no longer a simple allusion to the real world, but endowed with a rich poetic climate. He recreates space within the picture by a skilled interplay of pyrimidal structures and alternations of planes. This space comprehends all dimensions and suggestions; it adds yet more to the extraordinary pleasure given by his unusual colour harmonies.

Beyond the borders of France, Cubism, found difficulty in a large number of countries in finding a big enough public.

Paul Reth, already a Parisian by adoption, met with little success when a group of his works and of those by his colleagues was shown in Budapest in 1912. In France, he went forward with a nostalgic elegant version of Cubism, tending finally towards abstraction. Like Mondrian, Sluyters in Holland felt for a time the influence of Cubism.

In Denmark, William Lündstrom, by means of his adroit formal and colouristic explorations, prepared the way for abstraction. In Poland, which was already represented in Paris by Hayden, an exhibition by Mercereau was enthusiastically received; Filla became the moving spirit behind a generation's restless and vigorous pictorial researches.

On his return to the United States after five years residence in France, John Marin, who was, together with Hartley and Demuth a friend of the Steins etc., the leader of the *avant-garde*, moved progressively towards a wholly personal synthesis which in the end was accepted by the New York public, thanks to the far-sighted stubborness of Steiglitz, who, from 1909, gave an annual exibition of Marin's work.

He used an almost Fauve palette, somewhat more restrained in his beautiful watercolours, to compose, skillfully and passionately, strange, visionary syntheses inspired by the American way of life. In these, the fragmentation of the reality about him, and above all of the city landscape, sometimes carried very far towards abstraction, formed the basis for his creation.

Futurism in Italy, was the first movement, related to Cubism because it too was a response to the same need for freedom and to the climate of the time. It differed however because of its demand for conscious originality. This explains subsequent deviations and recantations. An organised, self-conscious movement

CARLO CARRÀ *Italy* Horseman and Horse 1915 G. Mattioli Collection, Milan

in which, alas, provocative manifestoes often took precedence over painting, its course was both helped and hindered by the dominating personality of Marinetti, who became its organiser and publiciser. In Paris in 1909, he published the first Futurist manifesto in which he explained the necessity, for Italian artists, of a breach with the overwhelming past.

Some of the artists whom he happened to bring together were more strongly moved by this feeling, than by an interest in the movements of their own time.

At the beginning of the century, Balla had been fired with an enthusiasm for Neo-Impressionism in France, and had, on his return to Italy, infected both Boccioni and Severini with it. Boccioni came to Paris, and so did Severini in 1906. This latter was a familiar of the painters of Montmartre, and was able, in 1911, to bring his friends into contact with Cubist circles. They, together with Russo and Carrà, were signatories of the Futurist Manifesto in 1910, and also, in the following year, of the technical manifesto of Futurist Painting. In 1912, Paris saw the first exhibition held by the group, which had now been joined by Prampolini, Soffici (for a brief moment), Ottoné-Rosai, Mario Sironi, and afterwards many others.

If the war, and the course taken by politics, meant the failure of the group as an official organisation, it still succeeded in spreading the taste for modernism in Italy though sometimes in adulterated form; above all, it made plain, even outside of Italy, the importance of ideas of space and simultaneity to modern art.

From Cubism, from which they also took the idea of making collages, the Futurists borrowed the idea of endeavouring to make a plastic synthesis of form and space, adding intensity of colour and luminosity, and exalting all the dynamism of modern life through a feeling of force and of motion.

First Severini, followed in 1912 by Balla (whose work provided with most complete exposition of what they were trying to do, and came close to abstraction), and a little later by Boccioni, succeeded in creating glistening and luminous paintings which gave the feeling of continuity of movement in multiple space – the movement of crowds, of animals, and of machines. These artists had a romantic mystique connected with

UMBERTO BOCCIONI *Italy* The Mother 1912
G. Mattioli Collection, Milan ▷

Gino Severini *Italy*, *France* Cannons in Action 1915
P. Guarini Collection, Milan

66

GIACOMO BALLA *Italy* Streamlines of Flowers 1914 A. Mazzotta Collection, Milan

CARLO CARRÀ *Italy* Bottle and Glass 1915 A. Mazzotta Collection, Milan

PABLO PICASSO *Spain, France* Seated Woman 1909
Collection Roland Penrose, London

GEORGES BRAQUE *France* L'Estaque 1908
Rupf Collection, Berne

JUAN GRIS *Spain, France* Still Life 1917 ▷
Private Collection

ROGER DE LA FRESNAYE *France* The 14th of July 1915
Private Collection, Paris

FRANCIS PICABIA *Spain, France* Udnie 1913
Museum of Modern Art, Paris

FRANÇOIS KUPKA *Czechoslovakia, France* Circles 1911 Study for the « Fugue »
Mrs. Kupka Collection

ROBERT DELAUNAY *France* Tribute to Blériot 1914
Private Collection, Paris

75

WASSILY KANDINSKY *Russia, Germany, France* Composition 1914
Solomon R. Guggenheim Museum, New York

the idea of power and energy, and this they interpreted by means of repeated distortions of planes and through the play of colour and the witty confusion of lines, in compositions which remained basically monumental in character. After the war, Severini paid homage to Classicism, before going back, in our own day, to an abstract geometry still much concerned with colour.

THE APPEARANCE OF ABSTRACTION. It was the role of other artists to draw conclusions from the premises of Cubism, and to carry forward its work. Delaunay and Kupka arrived at this instinctively in carrying out their own plastic experiments. Kandinsky and Mondrian evolved in a more considered way. Because of their age and experience, this evolution took on the aspect of true philosophical speculation. In fact, this « crossing the line », as it is now fashionable to call it, was within the grasp of most artists. The new generation has good reason to acclaim Impressionist paintings as « these dazzlingly coloured abstracts », in André Breton's phrase. Monet, in many of his works, and Van Gogh in certain landscapes, only suggest reality by slight references which they might quite easily have suppressed.
Even Signac, in his portrait of Fénéon, was pleased to have established « a rhythmic base of proportions and angles, of colours and tones. » Redon, in his shimmering visions, and other artists too, come close to the pure form of expression which many Cubists, from Picasso to Léger, found no difficulty in using. Tchurlianis and Rossine were also precursors. But the groups which now formed were marked by a more apparent consciousness of the problem. They explored it more deeply and brought all their energies to bear on it.

ORPHISM. - Delaunay was much indebted to Neo-Impressionism, and still more to Cubism. He succeeded, between 1910 and 1912, in creating the impression of movement and above all the transformation of space which so much engrossed him. He based his compositions on a rhythmic multiplication of planes and on the active part played by colour, using these in simultaneous contrasts. This led him to create his series of « Windows », « Discs » and « Circular Forms », the first specimens of what he came to call « non-objective painting ».
Through a more conscious line of development, Kupka, who was Delaunay's neighbour at Puteaux, and who participated in the meetings and discussions held there, embarked upon non-figurative painting from 1912 on, and exhibited pictures which showed what he described as « a kind of picturesque geometry of ideas, which alone remains possible ».
Apollinaire, always on the look out for novelty, constituted himself the champion of these new experiments, and christened them « Orphism ». Through the agency of Macke, whom he met in 1909, Delaunay took part in the first exhibitions at Munich of the *Blaue Reiter*. His work made a deep impression on some of the members of the group.
He was so much regarded as a leader that in 1913, at Berlin, Walden asked him to set out his ideas in his review, and showed a group of Delaunay's pictures in his gallery *Der Sturm*. Delaunay was also invited, together with Sonia Delaunay, to play a prominent part in the Berlin Autumn Salon.
Henceforth, with some moments of return to figuration, these two artists continued to work together. They show strong links with the machine-age. It was, above all, in his gigantic mural decorations for the International Exhibition of 1937 that Delaunay was able to show at their true strength the principles he had established of a rich and moving orchestration of colour linked to the animation of surfaces, where colour and rhythm, as the interpreters of the multiplicity of pictorial spaces, became the direct expression of the spatial and temporal dynamism which gave his work its quality of joyousness, its feeling of strength and energy.
Kupka, who was not properly valued until recently, remained quiet and solitary until his death. He persevered, without weakening and with serene philosophy, in the creation, sometimes arid but always renewed, of « a tightly closed imaginary universe which preserved no link with the physical world of living ».
The last member of this group which Apollinaire invented in his writings, was Picabia. He, driven by his

liking for the subversive, became together with Marcel Duchamp, the initiator of Dadaism in New York in 1915. After innumerable *volte-faces* inspired by his feeling for the Absurd, he returned to abstraction shortly after the Second Word War.

DER BLAUE REITER (THE BLUE RIDER)

Germany is usually considered to be the native ground of abstraction and of the *Einfühlung*. But, until the first decade of the century, little interest was shown there in new forms of art. Then, in the few years between 1911 and the war, Germany was taken with a passion for making up the lost ground which soon made it the place where all the most advanced currents in modern art confronted each other.

The *Blaue Reiter*, newly formed at Munich; later the *Sonderbund* and the *Salon of the Rhine* at Cologne; the *New Sécession*, the *Der Sturm* Gallery and the Autumn Salon at Berlin, all vied with each other to attract the best artists from all countries.

Kandinsky arrived from Russia in 1896, and had a long struggle, together with the faithful Jawlensky, before Munich began to take an interest in what he was doing. He showed with the *Phalanx*, with the *New Asso-*

LYONEL FEININGER *Germany, U.S.A.* Cyclists 1912
Gallery Ferdinand Moeller, Cologne

Amedeo Modigliani *Italy, France* Woman
Private Collection

ciation of Artists in 1909, with the *Blaue Reiter*, born of a schism, in 1911, and had to show much perseverance, sometimes only to be greeted by critical sarcasms.

The first, restrained, *Blaue Reiter* exhibition showed that there were still differences between Kandinsky and his chief colleagues, Mark, Macke, Kubin, Schönberg and Gabrielle Munter. But the album which appeared a little later was a true dossier of all the artistic experiments taking place in Germany, in Russia and in France. The 1912 exhibition, on the contrary, emphasised the many views held in common between the Germans, who had now been joined by Klée, and Delaunay, Léger, Picasso, Braque, etc., and also the Russians Nathalia Gontcharova, Larionov and Malevich.

Kandinsky, then aged 46, published in the same year his book *On the Spiritual in Art* and held his first retrospective exhibition in Berlin, was able to exercise a moral ascendancy over his young colleagues.

He always remained the pioneer along the road which he had deliberately chosen in 1910, after the initial impact of Fauvism and Gauguin upon him in Paris four years earlier.

Apart from his decision to cut himself off from nature so that his painting might respond only to the « interior necessity » which is the determinant in form and colour, Kandinsky preserved an openess to all ideas, and in this, his so-called « dramatic » period, which lasted up to 1920, he was engaged in a tumultuous outpouring, a brilliant release, with wild lines and brutal black striations.

Macke followed a similar principle of endowing colour with all the expressive and symbolic virtues, but his course was different because of the inner nature of the artist.

From Divisionism and Cubism, and above all from Delaunay, he retained a need for equilibrium, a feeling for order and for volume which only grudgingly gave place to the violent lyricism of Kandinsky.

The abstraction into which he entered towards the end of 1913 still remained, quite often, a joyful and poetic transposition of the pantheist fervour which he felt. He expressed this by a crystalline interpenetration of planes, and through an interplay of vibrant, turning forms with skilful contrasts of colour.

Though he too wanted his painting to become the direct expression of spiritual reality, Macke, who had been deeply marked by contact with Matisse and Delaunay, both of whom he had known in Paris, kept a constant concern for direct visual experience; abstraction remained a pleasure which he sometimes allowed himself. He preferred to borrow from reality in order to distil living silhouettes or allegorical forms, transcribed in the form of a subtle geometric schema. Simultaneous contrasts were used to give light and gaiety.

Both men would no doubt have played a large part in the future of German art, if the war had not come to cut off two growing bodies of work, each charged with hopes and radiant confidence.

In fact, the clear principles of the *Blaue Reiter* did not acquire their full importance until Kandinsky's return to Germany, and his appointment, in 1922, as professor at the Weimar Bauhaus. There he both diffused and applied his ideas of the entire autonomy of art, in which intuition became the essential means of comprehending and representing the universe, tackled as a whole. This required of both form and colour, intimately linked together, the fullness of their meaning, and it called upon all their powers of musicality and spirituality. The aspirations to wholeness in art, coincided with those of the school's founder, Walter Gropius. Gropius took up in more logical form the ideas of the end of the previous century, and announced in his programme that he wished « to re-establish the harmony between various sorts of artistic activity and between all the disciplines of craftsmanship and the fine arts, and bring them completely into line with a new conception of building. Our final aim is unitary works of art in which no distinction remains between the monumental and the decorative. »

In their turn, other artists were to give the Bauhaus admirable impetus and great influence - Muche, Schlemmer, Laszlo, Moholy-Nagy, and especially Paul Klée and Lyonel Feininger. With the two latter, and with Jawlensky, Kandinsky associated himself in 1924 to found the *Blaue Vier*, to hold exhibitions.

Unhappily, the political climate led to the Bauhaus being transferred to Dessau in 1929, and soon after closed altogether. The artists were driven into exile.

Kandinsky lived in France until his death, and the triumph which fate was to bring him and the unprecedented notoriety which was to be attached to his name remained alike unknown to him.

In his silent retirement, he continued to enrich his lifework, even during his active time in Russia. His fiery « improvisations » of before the war gave way, under the influence of Malevich and the Russian constructivists, to a dynamic and distinctly geometric architecture in which, later, circular elements played their parts. But he always showed a certain humour and a rich inventiveness which linked him to the verve of Russian popular art and life. In Paris, his impulse towards colour was set free. It triumphed during this period, called that of the « great synthesis ». Here poetic intuition mingled boldly with lyric enthusiasm. Klée, established in Switzerland, continued to carry on, indifferent to time and fashion, a wholly personal way of working whose ingenuous freshness and ability to renew itself are the best guarantees of its value.

AMEDEO MODIGLIANI *Italy, France* Portrait of Jeanne Hébuterne 1918
Private Collection, Berne ▷

EDOUARD PIGNON *France* Olive Groves 1955
I. Magliano Collection, Milan

ANDRÉ LHOTE *France* Leda and the Swan 1934 ▷
Stiebel Collection, Paris

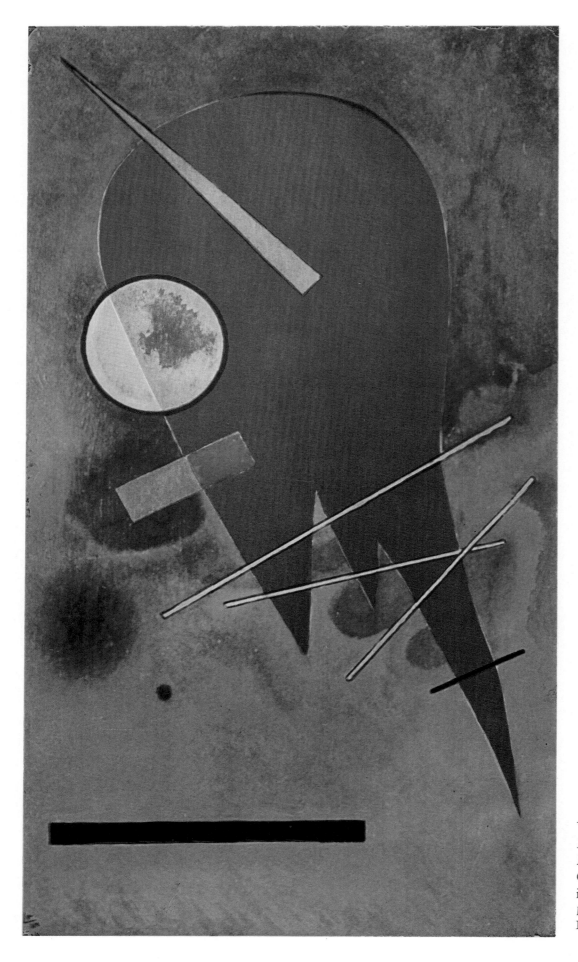

WASSILY KANDINSKY
Russia, Germany
France
Composition
in Red 1924
Mrs. Sacher Collection
Basel

84

24-5-40
J. G.

JULIO GONZALEZ *Spain, France* Head 1940 Chinese Ink, Coll. A. Gonzalez, Paris

Everything served him as the basis for the signs which he invented. Among them, sometimes, there arose the memory of his travels to Tunisia which had confirmed him in his resolution to be a painter. His little pictures, made to give visual as well as intellectual pleasure, open out to a limitless universe in which the most fugitive perceptions become harmonies, happiness and poetry.

Feininger returned in 1937 to the United States, where his influence soon became important. He faithfully exploited the feeling for space and the musical sense which were his own particular gifts. He borrowed from Cubism, or rather from the *Section d'Or*, the crystalline multiplication of planes, and reconstructed reality as a kind of dream architecture subject to strict harmonic organisation. The linear severity of this was tempered by the gentle, spiritual luminosity of his tonality.

Only Moholy-Nagy tried, in the United States after 1937, to revive the experimental spirit of the Bauhaus, whose moving force he had been. He continued, along the lines indicated by Lissitzky, his spatial researches in « object-paintings » in which he employed many different kinds of material.

TOWARDS A NEW LANGUAGE. – In the Parisian crucible, between 1912 and 1914, a Dutchman succeeded in bringing the personal deductions he had drawn from Cubism into focus. Now aged 40, Mond-

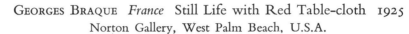

GEORGES BRAQUE *France* Still Life with Red Table-cloth 1925
Norton Gallery, West Palm Beach, U.S.A.

DUNOYER DE SEGONZAC *France* Antilope 1912
Pen and Ink, Private Collection

rian had already taken what he needed from Neo-Impressionism and Fauvism.

The problems of rhythm, which is also to be found obsessing the work of Picasso at this epoch, led him to the discovery of abstraction, and to the elaboration of a real metaphysic of painting.

Shut up in Holland by the war, he continued his researches. The *De Stijl* movement was born of his meeting with Van Doesburg, and this latter became its fiery propagandist.

Mondrian published numerous essays in the review, also called *De Stijl*, which Van Doesberg edited; Vantongerloo, Vilmos, Huszar, etc. were also concerned with it. A little after his return to Paris, Mondrian published a pamphlet which explained the doctrinal position of what he called « Neo-Plasticism ».

He was looking for an imaginative perfection out of which he wished to make an ethic applicable to the whole of society. He wanted to reduce painting to its essentials, to a kind of common denominator which would have universal validity. Beginning with pure rhythm, limited to horizontal and vertical movement, he conceived of an art in which all varieties of human expression could be condensed into the relationships between differently coloured planes, these relations being determined by an assymetric play of straight lines meeting each other at right angles.

For these relationships to been seen at their full value, the surfaces must be smooth, without the mark of brushstrokes and, like the rectilinear black outlines, uniformly coloured either in one of the three primary colours, in grey, or in white. Mondrian produced admirable work in this absolutely pure style, even though it seemed a renunciation of all the pleasures of painting, and even sometimes as its completely negation, like the work of the Dadaists whom Mondrian came close to on occasion.

At the end of a life which had known much austerity, and perhaps thanks to the triumph accorded him in New York in 1940 (which preluded the sometimes excessive veneration of which he is now the object) Mondrian permitted himself a certain loosening. Colour invaded his lines and broke them up, thus giving to his last works a more animated rhythm, a joyous exaltation.

Thanks to the work of Van Doesberg in Holland, in France, and in Central Europe, and thanks moreover to the Bauhaus, which took much from it, Neo-Plasticism had a certain success and recruited sufficient disciples for the *Circle and Square* group to be formed under the leadership of Seuphor and Torrès-Garcia in 1930; and in the following year *Abstraction Création* heralded a full development.

But it was only after the Second World War that the doctrinal rigour of Neo-Plasticism awoke an immense, almost world-wide, enthusiasm, which led to the admirable application of its principles in architecture.

No less symptomatic of the spirit of the time was the work of Ozenfant, also in France. In 1915 and 1917 he began a parallel development, with the help of Jeanneret. This he called « Purism ». Starting from Cubism, he too proposed to eliminate everything variable and accidental, and to keep only what was constant. Unhappily Ozenfant, through lack of true spiritual depth as well as through his opposition to all forms of abstraction, arrived at a method which left him no room for development.

Malevitch, too, returning to Russia from a visit to Paris in 1911, abandoned Expressionism for the Cubism of Fernand Léger. A whole group of artists followed him: Pevsner, Puni, etc. Stimulated by the lectures given by Marinetti, and by the numerous exhibitions then being held in Moscow, he soon went over to Abstraction and, after 1913, he adopted a style which he called « Suprematism » in his manifesto of 1915. Like Mondrian, he was imbued with theosophical ideas, and wished to make art into a pure, mystic effusion, stripped of all unneccessary elements and restored to primitive simplicity. This naturally led him to choose the simplest geometric forms: squares, circles, triangles, crosses, whose various permutations he proceeded to explore until he arrived at a kind of supreme renunciation, or act of faith, with his famous white square on a white ground of 1919. After the war, he was able to make his message still further heard with the publication, through the Bauhaus, of his book *The World of Non-Representation*, and he enjoyed, it appears, a decisive influence on the creators of the abstract film: Ruttmann, Richter, Eggeling, long before his name and his attitude received their present-day canonisation.

Other artists also appeared like comets in the feverish atmosphere of pre-war Moscow, before coming to

CHRISTOPHER WOOD *England* The Cross at the Market, Tréboul 1930
The Art Gallery, Buffalo, U. S. A.

JEAN MIRO *Spain, France* Woman Seated
Pierre Matisse Gallery, New York

STUART DAVIS *U.S.A.* Composition 1950 Downtown Gallery, New York

HENRY LAURENS *France* Crouching Woman 1944
Pencil, Gallery Louis Carré, Paris

live in France. In 1913, Larionov and Gontcharova, hastily amalgamating Cubism and Futurism, launched «Rayonnism», a movement which in the following year received Apollinaire's blessing in Paris. But soon, absorbed by their work on the decor for the *Ballet Russe*, they dropped out of sight until the recent fashion for abstraction restored to them, too, their position as pioneers.

London also, stimulated by exhibitions from abroad, felt, in 1913, a movement in favour of modern arts. Wyndham Lewis banded together a small group of friends and campaigned in his review *Blast*. One of his colleagues was Wadsworth, who even translated a piece by Kandinsky.

Thus « Vorticism » was launched. Even though the manifesto was not published until 1914, its two principal participators had been making, for several years beforehand an astonishing affirmation in a style of geometric abstraction. This they abandoned after the war. Lewis retained from it, however, when his work became figurative, a taste for structures with very heavy emphasis on the verticals.

In New York, the changes brought about by the Armory Show were yet more important, and their effects lasted longer, no doubt because of the unexampled vastness of the exhibition. With astonishing prescience, the informed public was especially interested by the work of Marcel Duchamp. This encouraged him to stay in the United States and to pursue, in this sympathetic atmosphere, his fruitful experiments in transposition of movement, as in his famous mystic-cum-mechanical piece *The Bride Stripped Bare by Her Bachelors* which was executed between 1915 and 1923. Duchamp, moved by a spirit of mischievous inventiveness which was never to leave him, also submitted his *Ready Made* to American exhibitions after 1914.

However, what interested Americans most was the discovery of their own *avant-garde* school of painting, of which they are justly proud to-day. These dissidents were all much indebted to the Orphism of Delaunay. Patrick Henry Bruce, after his time with Matisse, remained a solitary figure. Morgan Russel and Macdonald Wright, who had also lived in Paris, and now feeling themselves to be in full possession of their own means, created in 1912 an autonomous movement called « Synchronism ». They exhibited in Paris and Munich the following year, and again, with more maturity, in New York in 1916 after their return to the United States. However, Macdonald Wright was the only one of the three who was able to build on his pioneer position. He showed his qualities in his recent return to abstraction.

Cubist pictures by Hartley also figured in the show. At the same time he was taking part in the Berlin Autumn Salon. A little later he returned to the United States, won over for the moment by Abstraction, of which all his later work was to show some vigorous traces. Covert, resolutely abstract, also exhibited.

Sheeler's work was already taking from the Cubist example the simplification and the rigour which he employed to evoke the inhumanity of cities.

The still modest contribution sent by Stuart Davis was a preparation for the flowering of a talent which now takes its place as perhaps the most important in contemporary American painting. He was only a step away, in the Cubist collages which he continued to make till after the war, from his own masterly form of expression.

Near in spirit to Léger, he constructed his syncopated visions with robust rhythms, intense colours, frankly accentuated contrasts, and a robust sense of decoration. He is often entirely abstract, especially after 1938; his art still retains the liberty, the lively flavour of popular communication in the very image of American life.

CONCLUSION. - It would be difficult to cover all the experiments, all the attempts, which feverishly proliferated in all countries. This effort is sometimes carried to excess nowadays. How many « isms » there were. Arp and Lissitsky made a careful list of them in 1925. They sprang up and struggled for survival in the immediate post-war period, and most of them, like Strzeminski's « Unism » in Poland, and Berlewi's « *Mechanofaktur* », were doomed to prompt disappearance.

It is neccessary however to say that if the war came to cut short the energies of this wonderful period, time was still granted to open up all the new roads, and to provide them as a legacy to those who came after. Arp and Chirico provide two especially valuable examples in this regard.

José Clemente Orozco   *Mexico*   Mexican Village
The Detroit Institute of Art, Detroit, U.S.A.

Chirico has been turned into a hero by the Surrealists. But was he not justified in rejecting an attitude which he had already long before renounced in his work?

In fact, what is best in his work dates from before the war up to the moment of his arrival at Ferrare in 1915, where he turned academic. All the important pictures praised by Apollinaire were painted in Paris after 1912; in them he piled up unaccustomed associations of images and ideas which provoked a vague inquietude. He also created a true spatial magic, theatrical in nature, which he uses here to offer an unexpected possibility of escape. He seems to have had a talent for uncovering Spectres; anyway, he leaves great open spaces in his pictures which seem to conjure up invisible presences. Chirico was very conscious of all this, and wrote in 1913: « For a work of art to be truly immortal, it must completely go beyond the limits of the human: commonsense and logic are defects in it. In this way it will come closer to reality and to childhood habits of thinking... The artist discovers the profundity of his work in the depths of his own being. »

95

Without being perhaps so pronounced, the personality of Jean Arp was already at this moment distinguishable. He had taken part in the *Blaue Reiter*, and in the Berlin Autumn Salon of 1913, and was closely linked to Apollinaire and Delaunay. He embarked on an astonishing style of geometric abstraction, no doubt influenced by Sophie Taeuber, after his exhibition of 1915, and in the following year began his search for irrational objects which he was to pursue thenceforward.

If, in 1916, he amused himself by setting the Dadaist bomb alight, in company with Tzara, Ball and Hülsenbeck, his earliest polychrome reliefs, created in 1917, already marked him out as the astonishing creator of plastic forms who would be henceforth as much inventor as painter.

III

BETWEEN THE WARS
THE PERIOD OF RELAXATION AND DISILLUSIONMENT
1918-1939

While we must admit that the sectarianism of many of the defenders of abstraction has helped to reinforce an attitude of mistrust towards the between-war period, the severity with which it has been judged is not excessive. This is not just a question of fashion; it is a question of demanding the truly creative spirit to which our age has accustomed us.

It is true that the enormous vitality of the time before the war and its accumlated riches necessarily tended to dominate and overwhelm the period which followed. But this, instead of trying to put such a powerful aid to good use, insisted on either blindly neglecting it, or in trying to turn it from its real direction. Much windy eloquence was used, or misused, to show that Cubism and Abstract Art were finished, and, with the help of nationalism and later of political passion, to turn them into dangerous bugbears. Enticing promises were made of a return to Classicism, under the aegis of a new academism which no longer dared to show itself openly, and which disguised itself misleadingly as modernism. There were many temptations for the young and many backslidings by their elders, nearly all of whom had the excuse of a desire to forget the terrors of a war whose full weight they had borne. And, too, the war had, directly or indirectly, made many gaps in the ranks of the new generation. We know the names of the vanguard: La Fresnaye, Boccioni, Duchamp-Villon, Macke, Marc, Wouters, etc., but the bulk of these losses must remain unknown.

How much wastage of talent, how much ill-informed praise, how many false illusions there were! Exhibitions and facilities were offered to any comer, art became a dreadful Bartholomew Fair; and retains this aspect to our own day.

Allowed no rest by successive political crises, artists suffered still further collective frenzies, until, towards 1930, these were brought to an end by the economic crisis. « After-the-party blues », as Basler called them, gave several important painters the opportunity to regather their powers after too easy a plunge into relaxation. Under their influence both young and older artists saw the task more clearly.

If the convulsions of an anxious and divided Europe spread to the whole world, certain countries succeeded in escaping, at least partly, like Mexico, and the United States began to benefit from the arrival of painters from abroad. Thus, in the last years before the Second World War, modern art began to take up a stabler position almost everywhere.

THE AFTERMATH OF EXPRESSIONISM. - Among the new artists who were most successful in Paris between 1920 and 1925, three distinct groups appeared.

There were those painters of the so-called *École de Paris*, who became regarded as good investments, just as Utrillo had previously done, at the end of the war. These included Modigliani, dead on the very eve of

GIORGIO DE CHIRICO *Italy* The Jewish Angel or The Two Sisters 1916
Collection Roland Penrose, London

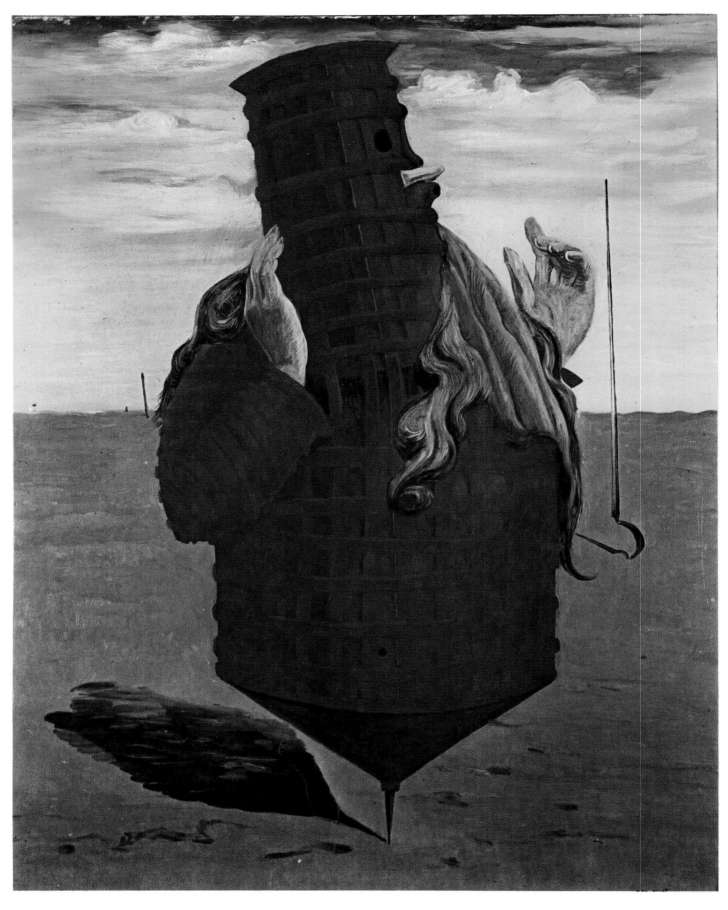

MAX ERNST *Germany, France, U.S.A.* Ubu Imperator 1923 Coll. Mr. and Mrs. Claude Hersent, Medon, France

ANDRÉ MASSON *France* The Battle of the Insects 1934
Coll. Pierre Matisse Gallery, New York

RENÉ MAGRITTE *Belgium* The Healer 1937 Coll. Urvater, Brussels

FRANCIS PICABIA *Spain*, *France* Hera 1928
Collection Gaston Kahn, Paris

Yves Tanguy *France, U.S.A.* The Blue Sea 1950
A. Mazzotta Collection, Milan

MARC CHAGALL *Russia, France* The Artist and His Model 1949
The National Gallery of Canada, Ottawa

WILFREDO LAM *Cuba* The Jungle 1943
Museum of Modern Art, New York

104

success, Soutine (Barnes bought a hundred pictures by him at the end of 1923), Kisling and Pascin, and also, by 1922, Chagall, from whom Vollard was soon commissioning illustrations.

They had all been friends and former companions in misery at the *Ruche*, and their styles and personalities were pretty well matured. By instinct Expressionist, by nature uneasy and tormented, often leading vagabond existences, they had, during their long years in Paris, felt the influence of contemporary experiment without always wanting to.

Chagall, with a subtle colouristic gift, was Cubist and almost abstract before the war. He returned from Russia more enchanted than ever with his own visionary and poetic gift. Henceforth he used its magic over and over again on the same themes, the same memories, and created again and again his delightfully childish fantasies and his tragic enchantments.

Modigliani learnt the directness and suggestive force of his line from Cubism as much as from sculpture. With inborn skill he used it to create fragile and pathetic transformations of reality. These, with the subtle, nostalgic tones of his surfaces went to make the somewhat affected, almost mannered harmony of his strange hieratic figures. These hid, beneath a tender reserve, his weight of introversion.

Younger, and painfully shut in upon himself, Soutine gave himself up to fire within him and made of painting a deliverance. A tachist before tachism was invented, but infinitely more sincere, his colour, even his use of paint, were the direct expression of the human warmth for which he felt a need, and which he unburdened more peacefully just before he died.

More dispersed, but sometimes forming ephemeral groups, such as the *Jeune Peinture Française* was the generation which the war had for so long monopolised and baulked of its hopes, just as its first successes were being gained. These artists, with their appetite for living, many with haunting memories of the war, some

MAX ERNST *Germany, France, U.S.A.* The Field of Honor 1952
Pencil, Illustration from « *Histoire Naturelle* »

ALBERTO SAVINIO *Italy* Self-portrait
Watercolour, Museum of Modern Art, Turin

SALVADOR DALI *Spain, U.S.A.* Living Still Life 1956 Coll. Reynolds Morse Foundation

having shared the teaching of Le Fauconnier in the distant days of the *Palette* art-school, at first embraced an apparent expressionism which was praised, sometimes with exaggeration, in the Press. But most soon gave up these borrowings, just as they hastened to abandon a constructive discipline which rarely went very deep. Urged by the critics to go in search of some kind of French tradition, they made plain their hostility to anything which might look like a theory; the Cubist mixture, brought into fashion by the *Exposition Internationale des Arts Décoratifs*, gave them good reason for their scepticism. Thus limiting their ambitions, they rediscovered with delight a quiet realism which they had never really wished to shake off, and dressed it up as « modern » by using a certain freedom of touch.

Few of them escaped the tranquil conformism which lies at the very heart of the period. And of all those who were so much praised, how many are still known to-day?

Of those who belonged to the group of friends called the *Bande Noir*: Boussingault, Luc Albert Moreau, Dunoyer de Segonzac and Dufresne, only the two latter have managed to keep a personal and vigorous accent in their work, the first by mastery of line, the second by his decorative sense and fresh lyricism of colour.

Among those who are already dead, Loutreuil had an undeniable feeling for humanity and La Patellière a poetic spirit of concentration. The rest have remained faithful, like Yves Alix and Waroquier, to a rigorous and sometimes rather strained style. Georg Grosz, because of the haunted feeling contained in his engravings and still more in his paintings, was the only one who for long merited the label « expressionist ». To-day he finds himself pleased to rediscover a certain sweetness in life.

Gromaire, who was linked both by age and by friendship to all this group, was for long condemned, despite his incessant protests, to appear in exhibitions and in textbooks as a representative of Expressionism. His slow but sure development, his flowering into maturity, are now removing the misunderstanding to which his early pictures, with their harsh distortions, might have given rise.

In fact, like Gondouin, whose shining promise was cut short by death, Gromaire is solely indebted to Cubism, and now draws from it a monumental synthesis where the rhythm of colour is combined with a powerful and well-thought out schematisation which puts him among the first rank of contemporary artists. A third group too achieved official recognition and soon attracted, sometimes to the detriment of those previously mentioned, the flattering notice both of the press and of official bodies. These were young artists newly-hatched from the schools and detached from events. They cared little about expressionism or aesthetic theories, and were often simply eager to pick up some fashionable tricks, and to achieve a place in the sun and make the most of what the period had to offer them.

ANDRÉ MASSON *France* Two Women. Study 1950
Private Collection

FERNAND LÉGER *France* Still Life with Butterflies 1951
Coll. Mr. and Mrs. Charles Zadok, New York

LUCIEN COUTAUD *France* The Seashore at Cheval de Brique 1955 Private Collection, Paris

BALTHUS *France* Saint André du Commerce, Detail 1952-4 Collection C. Hersent

GEORGES ROUAULT *France* Design for a Pottery Plate.
Gouache. Coll. Hahnloser, Bern

◁ FRANCIS GRUBER *France* Spring
Lundberg Collection, Tessin Institute

And what remains to-day? The best of those who comprised that small group of friends, recently christened «Poetic Painters of Reality». They followed the example of the Nabis in their attitudes as in their art, and kept their heads and their balance. With well-trained ease, they isolated themselves in the analysis of the power of colour. Among them were: Brianchon, remaining faithful to a musical sense of harmony and of subtle nuance, Legueult, with his remarkable gift for a free and joyous chromaticism, Oudot and Terechkovitch, withdrawn into an idyllic dream-world. Somewhat apart from this group, and tending towards a more immediate interpretation of reality, were Planson and Limouse, with their love of light, and especially Caillard, with his direct, profound sensibility. There were others, too, among those who joined up with the group later on: Chapelain-Midy, the prisoner of his own virtuosity, Aujame, with tendency towards a restless lyricism, Breuillaud, who has now achieved the freedom of abstraction.

And what is there left of Flemish Expressionism, so loudly hailed by the Belgian press when it made its first appearance at the *Sélection* Gallery in 1920 – a gallery which came for a time to enliven the local scene.

This small group of artists, which dispersed a few years later, certainly owed as much to Laethem-Saint-Martin, who formed them before the war, and to the almost mystical spirit preached by the poet van de Woestijne, who called for a return to a primitive communion with nature and the essence of things, as to a sincere need for revolt or a desire for the sort of plastic experience which was sometimes too readily attributed to them. Van den Berghe for a short while, Gustave de Smet with a melancholic *finesse*, and also his brother Léon,

RENATO GUTTUSO *Italy* People on the Street
Watercolour, Museum of Modern Art, Turin

GEORGES ROHNER *France* The Potatoe Pickers
Museum of Modern Art, Paris

and above all Permeke, did recover the feeling for popular imagery, and a strong simple language with rough, simplified handling and curt accents of colour. Moved by his own temperament, Permeke exploited this tirelessly and often knew how to draw from it a feeling of virility and of true human grandeur.

Things went quite otherwise with the Expressionism which was reborn amid the tragic chaos of the Germany of 1918. The feeling of rebellion which inspired this could not be doubted. But these vehement protests, which were already moving, in the work of Grosz and his friends, towards a destructive and subversive dadaism, had no concern with plastic problems or choice of means; with the foundation of the *Novembergruppe* they were already aiming at an art of propaganda.

In the end, while Otto Dix reverted to a cold, bitter realism, Grosz partly escaped this through his personal

116   JULIUS PASCIN *Bulgaria, France* Study of a Nude Pencil, Gallery Jourdain, Paris

CHAIM SOUTINE *Russia, France* Woman in Pink 1922 Petit Palais Museum, Paris

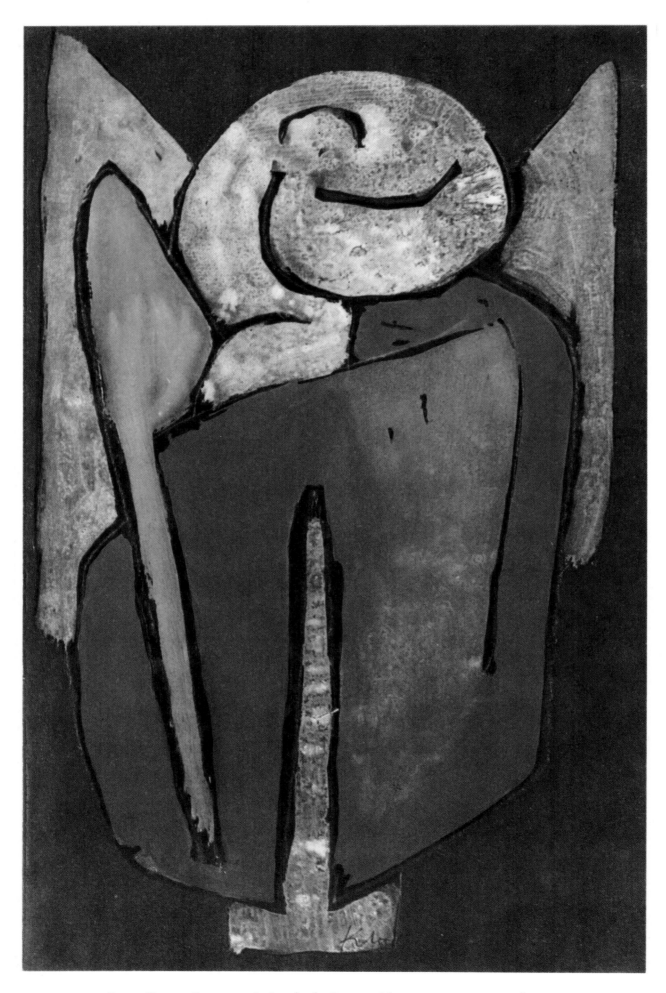

PAUL KLEE *Germany, Switzerland* Composition 1935 Private Collection

MARC CHAGALL *Russia, France* Mexico 1942 Baltimore Museum of Art, Cone Collection

JOHN MARIN *U.S.A.* Brooklyn Bridge 1932
Whitney Museum of Art, New York

KURT SCHWITTERS *Germany* October 1918
A. Mazzotta Collection, Milan

MARCEL GROMAIRE *France* Nude 1927 Stiebel Gallery, Paris

JACQUES VILLON *France* Man Reading a Paper Private Collection, Paris

MARSDEN HARTLEY *U.S.A.* Tropical Phantasy 1935
Collection Mr. and Mrs. William Lee McKim, Palm Beach, Florida

GEORGE L. K. MORRIS *U.S.A.* Fugitive 1956 Alan Gallery, New York

BEN NICHOLSON *England* Still Life on a Table 1947
City Art Gallery, Aberdeen, England

126

Robert Motherwell *U.S.A.* In the Sun 1946 Coll. Mr. and Mrs. William Lee McKim, Palm Beach, Florida

Jean Dubuffet *France* Two Mechanists 1944
Coll. Mr. and Mrs. William Lee McKim, Palm Beach, Florida

128

handling of line, through his talent for satire and a taste for the fantastic which was sometimes coloured with romanticism after his arrival in the United States.

Beckmann alone, who owed his formation to Corinth and who, by 1912, was already under the influence of Munch, continued to carry within himself, throughout all his wanderings, and right up to the time of his death in New York, an oppressive nightmare. This he often depicted objectively and cruelly, with a feeling for powerful structure, more highly coloured violence, and for nervous, energetic simplification.

The Expressionist revival crossed the frontiers and implanted itself almost everywhere, though under slightly different forms: in Holland with Wiegers influenced by Kirchner with the sturdy harmonies of Sluyters and the highly visionnary art of Kruyder; in Italy with Scipione; in Switzerland with Auberjonois, and Gubler; in Luxembourg with the vigorous Kutter; later in Jugoslavia with Peter Lubarda; in Austria with Boeckl; in England with Roberts while in Turkey Cevat Derelli advocated a certain moderation and in Japan Umehara recalled the oriental tradition. Across the Atlantic, at the same moment, an authoritative synthesis of Expressionism and the constructive principles of Cubism was being elaborated, and was becoming a monumental art in scale with the American continent.

The Mexican school took its beginnings from the Manifesto of Revolutionary Art published in 1921, and profited both from exceptional political circumstances and from the return to Mexico of several artists till then in exile. Among them were Rivéra, Siqueiros and Orozco-Romero, from Europe, and Orozco from the United States. They were joined by the Mexican Xavier Guerrero, by Carlos Merida from Guatemala, and by Jean Charlot from France.

That same year Diégo Rivéra undertook a huge fresco at the National Preparatory School, together with

FERNAND LÉGER *France* Cyclists 1944
Chinese Ink, Gallery Louis Carré, Paris

CHRISTIAN CAILLARD *France* Mexican Landscape, 1948
Museum of Modern Art, Paris

the whole group who soon constituted a syndicate. After this, thanks to the constant support of various governments, mural paintings continued to multiply in all the public buildings of Mexico and the provinces; more recently still, frescoes and mosaics cover, quite literally, the buildings of University City.

The movement soon achieved such prestige that first Orozco, from 1927 to 1934, and then Rivéra from 1930 to 1934, were summoned to the United States to execute important commissions for mural paintings. Siqueiros worked in the Argentine, in Uruguay, and especially in Chile. The fact that this movement associated itself, often with too great an insistence, with political considerations responsive to the propagandist objectives which were its aim, should not cause us to forget how closely its character was linked to the country itself.

Sometimes, in order to assume its popular role, it turns too much to monotonous preaching. But « European criticism », often with an axe to grind, has not done well to reproach it with its taste for the excessive, for its apparently unnecessary extremism and its almost caricatured violence, when these are in fact due to an instinctive Expressionism married to the Baroque.

It is only when one sees them in their setting, that one understands the powerful energy which animates these frescoes, and the breadth of view and imaginative fertility which presided at their creation.

There are few of these works which fail to respect their surroundings, and which do not impose by their air of grandeur. This applies as much to Rivéra, despite his innumberable figures, ordered by a sure orchestration of colours, as to Orozco, despite his fiery dynamism and his fanatical instinct for violence. It was the role of Tamayo, despite prolonged opposition, to show that a more complete synthesis might yet be achieved.

He associates an exciting plasticism, founded on rich tonalities, with an inspiration which owes nothing to politics and which is drawn from truly ancestral sources. In 1943, in his earliest mural paintings, he gave proof of a talent fully confirmed to-day. The vitality of the School of Mexico, founded upon its own originality is now to be seen in the precocious talent of Cuevas.

Under the pretence of following the example shown by Mexico, many artists from South America and the United States have usually succeeded in producing work of the most banal realism.

In Brasil, however, Portinari, leaving behind the first impulse given to him by Segall and Di Cavalcanti, has achieved a brilliantly coloured epic style, and has been able, benefiting from the extraordinary architectural flowering in the country, to show his skill in numerous commissions for murals. Ecuador fo lowed the same path a little later with the taut line of Maria Zaldumbide de Denis, the authoritative touch of Kingman, and more directly still with the feverish creations of Guyasamin with their dramatic contrasts.

DADAISM AND SURREALISM. – Dadaism, which sprang from a subversive spirit of negation, and was born of the agony of the war, took little interest in painting, with the exception of the solitary exhibition in Zurich in 1917.

Besides Arp, Marcel Duchamp and Picabia, it especially brought to notice artists who were in the process of renewing the means of expression offered by collage – such as Max Ernst, and especially Schwitters, who even raised collage to the status of principle of monumental construction with his *Merzbau*, those extraordinary assemblages of heterogenous objects which he assembled with rare visual sensibility.

Dadaism, despite its almost exclusively literary orientation, and despite its rapid decline after the regrouping which took place in Paris in 1919, still had the time, thanks to the very personalities of its founders, to breathe into artistic life that feeling for invention and that taste for total liberty which, after so short a time, our own age now seems to delight in rediscovering.

On the other hand, Dadaism's heir, Surrealism (whose first manifesto of 1924 was the work of poets and writers) did not wait long before, under the influence of André Breton, it took an interest in painting. In 1925, the first exhibition of surrealist painting was organised, showing the work of Arp, Chirico, Ernst, Klée, Masson, Miro, Picasso, Man Ray and Roy. The next year the *Galerie Surréaliste* was opened. The movement, despite internal dissensions spread to all countries and exercised a fascination over the restless young.

The two important international exhibitions which were held, one in London in 1936, and the other in Paris in 1938, then had the appearance of an apotheosis closely preceeding a funeral.

And, after a war whose horrors had exceeded those of which the most morbid artistic imagination seemed capable, Surrealism seemed definitely doomed. Nevertheless, the exile of its principal exponents to the United States and Mexico, gave it new life and an influence over young artists.

If the International Exhibition of 1947 in Paris marked above all its degradation, it could still, shortly afterwards, accredit Hantaï, and, not without reason, claim credit for much of « Tachism » and other recent techniques of abstraction which had borrowed from it and which visibly showed its influence.

The exceptional longevity of the movement; was due first of all to the authoritarian personality of André Breton, and to the fact that Surrealism was more concerned with a general idea, an advertised desire for non-conformity, than with the simple rejection of appearances in favour of the irrational and the subconscious. If the use of psychic automatism and systematic obfuscation renewed the springs of the imagination, and helped to rescue both fantasy and the feeling for inventiveness from any restraints, the means could not also coincide with the very nature of painting. From which arose the constant ambiguity in the choice of artists by Bréton, and the exclusions which he announced, and also the manifest desire felt by him and his associates to persevere in the work of demolition which led to « Anti-Art ».

The success gained was to be so complete that, through the bias towards surrealism, both conventional realism and *rompe l'oeil* painting recovered, alas!, their lustre and prestige. This perhaps explains why, despite so much clever drum-beating, the results achieved were in the end so disappointing that we must search among those who have escaped Surrealism's too-burdensome influence, rather than among all those beneath its aegis, for the few rare artists who have truly served its cause and that of modern painting.

We prefer not the honesty of Pierre Roy, or Dali with his erotico-obsessional machinery set off by undeniable technical virtuosity, or Tanguy soon imprisoned in his oneiric universe and lunar cosmos, with its spell-binding seething of larva, or the Belgian Surrealists, Delvaux and Magritte, careful and scrupulous craftsmen of the exploitation of the dream-world and its poetic confrontations, but those artists who give painting itself priority over strangeness of imagery: Masson, Miro, Max Ernest. Surrealism itself very rightly gave them prominence from its beginnings and put them forward as examples.

In an apparent orgy of line, in an interlace of sensuous curves feverishly scattered over the whole canvas, Masson seems to paint to deliver himself quite spontaneously of a poetic universe which he carries within himself. But this cursive, hasty language, which borrows from automatic writing, trembles with intense life. It is always animated by a subtle swarm of coloured forms, as in a melodic dream. Here we undeniably have the work of a painter of undeniable gifts, who knows how to control and organise the lyric outpouring which he allows to unfold itself in the full light of his pictures.

Miro is not less lucid and impulsive in his ever new deployment of poetic forms, and adds an elegant fantasy beneath which he conceals, as a Spaniard should, a hidden gravity. The strange gathered forms which he scatters over his empty sonorously coloured areas of colour, regain the accent of ancient totemic incantations and take on true magic powers.

Even more than Man Ray in his strange *montages* and photographs, Max Ernst showed an inexhaustible inventiveness in which irony and a feeling for drama each had their place, served by a mind which was eager to penetrate the complexity of modern life. In his rubbings and collages, and later in his paintings, Ernst was marked by his feeling for fantasy and the bizarre, and in them appeared elements whose confrontation was not due simply to chance, but also to a sophisticated instinct to confer on them a somewhat malefic aspect. His now fully achieved pictorial work mingles all spheres: the vegetable kingdom, the animal, the mineral and the human, and seems charged with a poignant and profound human resonance.

Of the generation of artists who made their appearance around 1933, and who exploited the same vein, Oscar Dominguez turned towards Picasso, while Kurt Seligmann and Oelze carefully, Wolfgang Paalen more swiftly, and especially Brauner (who had to moderate his taste for the outrageous), and Herold moved progressively towards a feeling for expressive form.

Lucien Coutaud, aided, like Labisse, by his feeling for decoration, stood apart from all groupings, and early began to create a disconcerting fairy-tale world in which strange vegetable silhouettes moved at their ease. Thanks to the support given him by the surrealists, the Cuban artist Wilfredo Lam first made his reputation in New York, though now he most frequently works in Paris. Lam evokes with rare incantatory power jungles peopled with menacing fetiches and phantoms. The Chilian Matta, poet of luminous efflorescences and anguished cosmic visions, has had a similar career.

From 1935 on, Surrealism established solidly-based official positions abroad, and these often took up attitudes of combat or protest. This was the case in Czechoslovakia with the group in which the moving spirits were Strysky and Toyen, and in Denmark with the *Konkretion* group which included Bjerke-Petersen, Carlsson,

MAURICE BRIANCHON *France* The National Guard Leaves Longchamps
Museum of Art, Algiers

RAYMOND LEGUEULT *France* Women on the Seashore 1956
Museum of Modern Art, Paris

ROLAND OUDOT *France* Nocturne
Private Collection

ANDRÉ MARCHAND *France* The « Arlésienne » 1945
Private Collection

C. TERECHKOWITCH
Russia, France
A Young Dancing Girl 1946
Museum of Modern Art, Paris

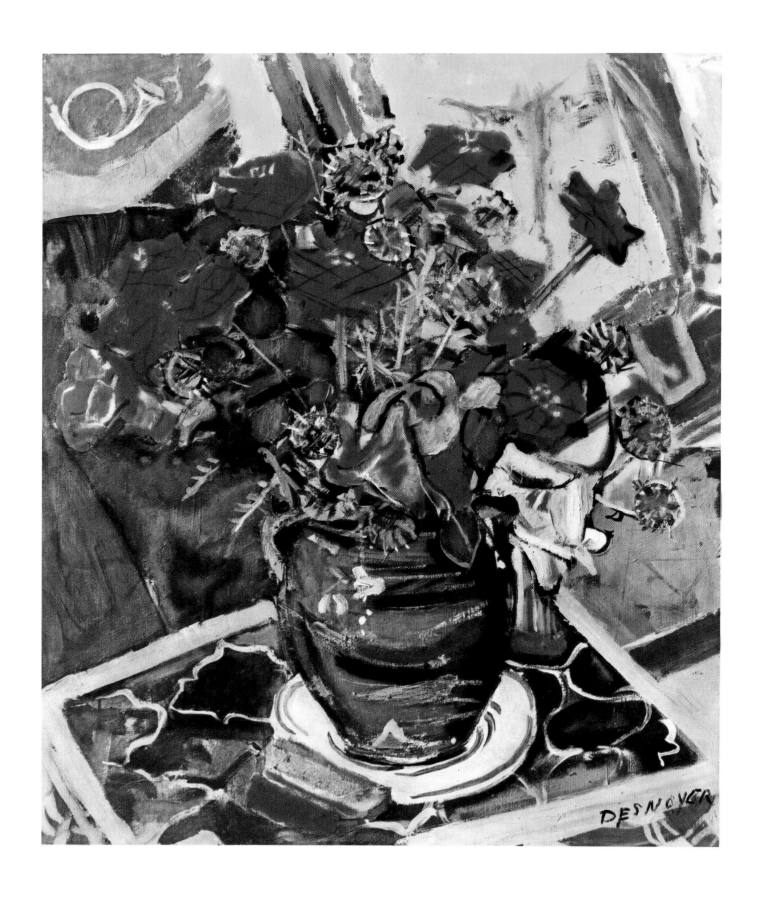

FRANÇOIS DESNOYER   *France*   Bouquet of Flowers   1956
Jonquet Collection, Paris

WILHELM NAY *Germany* Accord in Red and Blue 1955 Private Collection

ROBERT HUMBLOT *France* Still Life with Flowers 1959
Romanet Gallery, Paris

and, especially, Freddie who, after the war, with his aggressiveness little altered by events, was quick to bring new life to the movement, together with Arnell, K. Henning-Pedersen and Alfelt, and who helped the magnificent development of the *Imaginists* – Swanberg, Hultén, Kriland and Osterlin – in Sweden, where the famous Halmstadt group founded by Olsen in 1935 had rapidly declined.

In England, Penrose since 1936 firmly kept the surrealist traditions with Agar, Howard, Jennings, etc., which have since been brought back by Mesens, Banting and Melville.

In the United States, with the exception of artists who began the associates of the original Surrealists, such as Kay Sage and Dorothea Tanning, recruitment to the movement was more difficult, though it included Cornell, Onslow Ford etc., and, more recently, Copley and Kamrowski. But in the last few years there has been a resurgence of provocative dadaism with such young artists as Rauschenberg and Jasper Johns.

In the years immediately preceding the war, Japan in turn saw a flowering of Surrealism with Takimuti, Ichiro, Fukusawa, and Shitakumi, and even sent a few representatives to France – Susuki, Otsuka, and particularly Okamoto, a faithful Abstractionist. In Chile, the *Mandragora* group formed in 1938, with Arenas, Caceres and Kiesler; in the Argentine, Battle Planas initiated an action which still continues. Later, Finland with *Mäkilä*, Greece with Engonopoulos, Switzerland with Moeschlin, Australia, somewhat indirectly, with Drysdale and Nolan, Portugal after 1947 with Antonio Pedro, Azevedo and Vespeira, welcomed the Surrealist heritage. And Surrealism reappeared, as might have been expected, in yet more violent form, in those countries which had been weaned from it; in Germany it took on an often tragic aspect in the work of

MARCEL GROMAIRE *France* Study of a Nude 1951
Pen and Ink, Gallery Louis Carré, Paris

Jacques Villon *France* Still Life
Pen and Ink, Gallery Louis Carré. Paris

Ende, Zimmerman, Trokes, and Battke; in Austria it was often equipped with a kind of sarcastic humour in the painting of Hausner, Lehmden and Fuchs.

At the same times as the Surrealists, other artists were making advances into the realm of the imagination. These included Jean Lurçat in France. He, influenced by Cubism and by his time spent in Turkey, attained his full maturity, when he showed, during the last war, the full measure of his possibilities and renewed the art of tapestry, making of wool with a limited colour-range a full scale of expressiveness. There was also Sutherland, who achieved in England from 1938 a position of leadership, and revealed, with greater acuteness of form and colour than Paul Nash, a tormented, ravaged world, where nature was full of strange metamorphoses. This convention was also used, often aggressively by Francis Bacon in his curious figures and by the young Alan Reynolds in his landscapes.

In the United States, the little group of friends whom Breton had momentarily influenced during his stay in New York: Robert Motherwell, Arshile Gorky, de Kooning, etc., after 1945 soon returned to the road of Abstract Impressionism. Yet other artists, some years before the war, were inspired by the Surrealist gospel: some, like Peter Blume, to a quiet feeling for drama; some, like Aaron Bohrod, to unexpected invention; and some, like Kuniyoshi, to a feeling for the lyrical.

The painters of the so-called Social Protest group, formed around 1930, were marked yet more by Realist tendencies; these they prolonged with a kind of exacerbated imaginativeness. Painters like William Gropper, Jack Levine and Ben Shahn (formed by the School of Mexico and the best known of all of them) even had recourse to strongly anecdotic elements in order to give vigorous and eloquent expression to the striking loneliness of American life.

MAGIC REALISM. - As soon as the war was over, and even before, another movement had a great deal of success under different labels. It was called *Valori-Plastici* and began in Italy, where it was soon organised as a group, in 1922, under the name of *Novecento*; and was known as the New Objectivity in Germany, in 1927, and as the Regional Movement in the United States, and so forth.

The encouragement it received, both from the critics and later from certain governments, bore witness to the hopes it raised, which were only too often hostile to modernism, of bringing about what was called a return to order or to tradition. But, if it was helped and sustained by the spirit of reaction, Surrealism, too, must bear some of the responsibility, for, at the beginnings of both movements, we find the figure of Chirico. But this was already the post-war Chirico who, in company with Carrà who had also abandoned Futurism, was preaching a return to classic disciplines and methods as a means of attaining the eternal and the universal. In the pictures, men were replaced by lay-figures, and these were placed in interiors where the lines of perspective and the piling up of heterogenous objects effectively created a strange atmosphere. The purity of the forms and surfaces, and the richness of colour, recalled what the two artists had done in the past.

Completely removed from the propensity towards artificiality to be found in the artists of the *Valori-Plastici*, Morandi was to show that the humblest of familiar objects, when bathed in that tonal intimacy of which he had made himself master, were enough for true profundity of expression; and de Pisis discovered, and used sometimes to the point of abusing it, all the freshness of rapid, direct notation.

However, the idea made headway, and soon both Casorati the admirer of Piero della Francesca and Ubaldo Oppi were laying claim to Neo-Classicism. In the one case this was cloaked beneath a formal condensa-

ALBERTO MAGNELLI *Italy* Composition 1942
Pencil, Gallery de France, Paris

JACQUES DESPIERRE *France* The Seine at Rolleboise
Lithography, Gallery Marcel Guiot, Paris

MERLYN EVANS *England* Mask 1957 Chinese Ink, St. George's Gallery, London

ECHAURREN MATTA *Chile* Composition 1958 Private Collection, Paris

tion, in the other under popular or peasant themes. As soon as it was set up, *Novecento* became an official body, and introduced greater and greater Realism in the name of defending the modern. Among those who partly escaped this were Mario Sironi, through his dramatic force, and certain artists resident in Paris, such as Mario Tozzi and, especially, Campigli who joined a rich archaism to poetic invention and the use of popular themes. In turn, Soffici, restless of spirit, and an ex-Futurist, laid direct claim to a Neo-Realism transformed by a return to nature and the glorification of peasant life. This « recall to order », as he called it, was heard in neighbouring countries – in Poland by Malczewski, and also in Yugoslavia where the *Zemlja* (Earth) group was formed in 1928. The main interst of this group lies less in the work produced by Oton Postruznic, Franz Mihelic, etc., than in the setting up, through the agency of Krsto-Hegedusic, of the School of Peasant Painters at Hlebine which produced the authentic talent of the naif painter Ivan Generalic.

In Germany, too, Schlemmer, who was teaching at the Bauhaus, was indirectly responsible for the creation of the New Objectivity group, through his taste for human figures placed in severe and silent surroundings in which perspective made a discreet reappearance.

More than Grosz or Dix, who retained a need for dramatic tension, Georg Schrimpf personifies this tendency, for which the name Magic Realism, suggested by Franz Roh, is appropriate, because of the tranquillity of the figures, the feeling of emptiness surrounding them, and the severe character of the style in which they were painted.

In the United States, Hopper initiated the American Scene movement after the war, and evoked with insidious detachment the haunting melancholy of urban life, and Le Lorraine Albright from 1927 on was successful in imposing the grandiloquence of his virulently realist style. Meanwhile, a small group placed itself resolutely beneath the banner of Regionalism.

From their time in Paris, Wood, Curry and Benton wished to retain only the technique they had learned. Incited by the example of the Mexicans, whose work they sometimes imitated in their own frescoes, they decided to dedicate themselves to magnifying the image of their own country. If the two latter often lapsed into mere anecdote, Wood, who founded the artists' colony at Stone, preserved a primitive's purity of vision as he depicted the happy serenity of the local people and their occupations amidst the Iowa landscape.

148

South America was also drawn towards this orientation with equal enthusiasm. The Venezuelan Hector Poleo, to a greater degree than Argentinian Guido and the Mexican Ricardo-Martinez, became the best qualified and most gifted interpreter of it, using a supple and firm linear style, in which luminous harmonies were put in with a broad touch and where the figures were charged with a secret tension.

In France, the *Maitres de la Realité* exihbition of 1927, and the rediscovery of Georges de la Tour were certainly determing causes of the flowering, in the following year, of this tendency, which was supported by the *Forces Nouvelles* group. Essentially, this group consisted of three friends Humblot, Rohner and Jannot, together with Lasne (unfortunately lost in the war), Tal-Coat, who soon departed, and Venard, who only oined up with them provisionally in their last exhibition of 1941.

But these three were so much predisposed towards the tendency that all of them have continued to be more or less faithful to it right up to the present, preserving a taste for themes linked to nature and a predilection for forms concisely depicted with an austere palette.

THE FIRST SIGNS OF HEALTH. - While Russia, Germany, Italy, Spain, etc., were being turned into

GRAHAM SUTHERLAND *England* Sunset Between the Hills 1937
Coll. Sir Kenneth Clark, London

artistic deserts by politics, and while the rest of the world seemed to be urged by them to follow suit and deprive modern art of all it had gained, modernism was slowly regathering its forces in France and in the United States. These two countries became bastions of creative freedom and places of refuge for artists from all countries. Arp and Sophie Taeuber returned to France in 1926, and with van Doesburg, two years later, created the decorations for *L'Aubette* at Strasbourg.

In April 1930, the international exhibition of the *Circle and Square*, organised by Seuphor and Torrès-Garcia, brought together work by Mondrian, Arp, Baumeister, Kandinsky, Léger, Prampolini and Vantongerloo. This last founded, in the following year, together with Herbin, Béothy, etc., the *Abstraction-Création* group, and this soon had more than 400 members.

New artists began to confirm their talent or to make their first appearances, these included Beaudin, Suzanne Roger, Borès and Lapicque at the *Surindépendants*; Desnoyer at the *Temps Présent* Salon which was set up in 1935; Bissière at the *Académie Ranson*, where his evolution from 1936 on greatly influenced his students; and Walch, André Marchand, Despierre, Tailleux, Grüber, Pignon, Gischia, etc., at the *Salon des Jeunes Artistes* of 1937, or at the second *Salon de la Nouvelle Génération* in 1938 where Héraut suggested a search for a synthesis between Cubism and Surrealism under the aegis of Picasso. In 1938, the *Témoinage* group presented itself under the same banner at the *Galerie Breteau*. It had been formed previously in Lyons by Bertholle, Le Moal, Etienne Martin, etc. and was later joined by Manessier.

ROGER CHASTEL *France* At the Piano 1958
Pencil, Coll. Villand et Galanis, Paris

AFRO *Italy* Night Landscape 1953
Museum of Modern Art, Turin

The older ones among them acted as friendly guides to the younger, and as a link with the generation who had known fame for longer. Beaudin and Suzanne Roger were, like Borès, faithful disciples and friends of Gris, and continued as best they could according to their individual temperaments, the essential principles of Cubism which had to do with the construction of forms and with light. The first two worked towards sobriety, thoughtfulness and refinement of colour, the third was more dynamic and outgoing.

Desnoyer, who felt a natural attraction towards the chromatic richness and the expressive truculence of Fauvism, and Walch, with his instinctive *joie de vivre*, both took their inspiration from a deliberate schematisation. In the one this produced a living, powerful sense of construction, while the other was set free by it to give full rein to his sense of fantasy.

Bissière, arrived at a late maturity which had been hindered by many difficulties, gave up all contentiousness in order to spiritualise and refine his materials, and revealed, for a decade, the *plaint-chant* of his diapered colour schemes in which all reference to figuration had often disappeared. Fautrier was preparing in solitude his vigorous, brightly coloured textures, worked with a loaded brush and heralding, in his famous exhibition of 1945, the unleashing of Tachism.

PIERRE SOULAGES *France* Composition Charcoal, Gallery de France, Paris

Francisco Borès *Spain, France* Still Life in Blue 1951
Coll. Louis Carré Gallery, Paris

JEAN POUGNY *France* The White Armchair 1945
Coll. Louis Carré Gallery, Paris

154

CHARLES LAPICQUE *France* Lust 1949 Dotremont Collection, Brussels

MAURICE ESTÈVE *France* The Sculptor 1947 Private Collection, Paris

JACKSON POLLOCK *U.S.A.* Seven 1950
C. Cardazzo Collection, Venice

RUFINO TAMAYO *Mexico* The Civilisation Vanquishing Evil Forces 1957
Study for the Fresco of the United Nations Building in Paris
Museum of Art, Turin

WILLEM DE KOONING *U.S.A.*
◁ Portrait of a Woman 1960
Private Collection

GUSTAVE SINGIER *Belgium, France* On the Water In the Water II 1959
Collection Charles Laughton, U. S. A.

JEAN BAZAINE *France* Chicago 1953 ▷
Collection L. G. Clayeux, Paris

ANDRÉ LANSKOY
Russia, France
Atrocities of the Reds
1959
Coll. Louis Carré Gallery
Paris
◁

▷
MARIO CARLETTI *Italy*
The Church
"Madonna della Salute"
Venice 1960
Private Collection, Milan

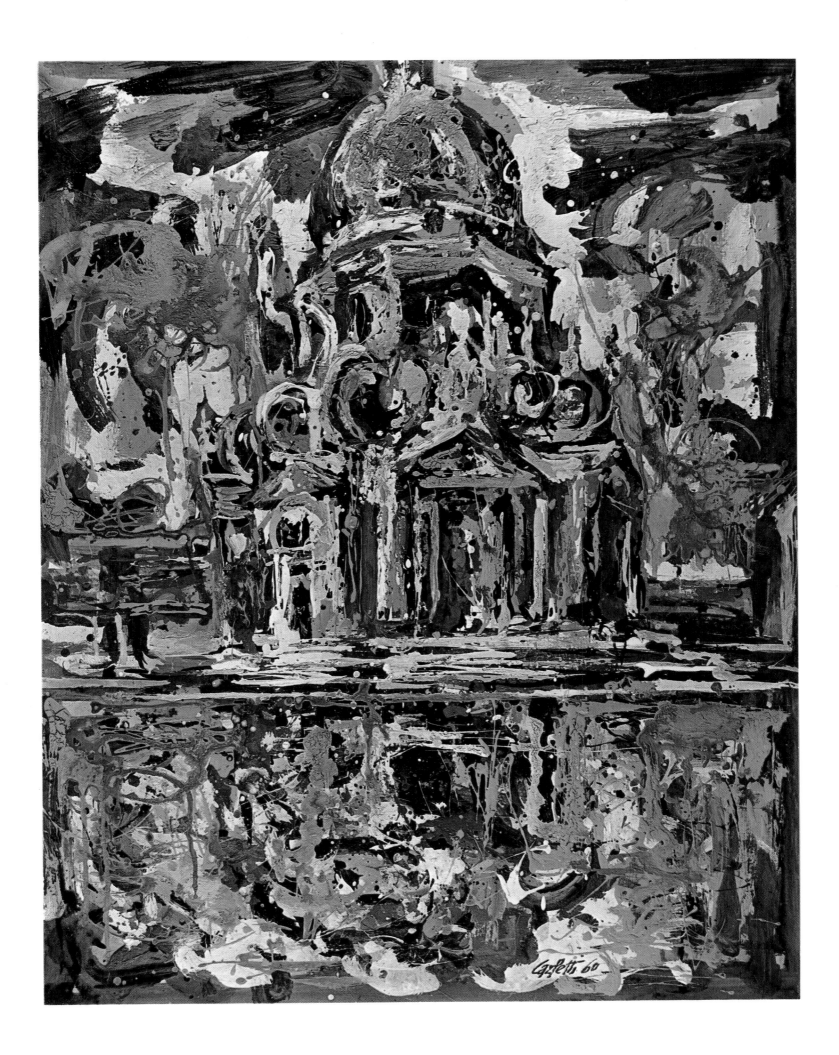

Bruno Cassinari *Italy* Night Fishing 1958
B. Grossetti Collection, Milan

164

During the years immediately preceding the war, several artists of already established talent embarked, to the great pleasure of the critics, upon the road to Realism, but for most of them this turned out to be merely a detour on the way to their own inner truth. Tailleux, and even more conspicuously Despierre, remained faithful to the teachings of Dufresne with an elegant, well constructed, harmoniously decorative style.

Tal-Coat, after some violences of expression, lightened and simplified his painting until now it retains only the faintest suggestive marks of the brush, in the best Chinese tradition. He thus embarked upon a personal manner which to-day possesses great authority.

André Marchand, and also Balthus, were, under the pressure of Surrealism and of events themselves, the inventors of a dreamlike Realism. For long their art was charged with tension and disquiet. With the one this preceded an absorption in the search for the greatest economy of means, in the other a move towards a lyricism of line and colour which has now led to an attachment to an intimately experienced Pantheism.

Gruber, with the stamp of genius already condemned to death, quickly marked out a personal, tormented, incisive, nervous style, which was at once passionate and torn, with tremendous persuasiveness in the subtle dissonances of its harmonies, and its splintered, piercing line. This line was to be used by many others after him, such as Carzou, who used it even before the war with a clever sense of the decorative, Minaux, and

GIORGIO MORANDI *Italy* Still Life 1952
Coll. A. Mazzotta, Milan

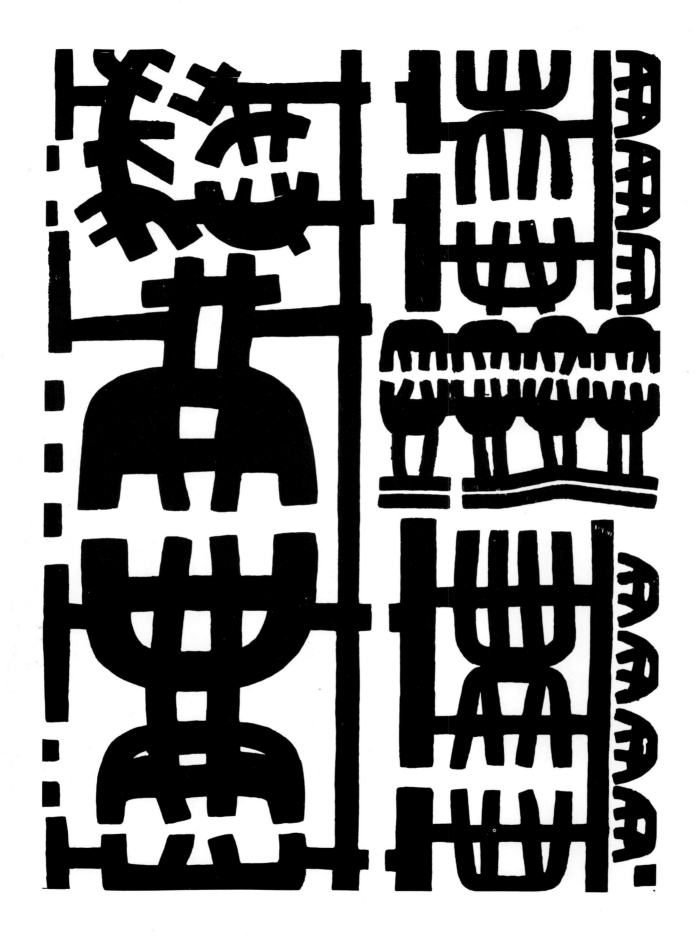

GIUSEPPE CAPOGROSSI *Italy* Surface 1951 Chinese Ink, Gallery of Art « Il Naviglio » Milan

NICOLAS DE STAËL *Russia, France* Landscape 1952
Coll. Mr. and Mrs. David Solinger, New York

Buffet who restored to it an apparent feeling of anguish in 1947, and used it thenceforth as the strict armature of an insistently schematised universe.

In Europe, Carlsund was vainly trying to introduce Abstraction into Sweden from 1931; Max Bill and Leo Leuppi with the group *Die Allianz* in Switzerland began to establish themselves after 1938.

In England, Ben Nicholson, who had been in contact from 1933 with *Abstraction-Création* and with Mondrian, created a brilliant personal formula, with refined simplication of both colour and form. This gives his work a noble purity and a diaphanous transparency. After the war, he attracted many young artists to him in St. Ives. In Israel Mordecai represented the tradition of the *Bauhaus*.

In Uruguay, where he returned in 1934, Torrès Garcia enriched his work with an inventive pictography, and his constant support for «Constructive Universalism» prepared a favourable reception for Abstraction in Brasil and the Argentine in recent years.

The United States was engaged, more resolutely than any other country, in the double defense of its own artists and of the art of the *avant garde*. Katherine Dreier, who in 1920 founded the *Société Anonyme* together with Marcel Duchamp and Man Ray, from 1926 on organised circulating exhibitions which included the work of Mondrian, Malevitch, Kandinsky, etc. The Gallatin Collection opened its doors in 1927, the Museum of Modern Art in 1929, the Whitney Museum of American Art in 1931. The *Society of American Abstract Art*, created by Morris, Boltowsky and their friends in 1936, brought together the work of such pioneers as Arthur G. Dove, Arthur B. Carles, Stella (who was a participant in the *Circle and Square*) and

JEAN DEYROLLE   *France*   Hiltrude 25-P
Gouache, Coll. Galerie de France, Paris

HANS HARTUNG *Germany, France* Painting T 50-5
Museum of Modern Art, Turin

also of other more recent converts such as Burgoyne and Diller, who were faithful disciples of Mondrian, George Cavaillon and Carl Holty, who owed their formation to Hans Hofman, and of the refugee artists, like Hofman himself, who came in ever greater numbers to swell the ranks and who included Josef Albers, Fritz Glarner, etc. The Museum of Non-Objective Painting, founded in 1937, and now known as the Guggenheim Museum became the Mecca of Abstract Art, and its collections were shown throughout the world.

IV

THE SECOND AGE OF MODERN ART
THE TRIUMPHAL ADHESION OF THE YOUNGER GENERATION
1941-1961

Through a surprising turn of events which showed how closely similar was the preparedness of spirit on both sides of the Atlantic, the entry upon the scene of the younger generation happened simultaneously in France and in the United States, and this generation showed in both places an assurance which forced it into notice despite particularly unfavourable circumstances and the tragic upheavels of politics.

In Paris, it was right in the midst of the Occupation that the group of *Jeunes Peintres de la Tradition Française* formed by Bazaine in 1941, and which included Manessier, Pignon, Estève, Lapicque, Le Moal, Singier, Gischia, etc., saw a sudden increase in its prestige due to various exhibitions, such as *Les Etapes du Nouvel Art Contemporain* and *Douzes peintres d'aujourd'hui* which I myself organised in 1941-42 and in 1943, or the *Dix peintres subjectifs* exhibition shown by Bernard Dorival in 1944. They also made their mark in successive *Salons d'Automne* and *des Indépendants*, and the movement culminated in the *Salon de Mai* which I founded with them at the Liberation.

At the same time, in New York in 1941, that Pollock had his first exhibition with Peggy Guggenheim, the Museum of Modern Art made known the work of Morris Graves in 1943 and 1944, and, at the Willard Gallery, Mark Tobey established his reputation and Motherwell had his earliest successes. These were all preludes to the flowering of American art in which Arshile Gorky and de Kooning played a part and obtained a world-wide audience.

The flow of artists from abroad come to seek refuge and the means to live in America, and which had already been going on for several years and had included Grosz, Hofman, Glarner, Berman, Tchelitchew, Feininger, Moholy-Nagy and Ozenfant, suddenly grew in volume after 1940. It was enriched by such eminent figures as Mondrian, Chagall, Léger, Lipchitz and Zadkine, and the Surrealist group complete with Dali, Max Ernst, Masson, Seligmann, Tanguy and André Breton. They made of New York the new Babel of the Arts, and conferred upon it, thanks to their intense activity in the United States and in Latin America, and through schools and universities, and numerous galleries, museums and para-official organisations, an

RAOUL UBAC *France* N. N. in Cameo
Chinese Ink, Private Collection, Basel

GERARD SCHNEIDER *France* Painting 65 B 1954
Private Collection

undeniable pre-eminence up to the moment of their return to Europe in 1946 or 1947.

After the war, there was a real crusade in favour of modern art throughout the world, and this was helped by the powerful means of information and propaganda available in our epoch: reproductions, films, magazines and publications devoted to artistic exchanges, and also by the prodigious extension of cultural exchanges: travelling exhibitions throughout the world, and huge assemblies of painting such as the Venice *Biennale*, the Sao Paulo *Biennale* set up in 1951 and the recent Paris exhibition devoted to the younger generation. This triumphal upsurge caused frontiers and barriers to be forgotten, as at the Brussels Exhibition. With its help the new generation of artists have succeeded in imposing their point of view, new national schools of painting are springing up everywhere, even in the most distant countries, and already established schools have witnessed a tremendous renaissance, as in Germany, Italy, Japan and Spain. Aesthetic conceptions and museums alike were renewed by the fountain of youth, and ceaselessly multiplied; the capitals of all continents were emulous and ingenious rivals when it came to helping and favouring the development of art.

It is true that all these endeavours, unprecedented until now, contain inevitable dangers due to the attraction exercised by fashion or by theory, to speculation or to hasty misjudgement, but this should not put what has been achieved in doubt. Their success has placed all artists under the banner of a common search for an international language at the service of all mankind.

171

THE RESORT TO INTELLECT. - By an unexpected paradox, it was the heavy constraints of wartime which led, in France, to a new grouping of young painters, and which hastened their maturity by demanding from them a clear knowledge of how they stood. Face to face with an occupant who was known for his contempt for spiritual values, artists had already enough experience behind them – for most were nearly 30 or even more than 30 – to have little difficulty in uniting and in reaching agreement on the essentials of the inheritance to be saved. It was less a matter of their opposing the course of events and of marking their opposition with tranquil courage, than, in the chaos of the moment, of finding the orientation which would help them to nourish and deepen their work.

After wise reflection, as the notes afterwards published by Jean Bazaine bore witness, they arrived at conclusions which had already been foreshadowed in all of them by their previous developments. It was a matter of urgency with them to return to the hey-day of modern art, to rediscover and assimilate the fundamental principles of Fauvism, Cubism and Abstraction, and to take up again from the beginning problems of space colour and construction after twenty years of neglect.

The conditions defined with magnificent rigour for literature by Camus in 1944, were equally applicable to the pictorial researches then taking place: « In place of taking every possible liberty – calculated insanity, automatic inspiration – from the uncertainties of the universe or of language, the artist conforms to an interior discipline. Self-domination, not anarchy, now springs from despair. There is no longer a tendency to deny reason to language and to leave it unbridled to disorder. Instead it is to recognise the power of language, to return, through absurdity or through the miraculous, to tradition. To put it another way, and this idea is essential to our epoch, the artist, from a philosophy of falsehood and non-significance, takes, no longer an apology for instinct, but an argument for the use of reason ».

As with Matisse, Villon and Delaunay, whose liberating efforts now found the best possible continuation, it is this conscious determination to restore the power of reason without giving way to mere transcription of the external world, which gives its value to the work of Manessier, Bazaine, Pignon, Estéve, and Lapicque, and to that of their companions of the same generation; and it is this which brings what they do into so close a relationship despite differences of temperament and in the means which they adopt. The degrees of legibility which in appearance mark them off from each other are unimportant, and only sectarianism would reproach them with this or use it to cast doubts on their sincerity. Unimportant, too, is the vibrant scattering and breaking up of colour which seem to link some of them with Impressionism, and which also has been made a cause of reproach. These are merely verbal quarrels which will soon seem as foolish and old-fashioned as those stupidly undertaken in order to make opponents, of abstraction and figuration. Excessive dogmatism can only lead to dangerous confusions. If Lapicque proposed in 1940 the solution of « a blue armature, sometimes figurative and sometimes abstract, allowing vistas of colour to appear... » as he himself describes it, this was as a result of mature thought on the subject of pictorial space and not an abstract enunciation of principles in the manner of those who, some years later, condemned themselves by prefering to empty their work of all emotive content in order to apply themselves to an elementary geometrisation of surfaces. The common effort produced a new non-realist language, which adamantly refused to confirm the fiats of Abstraction, but which sprang from hard thought about the possibility of an all-inclusive way of painting. However, the search for power of colour, for internal luminosity and powerful lines of force, as well as the need for an interior geometric of forms and for an enraptured lyrical transformation of the world, led most of the painters of the group to sheer away from too direct reference to the world of appearances.

It would be difficult to evaluate the individual contributions made. It is worth pointing out only that the two eldest, Lapicque and Bazaine, went forward the most boldly, the former by making intelligent inferences, the latter taking something from Gromaire through attentive and perceptive analysis, and that Gischia had for long been led, by his erudition and the rigourousness of his reasoning, to examine the problems of monumental architecture in painting, and that these three were sometimes able to influence the decisions of the rest of the group when it was formed in 1941. They achieved the adhesion of André Marchand, Tal-Coat

172

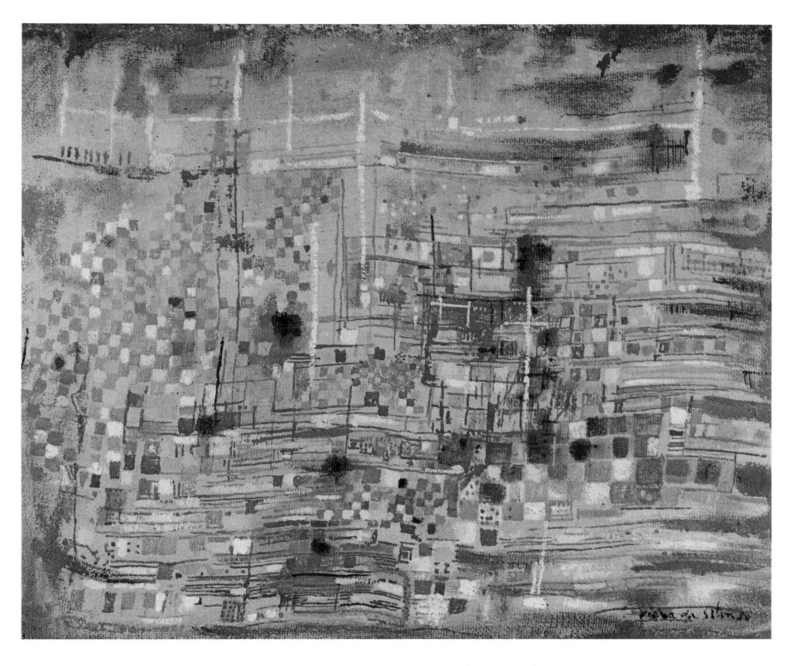

MARIA HELENE VIEIRA DA SYLVA *Portugal, France* Abstract
Coll. Mr. and Mrs. David Solinger, New York

and Gruber, and also, provisionally that of Robin, with his frank humility, and of Fougeron.
However, gradually, as the years have gone by, personal positions have become clearer, and the promise of certain artists, such as Bertholle or Le Moal, who had for long to struggle against circumstances, has been confirmed. Gischia now perseveres with formal simplification of great nobility, thanks to both its tension and is tonal sobriety; Lapicque confines himself to the exclusive exploration of movement and of colour laid on in opulent touches; but it is Bazaine who retains his position of leadership and who has even seen a notable increase in his influence of recent years. His painting, by means of extremely skilful chromatic complexity, and through the eddying fragmentation which he introduces into his canvasses in order to get a feeling of free, sometimes nervously syncopated pulsation, more and more offers a real communion with the world and thus defines itself as a style from which part of our age will hasten to profit.

173

JEAN LE MOAL *France* Composition 1958
Coll. Walstrom, Oslo

Bertholle, moved by his taste for the magical, and Le Moal, who has undergone a rich recent development, also convey this cosmic intuition in the fullness of its logic and human warmth. And Bryen and Ubac, and even Vulliamy, use it to free themselves at last from the *angst* which for so long held them prisoner to attraction of Surrealism, though the first preserved his animated sensibility, and the second his feeling of intimacy with his materials.

The patient and lucid rise of Manessier, who, like his companions, makes use of the example of Bissière, is certainly both revealing and exemplary of what it is possible to attain through this double exploration of the self and of the means of pictorial expression. His work is the image of the worth of our own generation. Manessier, guided by a sincere mysticism, achieves, through silent reflection and concentration, and without the least artifice, the spiritual vibration of colour and the majestic elevation which give his work its unique character, and its impression of radiance. This search, conducted with tremendous honesty and intelligence, for the sublimation of reality, makes him one of those rare artists who really achieve a kind of reincarnation of the universe, through a constantly renewed freshness of perception, and through a feeling of tenderness towards life, and sumptuosity of texture lovingly elaborated.

No less faithful to his own evolution, Pignon has continued, with absolute honesty, to maintain, and even to do his best to increase, the possibilities of contact with the external world. Deliberately as well as by temperament, he personifies with tremendous skill and with a feeling for monumental structure the new relationships which are being established between nature and man, and transcribes these in luxuriantly vital major rhythms, the powerful flow of which is reinforced both by the variety of the kinds of pictorial spaces he evokes and by the effective sobriety of his harmonies. Adopting similar attitudes, Burtin, Mouly and particularly Dayez, employ a measured style, with attractively restrained tones, whilst, among the painters of the younger generation, Rebeyrolle surrenders himself to the dominance of this vitality.

Standing somewhat apart, Estève also pursues, with remarkable and farsighted continuity, his attempt to achieve the maximum pictorial autonomy. Working by means of successive eliminations, he comes at length, thanks to a very personal feeling for the brushstroke, to a total fusion of colour and form which gives his work the supple and vigorous unity of a living organism. His begins with what he perceives through the senses, and, with outstanding intelligence, constructs a language of moving forms, with pure saturated tones which create light and space, and suggest to the spectator the sparkling fairyland of a universe of the mind affectionately and thoughtfully brought into being. Bolin, working with finely modulated planes, has in turn, tried to restore, quite directly, the outgoingness of colour-light.

Singier, who is the adherent of a yet more total pictorial autonomy, and an innovator by temperament, calls upon the resources of a well-informed and trained instinct in order to assemble, bring lightness to and vary his huge stretches of colour. His subtle taste gives them a calm intensity, both of form and space, which makes one think of limitless horizons where shine small and mysterious beacons.

Other artists attached to the group helped to give the *Salon de Mai*, at its creation, its original aspect. For example, Geer Van Velde, setting his own lofty and gentle serenity against the inventive, highly coloured tumult of his brother Brahm's work, offers the image of a world which is distilled, silent, dematerialised, and entirely recreated through the agency of a transparent spirituality which sounds the very depths of man's nature; Chastel and Vieira da Silva are equally poets of sublety and of the light within – Chastel boldly trans-

VICTOR VASARELY *Hungary, France* Sian II 1951-3
Coll. of the Artist

LEON GISCHIA *France* Face 1957 Gallery Villand and Galanis, Paris

SERGE POLIAKOFF *Russia, France* Painting 1960 Knoedler Gallery, Paris

CORNEILLE *Holland* Field Favourable for Birds 1960
Private Collection, Paris

FRANZ KLINE *U.S.A.* Cage I 1959 ▷
Coll. Mr. and Mrs. David Solinger, New York

Fritz Bultmann *U.S.A.* Leaves 1959 Coll. Mr. and Mrs. David Solinger, New York

MARIO PRASSINOS *Greece* Drawing 1958
Coll. Galerie de France, Paris

poses living forms, while Vieria da Silva bears us off into imaginary spaces where all the perspectives are linked and exaggerated into a psychological vertigo which still preserves the unity of the picture surface. Also to be met with in the Salon are Moisset (whose work is more anguished), Kolos-Vary, Anita de Caro, Szenès, Elvire Jean, Rouvre, Lombard and Lagage, all faithful to non-figuration and subtle harmonies. Also to be seen there on occasion are certain solitaries, such as Hillaireau, with his unpolished and sensitive receptivity, Pougny, whose tenderness expresses itself in melodious colour-harmonies, and Alberto Giacometti, who has recently been revealing in the nervous, multiple linework of his figures a true horror of the void. In the following generation, there are already many artists who have given the best possible proofs of maturity, and who have taken the same line, associating experiments into the means of pictorial expression with visual emotion before nature in order to achieve carefully constructed primitiva: from Prassinos with his impassioned lyricism to Dimitrenko who penetrates into the living reality of landscape, from Lagrange to Marzelle, both with a feeling for the rich rhythm of colour, from Cortot and Ravel, both in love with a certain preciosity, to Busse, with his tauter, more determined style, from Calmettes to Messagier, with his subtly evanescent forms, and from the affirmative style of Lesieur to Cottavoz's management of heavy impasto. Dufour and Lapoujade, who are openly abstract in reference, achieve, quite remarkably, a powerful appearance of sensual suggestion through their rich and skilful modulations.

As soon as hostilities were over, international artistic life awoke again, with an impatient curiosity which had grown during the years of isolation. Artistic exchanges took on an exceptional intensity. If the principal exhibitions were devoted to the great pioneers of modern art, and especially to Matisse and Picasso, the *Jeunes*

Peintres de la Tradition Française who were soon, thanks to the constant and vigilant support of Bernard Dorival, to be represented in the *Musée National d'Art Moderne*, took part in numerous travelling exhibitions organised by Francis Gobin under the name of *Action Artistique*, and put under the direction of Philippe Erlanger and Roger Seydoux. They thus quickly became known abroad despite the absence of specialised publications and the reserve shown towards their work in New York, and they thus influenced other capitals.

Friendly links were established with neighbouring countries, such as Belgium, Italy, Germany, England, etc. The *Salon de Mai* from its beginnings welcomed groups of foreign artists and was in turn asked to travel, even going as far as Japan.

In 1945, a representative group of works by Manessier, Pignon, Marchand, Tal-Coat, Singier, etc., was shown in the *Palais des Beaux Arts* at Brussels, and at the *Galerie Apollo* the *Jeune Peinture Belge*, whose principal participants were van Lint, Anne Bonnet and Bertrand, who had already been grouped together in the *Route Libre* in 1939, took a vigorous new impulse from their French neighbours of the same generation. Just as the French artists had, they turned more and more openly towards abstraction after 1950, without sacrificing any of their calculated vitality, their fullness of accomplishment or their fine sensibility. Luckily, they were followed by a whole group of younger artists: Burssens, Vandercam, Bulcke, and Dudant.

To begin with, things went the same way in Italy, but now seem to be taking a different course. In 1946 Birolli came to Paris and found there healthy influences to strengthen his generous power of expression and his constructive energy; he enriched, until his unfortunate death, the richness of his chromaticism. Birolli soon aroused the wish to follow the same course among those who had belonged with him to the *Corrente*

JEAN PIAUBERT *France* Gravel 1960
Coll. of the Artist

group before the war: Santomaso, Corpora, Morlotti, Vedova and Moreni. These artists formed in 1947 the *Fronte Nuovo delle Arti*, and this constituted, with the addition of Afro and Turcato, the *Group of 8* at the Venice Biennale of 1952. Lionello Venturi was justified in hailing with pleasure a certain spiritual relationship with their French contemporaries which sprang from their refusal of an imposed and total abstraction, their formal coherence and coherence of vision.

But, except for Cassinari, who continues in isolation a kind of poetic naturalism, most of them soon moved towards the informal, which had found its predestined climate across the Alps. Santomaso relinquished a way of painting filled with luminous reminiscences of nature in order to search for a way of seizing his perceptions as immediately as possible. Afro retained his typical refinement and his suggestive structure of colour and light in order to reflect his psychic emotion. Corpora abandoned his web of pure colours to seize more closely a cosmic imagination and to reveal, as Argan put it, « a cluster of intensities ». Vedova set free his aggressiveness and his unquiet lyricism in tumultous canvasses where broken blacks confront multicoloured rifts, and Moreni exalted his pantheistic outpouring.

Though they must be considered, together with Spazzapan, whose fiery lyricism is more directly abstract, and with Music who has discovered how to preserve a tender feeling for nature amid his spatial preoccupations, as among the most representative figures in current Italian art on a national or international scale, they did not rouse a favorable response among the younger generation of painters, who too readily allowed themselves to become weathercocks of fashion, as a result of the vain intellectual agitation, the frenzy for the *avant garde* and the experimental which has for some years taken root in Italy. Few artists – though these include Romiti, with his delicately serial efflorescences, Scanavino with his disquieting linear networks, and Dorazio with his monochrome spaces – have succeeded in surmounting the dadaist taste for scandal and provocation which inspires almost all artistic movements and excites them to over-large claims and to non-conformity, according to the usual formulas of « anti-painting »; thus, in the group called *Origins*, Burri is to be found adroitly manipulating metal and sacking in order to endow them with existential power; Fontana who was, in 1951, with Severelli and Crippa one of the founders of « Spatialism », makes holes in his canvases or stripes them with slashes; and there is the ferocious humour of Enrico Baj, the creator of the *Nuclear Movement*, and more recently the *Azimuthi* and *Miriorama* groups.

Artistic life revived slowly in a Germany devastated by Nazism and war, and experienced great difficulties in organising itself despite the geographic and political dismantling. However, some interesting German painting appeared in the *Salon de Mai* of 1950, and the review *Documents* was able, in 1951, to produce an important dossier on the active renaissance which had already come into being.

Apart from the rare artists of an older generation who had succeeded in surviving clandestinely, such as Baumeister and Bissier whom we shall return to on the question of calligraphic painting Buchheister charmed with precision and Theodore Werner the co-founder of *Zen 49* who tries to translate his philosophy of life into plastic terms and to reconcile his sense of the cosmic with his inner expression, it is a part of the generation contemporary with the *Jeunes Peintres Français*, who are beginning to confirm their reputation and to choose, under French inspiration, an often similar course to which they now hold authoritatively. Winter, one of the most gifted, recalls the lessons of the Bauhaus, and builds on sonorities appropriate to his forms and colours in order to conceive of his creation as a new birth of nature and to deploy the rhythmic power of his linework in order to evoke, as Haftmann puts it « diagrams of energy, fields of force, delicate crystalline shapes». Close to him are several members of the *Zen* group. Berke with his more violent lyricism, Trier with his expressive, arabesques, Fietz who sets up formal, mobile arrangements on subtly harmonious grounds, Thieler and also Fassbender who skillfully set out the explosive energy of their coloured forms, Fathwinder with his beautiful diapered textures, and, among the youngest, the dreamer Platscheck, who describes his vision in his book *New Figurations*.

Two other artists, somewhat isolated but none the less vigorous, show the same general tendencies: E. W. Nay, who was previously influenced by Kirchner, is now master of a special dynamism of planes and spatial organisation amidst a fullness of pure colour; Meistermann, religious and constructive in spirit, gives a hermetic direction to his creative work which, thanks to its intuitive richness, suggests another reality. The Nordic Countries are approaching France as an equal mecca for many artists who come to work there, in particular, the strongest group contain Andersen and Olsen, Perdur from Iceland, also Sigurdsson and Truggvadottir. The Norwegian Holt, the Swedes Bjorklund and Bergman, all attracted to abstraction by Nemes of Stockholm, teacher of the younger artists who were first drawn to surrealism. It would be presumptous to assign to French influence direct responsibility for the direction chosen in so many countries. The extraordinary upsurge of painting which appeared throughout the world after the war is still too near, too complex and too subject to incessant change for one to risk a complete summary. Nevertheless it is possible to see, among more or less corresponding generations, similar attitudes in favour of a fully elaborated art, built upon reflection and sensibility. Thus in Switzerland we find Rollier, with his

GEER VAN DE VELDE *Holland, France* Composition 1960
Collection of the Artist

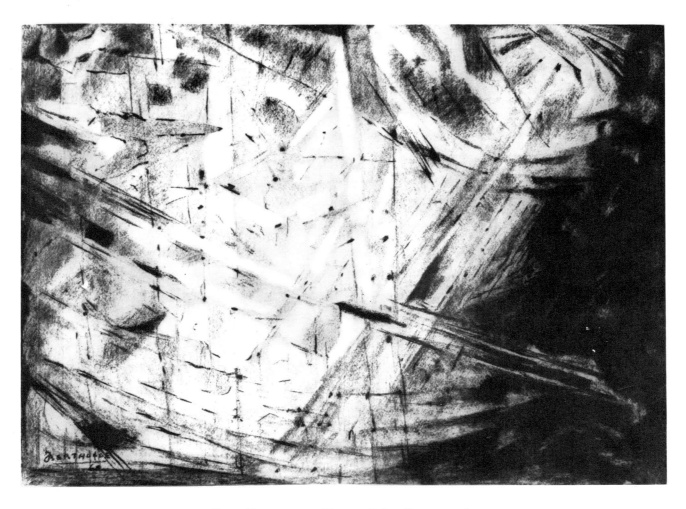

JEAN BERTHOLLE *France* Fairy Scene 1960
Gallery Jean Bouchet, Paris

fiery streaks of light, and Seiler, now a Parisian, with his natural schematisation; in Austria Weiler influenced Wickenburg by new richness of forms; for Portugal, Botelho with a synthetic lyricism, later followed by the excellent team of Vespeira, Azevedo, Ribeiro da Fonseca, once that they abandoned the spring board of surrealism; in England, besides Hayter with his long experience of print-making, there is Lanyon with his sure plastic invention, Hilton, with his luxuriant *matière*, and Bowen, Gear and Napper full of feeling and subtlety; in Australia there is Kemp and Miller, in Turkey Sabri Berkel and Aris Kaptan, in India Raza with their fondness for stylisation; in Yugoslavia there is Stane Kregar with his brilliant colour schemes and also the more intimist Stojan Celic, Miodrag Protic and Omcikous; in Poland there is Potworowski, in Finland Gösta Diehl, who is a little too symbolic, and Grönholm; in Greece there are Condopoulos, Moralis and Spiropoulos, and the very Parisian Israelis: Lan-Bar with his original architecture and Bella Brisel with an expert latent poetry.

For long isolated by the war, and having to live on their own resources, the artists of Latin America hastened to travel abroad, or looked out for the latest developments in the publications and manifestoes which reached them. The important travelling exhibition *Manet Till To-day* which I put together in 1949-50, arrived a little behind the times, when geometric abstraction was already, as in Paris, making fervent converts. Among the generation formed before the modern European spirit, part maintains its attitudes and its authority – in Cuba Amelia Pelaez with her masterly sense of construction, Venier in the Argentine, Danilo di Prete and Burle-Max, with his vigorous dynamism, in Brasil, Vicente Martin in Uruguay and so forth; other artists are turning deliberately towards a maturely studied transposition, such as Rendon with his fine sincerity or Kingman in Ecuador, the more voluble Portocarrero in Cuba, who calmly accepts an abstract style; the soberly refined Petorruti and Jonquières in the Argentine; the resolutely constructivist and geometric Dacosta, and Carreno with his sure audacity of line and Milian in Cuba, and Davila, with his natural feeling for composition, in Peru.

A whole group of young artists, whose talent, is to-day plainly recognised, early joined up with the preceding; frequently they had had the benefit of an adequate preparatory visit to Paris. Most of them have already boldly shown their wish to interpret the cosmic potentiality of the grandiose American nature, and to take advantage of the immediate expressive possibilities of the brush-stroke and of correspondence of tones. The new Venezuealan School is decisively pursuing this route, Hurtado with his ample rhythm, the more, spontaneous Jaimes, Guevara-Moreno with his sumptous harmonies, and above all Vigas with his extremely keen sensibility and profound feeling for spiritual needs. Very close to these ideas are Torrès-Aguero in the Argentine, Nieto and, in particular, Szyszlo (who is a powerful animator of coloured surfaces) in Peru; Villacis in Ecuador and Maria Luisa Pacheco in Bolivia prefer a rich *matière*; in Colombia Villegas shows a subtle poetry, and there are Enrique Grau and, with a firm attachment to figuration, Obregon with his supple monumental orchestration, the marked work of young Correa; in Cuba Consuegra and Camacho with their youthful imagination, in Chile Zanartu who has become, like Matta, a Parisian by adoption and creator of a living formal cosmogony; and finally in Brasil there is a whole group of painters with remarkable chromatic sensibility – the eloquent Inima de Paula, Loio Pérsio, Thereza Nicolao with her delicate nuances.

If many young artists from the United States came to live and work in France, few of them knew how to find a something quintessential in the Parisian atmosphere which favours restraint and finesse. John Koenig did it with great distinction, Buffie Johnson with a musical feeling, Chelimsky with a taking interior rhythm; Hultberg evoked a recreated world, Youngerman was more oriented towards geometry, Ronnie Elliott showed a gently flowering lyricism, and above all, there was Guston who clothed his colour in a precious luminosity and made it witness to an active personality. Sam Francis, adopted by Paris which soon gave his talent a prominent place, tenderly spreads his diapered network.

THE FLOWERING OF GEOMETRIC ABSTRACTION. - This new tendency, submerging the international artistic scene, knew an unprecedented vogue between 1949 and 1954, thanks to the ill-conditioned support given to it by the review *Art d'Aujourd'hui*, which spread its partisan tyranny to many countries.

On the return of peace, abstraction emerged from the shadows to which it had been banished by the Nazi occupier and began to arouse a lively interest in Paris which was confirmed by the setting up in 1946 of the *Salon des Réalités Nouvelles*. The Committee of this, with Fredo Sidès and Del Marle, maintained the severest possible orthodoxy and banished even the most inconsiderable references to reality. Galleries and critics everywhere rendered their homage to the pioneers who had recently vanished: Delaunay in 1941, Mondrian and Kandinsky in 1944, Freundlich who died as a deportee in 1943.

In 1945 Drouin organised the first exhibition of *Art Concret*, and Seuphor in 1949 assembled in his excellent and exhaustive book and in the important exhibitions held at the *Galerie Maeght*, the pioneers and survivors of the *Circle and Square* and of the *Abstraction-Creation* group. Several of these enjoyed success: Herbin whose long perseverance at length overcame circumstances and began to attract respect, Doméla with his pure rhythms inscribed with craftsmanlike ingenuousness in his picture-objects, and especially Magnelli who marked out with undeniable mastery a personal style – very distilled, with a lofty sobriety, with refined colour areas set by the dynamism of multicoloured lines.

Profiting from these favorable circumstances, a small group of artists, constituted at the opening of the *Galerie Denise René*, soon began to attract attention. As I emphasised in a pamphlet published by *Les Amis d'art*, entitled *For or Against Abstract Art*, the ambition of these artists was to turn to their own use all the heritage of the pre-war period and to incarnate the aspirations of the younger generation.

Arond Vasarely (who had been taught by Moholy-Nagy in Budapest), were Dewasne, Deyrolle and Pillet, and Mortensen. They wanted to make a synthesis between constructivism and Neo-Plasticism, seeking the integration of movement and form through spatial organisation of colour and rhythm, and by a logical ordering of the picture-surface.

The apparent simplicity of the solution they advocated, the spectacular successes which they achieved or inspired in creating these new relationships between architecture and colour in space, their frequent group exhibitions abroad, their exclusive dogmatism and peremptory statements of position, the teaching given by Dewasne and Pillet at the *Académie de l'Art Abstrait* between 1950 and 1952– all of these brought them a re-sounding notoriety, still further swelled by *Art d'Aujourhui* of which Pillet was in fact general secretary.

Vasarely's inexhaustibly inventiveness in animating spaces and multiplying them, and the rigorous contrasts which Mortensen extolled, attracted more followers than the quiet, sure poetry of Deyrolle, the effective subtlety of Marie Reymond or the sensitive and remarkable attempts made by Piaubert to maintain in his work a dialogue between forms and tones, or the intelligent experimentation of Lenormand and Idoux.

This order, responsive to the needs of plastic creation alone which they brought to painting, and the arro-gance of their crisp geometric shapes and bold, uniformly distributed colours, acted in fact as a salutary dis-cipline for many artists. To this it was at once easy and essential to submit. A sudden infatuation sprang up in France and throughout the world; a legion of zealots was enrolled – among already mature artists such as the Germans Ritschl and Vordemberge-Gildewart, who, like the Australian Balson the Portugese Neg-reiros, were admirers of Mondrian, as well as among younger painters, such as the Swede Baertling, the Dane Gadegaard, the Icelander Skulason, the Luxembourger Probst, the Dutchman Ongenae, the Belgian Delahaut (who, since 1956 has been, with the young artists Bury and Vandenbranden, one of the moving spirits in the *Forms* group), the Finn Carlstedt, the Cuban Arcay, the Canadian Leduc, the Americans Kelly and Breer, the Austrian Mikl, and the Yugoslav Picelj with the *Exat 51* group. Around Soldati and Reggiani, and the *Movimento Arte Concreta* founded in Italy in 1948, were grouped Mazzon, Monnet, Bor-doni, Nativi, etc. The movement organised in England after 1951, with Martin, Heath, Hill, etc., soon freed itself from obedience, thanks to the spirit of insularity, and Pasmore, following the example of Paul Vézelay, embarked on a personal style of great refinement, with moving inflections.

Latin America showed itself all the more receptive because of the architectural activity there; this often led to very successful immediate applications of the idea of a true integration of the arts, as witnessed by the work of Vasarely at Caracas City University, or that of the Venezuelans Alejandro Otero and Soto who conducted intelligent experiments with cinetic structures and the suggestion of movement in space, as did the Israeli Agam and the Swiss Tinguely. The period spent by Degand in Brasil led to the birth of an im-portant school with Flexor, Cicero Dias, Ivan Serpa, Carvão, Fiaminghi and Lima, almost all of whom were members of the *Concrete Art of Sao Paulo* group.

Colombia and the Argentine did not remain inactive, the former with Villamizar and Ramirez, the latter with Ocampo and Sarah Grillo with her agreeable finesse, Hlito, Kosice, and Maldonado who was to become professor at Ulm. Things went similarly in Buenos Aires where Arden Quin, before making his appearance in Paris, launched the *Madi* movement in 1946 and advocated works with irregular forms.

However, the apparent success of geometric abstraction in Paris was speedily checked, and the pretensions of its adherents miscarried because of their too-apparent desire to monopolise a heritage which were visibly larger than they were. In 1950, Charles Estienne, who till then had defended them, attacked their new con-formism in *Is Abstract Art a Form of Academism?* and thenceforth conducted an impassioned campaign against the preconceptions in favour of a cold plastic logic and a decorative formula borrowed from the most ele-mentary mathematical procedures.

But several artists linked to the group, or standing entirely apart from it, now received growing credit for their individualism. Like Charchoune in his naive and attractive illuminations, they had already for some time previously shown a talent for combining free geometrisation with an instinctive taste – which came to them from their Slav descent – for kneading and mixing their material till it made an appetising broth of colour. Their development was essentially founded on their temperaments: de Staël with his sometimes brilliant lyricism, and with the restless, generous ardour which at one moment led him to campaign against the Committee of the *Salon de Mai*, and with his tumultuous use of impasto which he succeeded in sublimating into an absolute purity of style, almost using a trowel to construct, lightly and lovingly, the areas of colour which were the outpouring of his inner tensions; Czobel, whose penetration of spirit still calls for greater attention, Poliakoff who shows immense virtuosity in balancing his rough brush-strokes against each other, Lanskoy, with his more studied elegance concealed beneath no less bravura, and with his skill in escaping from his own anxious impatience through a sensual, joyful outpouring.

FROM LACK OF FORM TO CALLIGRAPHIC PAINTING. – The growing opposition which showed itself in Parisian circles to geometric abstraction, opened up new roads in so many different directions that it is often difficult to define these with precision, so much do they overlap, and so great has the confusion now become.

The first to make their mark on history where the protagonists of *Formlessness* who were brought together by Tapié between 1951 and 1952, with the support of Estienne and the encouragement of André Breton, who quite rightly thought that this gave Dadaism and automatic writing an opportunity for returning to power. Did not Wols, with his organised delirium and his use of accident carefully elaborated in a strange, dense swarm of lines, achieve an enthusiastic reception with his big exhibition at Drouin's in 1947?

In the same gallery, repeated exhibitions by Dubuffet proved in the end that the unexpected content of *l'art Brut*, taken from graffiti and the productions of children or the insane, could serve the artist as a pretext for constantly renewed adventures in the exploration of visual possibilities.

Thanks to the support given him in Canada and the United States, the movement was not slow in growing, and received many names « Other Art », « Tachism », or « Lyric Abstraction » – according to the direction which each critic saw it as taking. It achieved a great international prestige, which has just begun to fade. It was also, during these same years, that the new American painting became known in the leading European countries: Italy, England and France in turn, and made its originality felt, especially that of Jackson Pollock, the representative of action painting. This latter made his debut in New York during the war, and by 1947 had passed the stage, still close to Gorky and de Kooning, of a use of heavy impasto in which he expressed his own emotional violence and transcended the influence of Picasso and Surrealism, the better to express directly his turbulent energy. It is of no consequence that the « drip » technique (allowing the paint to pour from a hole in the bottom of a tin) was suggested to him by Max Ernst, and has the appearance of a barbaric negation of all pictorial skills. It restored to gesture its exteriorising force and fitted Pollock's own expressive potential. It enabled him, with rare intuitive skill, to bring together in eloquent surfaces, according to Dewey's theory, his intense need for action and his immediate sensations.

But this improvisation, as the artist was soon to feel, carried within it its own condemnation, and was to become a fallacy and, in New York itself, a selfish regional academism. This has proved no obstacle to the imitators of the style, from Mathieu and Quentin in France to their numerous imitators in Germany, Italy and Japan. They continue their mimicry and their trances « of gesture ». Davie in England is more reserved, and contents himself with making use of this new freedom in order to express in brilliant colours his need for exuberance and vitality.

Also descended from Surrealism, as was shown by its name and by the manifesto *Global Refusal*, published shortly afterward by Borduas, was the Canadian *Automatism* group which made its appearance in Paris in 1947, and whose principal participants successfully integrated themselves with the capital's artistic life: Riopelle lives there at this very moment and Borduas did so for several years before his death. If intensity of the inner life is what one is looking for, both of these artists brought with them from Montreal a feeling for

JAIME LOPEZ CORREA *Columbia* Vendors 1957
Private Collection

ALFRED WICKENBURG *Austria* Gothic Variations 1957
Private Collection, Vienna

JANNIS MORALIS *Greece* Funeral Composition 1958 Private Collection, Athens

MORDECAI ARDON *Israel* Left Wing of the Triptych "For the Fallen" called "The Traps"
Stedelijk Museum, Amsterdam

illimitable space and for the forces of nature; Riopelle in particular expresses them with a precise sense of organisation, in the guise of eruptive violence of colour and light, in which the brushstroke itself participates with life-giving energy. The work of two other American artists was to find an even more favourable response in Europe because of positions currently being taken up. These were Gorky, who practised what has been called« Abstract Surrealism », and de Kooning, who works in the more general Abstract Expressionist manner.

Stimulated and directly helped by the Surrealist group during their sojourn in New York, Gorky gave way more and more to his cult of analogy and psychic reflexes. His tormented sensuality was thus able to exteriorise itself more and more in a strange world of volcanic, inorganic forms, in which unfamiliar harmonies concealed a hidden luminosity and a troubled feeling of metaphysical appeal which in the end led the painter to commit suicide. Also making use of a similar atmosphere of hallucination are Baziotes and Gottlieb, but they are too frequently content with elementary symbolic rituals.

De Kooning, if he was once tempted to explore these problems, has from 1948 on displayed his own violence of temperament, expressed, with somewhat too accomplished virtuosity, through unrestrained colour, through the allusive or abstract figures which dart and collide in his heavy *matière*, and in expressively powerful modelling emphasised with an ample, directly emotional and active brush-stroke. His splendid vehemence has brought him immediate authority over young painters in many countries, above all after his series entitled *Excavations* and *The Woman*, with their virulent expressionism. His technique of the whiplash line, his dynamic way of crushing the brush into the impasto and turning it « spoon-fashion » have gained followers, especially in Germany with K. O. Götz and Sonderborg.

But this expressionist renewal, carried through in France on an almost classic plane by Clavé, had long since presented its letters of credit in Europe, and these had already become patents of nobility. During the war, which trapped them in Copenhagen, the two Icelandic painters Gudnason and Skulason had, by the example they set, encouraged dissident members of the old *Konkretion* group, who now centred themselves upon the magazine *Hellestern*, to practice automatism without concealment, and to express with unrestrained colour and explosive form, « the complex violence of the war between the elements and between man and his elements », as one of them wrote.

Asger Jorn is the leader of this movement which, after 1945, took the name « Höst ». In 1948, he exhibited at the Galerie Breteau and played a part in the new magazine *Cobra* which, under the leadership of the poet Dotremont, did in 1951 bring together beneath the same banner the Dutchmen Appel, Corneille, Constant, and Rooskens, and the Belgian Alechinsky, almost all of whom were soon integrated into Parisian life and appeared in the *Salon de Mai*.

A tragic potential, near in spirit to the insensible lava-flow of Hasiasson, illuminates the work of Jorn, who often, like his compatriot and friend Egill Jacobsen, turns towards the mythical feeling in primitive Scandinavian art. But among the younger artists, this sort of painting, sprung from a total spontaneity, but displaying a sure mastery in the work of Corneille, in that of Lataster, who recently joined the group, and above all in that of Appel, whose canvasses are always loaded with a richly evocative *matière*, takes on the aspect of a frenetic need to possess the universe, with brilliant chromatic fanfares and angry dissonances.

It was after casting a glance at what was happening in Paris, where he had an exhibition in 1946, that Motherwell began to abandon the influence of Picasso and Matisse, and also that of the Surrealists which affected him during the war, and to look for a language which he conceived of as international and human in character. He created an interpretative synthesis which was calmer and more intellectualised, and in which formal signs occupied an important place.

In San Francisco, which was open to influences from the Far East, a parallel movement, wrongly called the School of the Pacific, was making its appearance. It, too, carried the marks of Hofmann's many years teaching in the United States – though he was less successful in applying his lessons to his own painting which is animated only by a healthy *joie de vivre*. Hofmann wanted to go beyond Expressionism and indeed the act of painting itself, in order to restore all its permanence to the human spirit by preserving only the most fundamental inflections and the energy of rhythmic necessity.

Still and Rothko taught till 1950 at the California School of Fine arts, where they inspired many young artists. This alone justifies the temporary existence of a School of the Pacific. Soon enough New York did acclaim their extremism, and arbitrarily promoted them to leadership of a trend in harmony with Far Eastern philosophies. Still formulated his spatial experience in great splashes of black, with patches filled with intense colour; the purifying asceticism of Rothko led, finally, to canvasses in which nothing appeared but simple, subtly harmonised bands of colour, in the manner of Max Bill.

These appeared as radical innovations and were described, in addition, as meditative exercises. All these qualities are now no longer attributed to them. Nevertheless Still and Rothko have imitators in many countries: Zack and Sima in France, Greis, Hoehme and the young Brüning in Germany, Mortier in Belgium, Manabu Mabe in Brasil, and the Japanese Yoshishigé, Saïto, Sugaï and the young Imaï. But it seems that in the United States there is a brighter future for those who, like Brooks, Stamos, Tworkov and Vicente, have preferred to work in more circumspect and disciplined fashion to enlarge the strictly pictorial possibilities of lyric abstraction, as Zaritsky has for long done, with a natural freedom, in Israel, and Kotik in Czechoslovakia. It is thus too that the new Spanish school - both the old Barcelona *Dau al Set* group with Ponc, Cuixart, and above all Tapies with his dramatic and incantatory power, and also the new Madrid *El Paso* group with the young painters Millarès, the very gifted Feito, Nieva, with his interest in the mineral, Saura and Canogar, etc. - must orient iself to survive the disproportionate triumphs accorded it. Thus it will succeed in escaping from the ambiguity of means which currently delights it - an ostentatious despair and a provocative dadaist rejection of the world.

Of the mythical School of the Pacific, which came into being at a period of excessive nationalism, there still remains Tobey, who lives in Seattle. He, with his forceful personality, would be sufficient in himself to lay the foundations for a real meeting of East and West. By going to the Orient, he has attempted to assimilate both aesthetics in order to make a spiritual synthesis. He was the pioneer, during the war, of the technique of «White Writings» - the calligraphy of white lines - a living and imaginative transposition of Chinese characters, and also of those dense networks of miniscule graffitti or filaments, with needle sharp pulsations, which he employed later and which secrete a silent and suggestive poetry of space.

Following Tobey's example, Tomlin reduced and refined his constructivist puzzles in order to knot his meshes into gentle melody. Even before Tobey achieved, in 1951, full recognition, Kline was bringing his own style to perfection. He in turn creates impressive calligraphies with lively tensions between the whites and the blacks, placed on a subtly worked ground. In the United States the junction was made between the dynamic exteriorisation of Expressionism and the calm concentration of thought characteristic of the Oriental tradition. This school is to-day typified by numerous painters: from Alcopley to Childs, and from Appleby to Don Fink. Without a tittle of influence from the art of the Far East - though this was to show itself later - an almost similar development was to be seen in Paris among certain artists who achieved success in the years 1947-1948: Hartung, Schneider and Atlan, soon to be joined by Soulages.

They define, each in his own way, the kingship of the sign - signs which are eloquent, heaped up, gashed out in black like an appeal from the depths of darkness. There is perhaps nothing romantic about them, but rather, an energetic affirmation in the face of the anguish of our times. In a way linked to existentialist ideas, they find no difficulty in blotting out the external world in order to discover what is truly essential and in order to bear witness to their own will to live.

Hartung has employed, for a good many years and with exceptional continuity, a masterly, dynamic counterpoint between the blot and the line. This he instinctively discovered while still very young, and he found how to perfect it during his stay in Minorca from 1932 to 1934, putting to good use, as Picasso also did, the things he learned from interlace, from damascening and from Hispano-Mauresque pottery. He excels in giving the psychic impression of « acting upon the canvas », to use his own words, and transcribes with his fingering

MIODRAG PROTIC *Yugoslavia* Still Life with Pitcher 1955
Private Collection

the contained elation which bursts out in firework fashion or in a black structure barely sketched upon a lu-
minously transparent ground, like a supreme parade of the spirit.

A similar, but more passionate, musicality emanates from the work of Schneider. This is ruled by a savage
ardour of touch, an admirable unfolding of colour which shows active contrasts of harsh black striations.
These, become static and massive in the work of Soulages, communicating an oppressive feeling of tension by their monumental lattice work, fringed with thunderous outbursts of colour, and all staged amidst a
strange chiaroscuro. Profoundly impregnated by the Jewish-Berber atmosphere which has surrounded him
for so long, Atlan has taken from it, quite naturally, a fascinating universe, richly supplied with unexpected
forms which distil a magical essence by their muffled incandescence enclosed by nervous strokes.

In Germany, Baumeister, after a prolonged Constructivist period which linked him to the *Abstraction-Crea-*

OSWALDO VIGAS *Venezuela* Fertile Stones 1960
Gallery La Roue, Paris

tion group, was, well before the war, one of the first to take refuge in the fantasmagoric poetry of inner reality, in order to escape the threatening demands of the epoch. Under this impetus, he sought, in ethnography and in ancient civilizations, for the constantly renewed elements of a personal style, boldly incised on a rugged *matière*, and alternating with quadrilobate imprints. His friend Bissier also, and elegantly, looked for an intimist language based on prolonged thought and on signs-symbols which could be raised to the point where they took on universal value. More recently, Grochowiak embarked on a similar course.

In Italy, Capogrossi, since 1950, has made exclusive use of the imprint, here taking a trident shape. This he tirelessly scatters upon his surfaces with an undeniable rhythmic sense. The Austrian Hundertwasser opts for the spiral and composes mosaics as ingenious as labyrinths. The Pole van Haardt traces his line in the richness of the impasto. In Canada, Pellan shows a virtuoso use of the resources of an inventive pictography, which is also taken up on occasion by the film-director Mac Laren.

As a result of this propensity, now more and more widespread, to ask a superior simplification of the work of art so that it comes close to the pure ideogram, possessed of only semantic value, Western painting, for the first time in its history, comes upon the international scene in a frame of mind wholly receptive to the ideas of the Far East. Zao Wou Ki had no sooner arrived from Hangchow in 1948, than he was rapidly accepted in

Paris, with his refined harmonies, his more and more allusive way of communicating, and his frail signs skilfully distributed among the subtlest possible glazes.

In Japan, thanks to the influence exercised by Tenrai Hidai, a movement towards emancipation sprang up, even before the war, among his pupils. Gakin Osawa and Yukei Tejima determined to use calligraphy intelligently as a true means of plastic expression. This evolution confirmed its course in 1952 with the foundation of the *Bokuzin-Kai* school, with such *avant garde* calligraphers as Yuichi Inoue, Shiryu Morita, etc. This latter, especially, plays a preponderant role, thanks to the magazines *Bokubi* and *Bokuzin* which he directs, and in whose pages are published many reproductions of abstract works by contemporary American and European artists, side by side with the Japanese painters Toko Shinoda, Bokushi Nakamura, Yoshimichi Sekiya, Sogen Eguchi, Futoshi Tsuji, etc. Their vibrantly supple and expressive calligraphic work in black and white, sometimes mingled with grey, after having travelled their own country, made on several occasions, after 1954, the circuit of the great centres of painting, and was received with lively interest; it aroused a desire to emulate them among such young French painters as Degottez, and Laubiès, who was specially predisposed by his time in Indo-China.

Though this spectacular alliance may prove fruitful and may lead to a better comprehension of painting considered above all, as Seuphor puts it, as a « spiritual act », it can also be compromised and harmed by excessive imitation. Certain Japanese, and other artists in the Far East, show a too immediate westernisation, which seems no less vain than the pretensions of certain of our own European calligraphers who, having discovered their vocation thanks to this new fashion, find themselves obliged, in order to serve the cause, to become disciples of Zen Buddhism – as if merely reading some textbook could give them the essence of this rich graphic tradition and initiate them into a lofty form of mysticism.

In Japan itself, Shuji Takashina, a Consistent advocate of the most daring modern tendencies recently has not hesitated to recommend, in his magazine *Soh*, the example of the young painter Takayasu Ito who, as he puts it, « is trying to break with western influence in order to create his own artistic universe, and who seeks to construct paintings which are subtley unified without losing the expressive force of brute matter ». While they submit themselves to the absolute power of an abstract style, Mohsèn Vaziri and Sohrab Sepehri in Iran; Saïd Akl and Chafick Abboud in Lebanon; Gharbaoui with his luminous enchantments, Aherdane with his poetry of introspection and Arama in Morocco; all spontaneously integrate their work with the age-old traditions of their countries – the riches of Arab art, its colour and plastic imaginativeness.

Across the Atlantic the newest generation of painters is starting to react both against geometric rigour and the liberties of complete absence of form. They allow that their intuition needs to have bounds, a living structure, a conscious handling of materials. We find this attitude in the Argentine with the most dynamic representatives of the *Buenos Aires* group, Krosno and Strocen, and those of the *Group of the South*, Moròn, Canas, Linares; and in Peru with the highly gifted Orellana.

Most of these artists have already had the opportunity, or are currently engaged in, forging their own spirit of independence in the Parisian melting pot, which alone is capable of galvanizing their ardour, of confirming their convictions without causing them to turn from their own past, of sharpening their judgement without forcing them to make a choice, and inspiring them with the simple courage to remain true to themselves. If this freedom of choice, this respect for human measure and human dignity, must be paid for with certain privations and sacrifices, this is a fate which Paris, throughout history, has imposed on many artists, native and foreign, who, at the start of their careers, have been obliged to suffer difficult circumstances in their way of living and in their work, being lost, forgotten even, amidst a ceaselessly swelling multitude.

But these difficulties once overcome, they are better equipped to escape the lures of fashion and to confirm their own individualities, by profiting from the special atmosphere of stimulus and lucidity to be found there. Thus, from year to year, the ranks of the new generation of artists are swelled. Already they are being summoned, as we have seen, to take responsibility for various new developments. New names are to be heard, significant of new possibilities. Several of these new artists, who started with an abstract expressionist mean.

of expression, or with complete lack of form, have now acquired sufficient maturity to go beyond these, to attempt on their own the risks of better conducted explorations, and to discover the first elements of synthesis, often thought of as impossible, between the newest tendencies which have made their appearance.

If they continue to explore their own inner lyricism, to use the structure of gesture and to develop spatial textures, they are also searching for more coherent forms, for a skill in the use of light and an educated employment of their media. They voluntarily limit themselves to a quiet and restricted range of colour. Alechinsky has pushed scruple to the point of going in person to study calligraphy in Japan, and pours out with rare intensity his rolling rhythms; Gillet expresses with restrain, in his whirling projections, a powerful energy; Doucet joins finesse to power, Barré emphasises sobriety, Marfaing displays controlled vigour, Nallard conceals fervour beneath a rich use of his *matière*, Huguette Bertrand and Lafoucrière use persuasion, Debré, Pouget and Romathier are more extrovert.

It is still too soon to single out those who are destined for success – the more because side by side with them there is a growing number of artists who are Parisian by adoption and who are now playing an ever greater part in this conquest of a pictorial language suited to our own times. They include Istrati, with his suggestive effervescence, Francis Bott with his mysterious density, Kallos, who interprets the ambiguities of light, Maryan with his inexhaustible talent for formal invention, Tabuchi with his heavily symbolic poetry, Moser with his sumptuous freedom, the more restrained Muller, the refined talent of Serpan, and the more instinctive one of Pelayo. They have come from every corner of the world to take part in this great gathering together of life and spirit: Kalinowski from Germany, Palazuelo from Spain, Tsingos from Greece, Néjad and Bitran from Turkey, Hamoudi from Iraq, Rezvani from Iran, Bezabel and Schatz from Israel, Lebenstein from Poland. And many others still from North and South America and from Asia.

Perhaps they will one day return to their own countries, carrying with them the memory of having found in Paris tihs complete view of all the world's horizons, which will give them the feeling, illusory no doubt but to-day, how fortifying, of having for a moment approached a true human communication.

Rabat 3rd May 1961

BIOGRAPHICAL NOTES

ABBOUD CHAFIK, 197.   *Lebanon*
Born in Bifkaya in 1926. Lived in Paris
from 1947 to 1949. First exhibition in 1950.
Working in Paris since 1951 and is active
as an abstract painter.

ACEVEDO FELICINDO IGLESIAS Y, 33. *Cuba*
Born in Orense, Spain in 1898. Settled in
Cuba as a grocer. Began to paint in 1939.

AFRO (BASADELLA), 151, 183.   *Italy*
Born in Udine in 1912. Studied in Venice
First exhibition in 1934. Scenic designs in
1936 and 1937. United States in 1950. A
founder of the *Huit Peintres* Group at the
Venice Biennial in 1952. Lives in Rome .

AGAR EILEEN, 141.   *England*
Took part in the Surrealist Exhibition in
London 1936 and in the New York Exhi-
bition.

AGUELI IVAN, 29.   *Sweden*
Born in 1869. Became acquainted with
Gauguin in Paris. Visited India and Egypt.
Converted to Islamism. Died in 1917.

AHERDANE MAHJOUBI, 197.   *Morocco*
Born in Oulmès in 1921. Took up drawing and painting in 1957. Also a poet.

AKL SAID, 197.   *Lebanon*
Born in 1925.

ALBERS JOSEF, 169.   *United States*
Born in Bottrop, Westphalia in 1888. Was
a student and later professor at the *Bauhaus*.
Went to the United States in 1933, appointed professor at Black Mountain College and Yale University. Now living in
New Haven.

ALBRIGHT IVAN LE LORRAINE, 148.
          United States
Born in 1897. Worked in Chicago.

ALCOPLEY, 194.   *United States*
Born in Dresden in 1910. Went to the
United States in 1937 and to Paris in 1952.

ALECHINSKY PIERRE, 21, 193, 198.
          Belgium
Born in Brussels in 1927. Studied in Brussels. Promoter of *Cobra*. Paris in 1951.
Member of the Committee of the *Salon
de Mai.*

ALIX YVES, 108.   *France*
Born in Fontainebleau in 1890. Artistic
training at the *École des Beaux-Arts*: later

at the *Académie Ranson*. Exhibited with the
Indépendants in 1912.

AMIET CUNO, 29, 51.   *Switzerland*
Born in Solcure in 1868. Worked in Mu-
nich: later in Paris at the *Académie Julian*.
Associated with Gauguin in Brittany.
Switzerland in 1893. Took part in *Die
Brücke*. Settled in Oschwand in 1898.

ANDERSEN MOGENS, 184.   *Denmark*
Born in 1916 in Copenhagen where he
received his artistic training. Settled in
Paris after the war.

ANQUETIN LOUIS, 29.   *France*
(1861-1932).

APPLEBY THEODORE, 21, 194. *United States*
Born in New Jersey in 1923. Lived in Yokohama: later in Paris.

APPEL KAREL, 193.   *Netherlands*
Born 1921 in Amsterdam where he studied. 1949 took part in *Cobra* and *Reflex*.
Paris in 1950. 1956 he produced decorations in Amsterdam and The Hague and
for the UNESCO building, in Paris.

ARAMA MAURICE, 197.   *Morocco*
Born in Meknès in 1935. Artistic training
in Paris. Director of the *École des Beaux-
Arts*, Casablanca.

ARCAY WILFREDO, 187.   *Cuba*
Born 1925 in Havana where he studied.
Went to Paris in 1949.

ARDEN QUIN CARMELO, 187. *Argentina*
Born in Uruguay, 1913. Artistic training
in Montevideo, Buenos Aires. 1944 published the manifesto of the *Madi* movement and became a promoter of same in
1946. Paris in 1948 where he founded the
Madisme scientifique. 1953 to 1956 returned
to South America. He later returned to
Paris.

ARDON MORDECAI   *(see Mordecai)*

ARENAS BRAULIO, 141.   *Chile*
Founder of the *Mandragora* group in 1938
in Santiago de Chile.

ARP JEAN, 94, 96, 131, 150.   *France*
Born in Strasbourg, 1887. Artistic training
in Weimar and Paris. Took part in the *Blaue
Reiter*. A founder of *Dada* in Zurich. Settled in Meudon in 1926. Awarded the Venice Biennial Prize for sculpture in 1954.

ATLAN JEAN, 194, 195.   *France*
Born in Constantine in 1913. Prepared for

a degree in philosophy in Paris. Devoted
to painting in 1941. First exhibition at the
Gallery Maeght in 1947. Died in 1960.

AZEVEDO FERNANDO, 141, 185. *Portugal*
Born in Porto in 1923. First exhibition in
1943. One of the founders of the Surrealist
group in Lisbon.

BACON FRANCIS, 143.   *Great Britain*
Born in Dublin in 1910. Self-taught:
worked with Sutherland. First exhibition
in 1946.

BAERTLING OLLE, 187.   *Sweden*
Born in Halmstad in 1911. Lived in Paris
and Europe. Worked with Lhote and Léger in 1948. Now living in Stockholm.

BAJ ENRICO, 183.   *Italy*
Born in Milan in 1924. One of the founders of the *Nuclear Art* movement.

BAKST LÉON, 16.   *Russia*
Born in St. Petersburg in 1866. Formed
the *Mir Izkoustva* group. Specialized in
scenic designs. Paris with the Diaghilev
Compagny in 1910 where he died in 1924.

BALLA GIACOMO, 58, 64, 67.   *Italy*
Born in Turin in 1871. Discovered Impressionism and Divisionism in Paris. Signer
of the Futurist Manifesto in 1910. His influence lasted long after the First World
War. Was a figurative artist after 1935.
Died in Rome in 1958.

BALLIN MOGENS, 29.   *Denmark*
Born in Copenhagen, 1871. In Paris associated with Gauguin and Verkade. He
gave up painting to set up a goldsmith's
workshop in 1899. Died in 1914.

BALSON RALPH, 187.   *Australia*
Born in England in 1890. Australia in 1913.
Took up painting late in life. First exhi-
bition in 1940. Now living in Sydney.

BALTHUS, 111, 165.   *France*
Born of a family of Polish origin in 1908.
Childhood in Switzerland. Met Bonnard
and Derain. Appointed director of Villa
Médicis in 1961.

BANTING JOHN, 141.   *Great Britain*
In 1936 he took part in the Surrealist Exhi-
bition in New York. Active in the British
Surrealist Group during the war.

BARAM SIOMA, 183.   *Israel*
Born U.S.S.R. in 1919. Worked in Israel.
Working in Paris for several years.

BARRIOS ARMANDO, 184. *Venezuela*
Born in 1920 in Caracas where he studied.
Visited Paris frequently. A promoter of
the Museum of Fine Arts in Caracas.

BARRAUD MAURICE, 58. *Switzerland*
Born in Geneva in 1889 where he studied.
Made his début in the art field in 1911.
Died in Geneva in 1954.

BATTKE HEINZ, 143. *Germany*
Born in Berlin in 1900. Lived in Paris and
Florence where he settled in 1935. Now liv-
ing in Frankfurt-on-Main since 1956.

BATTLE PLANAS JUAN, 141. *Argentina*
Born in Catalonia in 1911. Went to Ar-
gentina in 1913. First exhibition in 1939.
One upholder of Surrealism in Argentina.

BAUCHANT ANDRÉ, 133. *France*
Born in Châteaurenault in 1873. Nursery
gardener before the war. Began to paint
at the age of 46. First exhibition under
Jeanne Bucher in 1927. Died in 1958.

BAUMEISTER WILLI, 150, 183, 195.
Germany
Born in Stuttgart in 1889 where studied.
1912 took numerous trips to Paris. Profes-
sor in Frankfurt-on-Main 1928 to 1933.
His property was confiscated by the Nazis.
Worked secretly. After 1946 he gave courses
in Stuttgart. Died 1955.

BAZAINE JEAN, 161, 170, 172, 173. *France*
Born in Paris in 1904. Received degree in
letters, attended *Beaux-Arts* school. First
exhibition 1932. Friend of Bonnard and
Gromaire. Published *Notes sur la peinture
d'aujourd'hui* in 1948. In 1952 member of
the jury at the Pittsburgh Exhibition. Produced stained-glass windows and mosaics.

BAZIOTES WILLIAM, 193. *United States*
Born in Pittsburgh in 1912. Studied at The
National Academy of Design in New York.
Professor in 1936. In the Surrealist exhibi-
tion New York in 1942. First exhibition
in 1944. Together with Motherwell, Roth-
ko, etc. formed « Subjects of the Artist »
School in 1948. Now teaching at Hunter
College, New York.

BEAUDIN ANDRÉ, 150, 151. *France*
Born in Mennecy in 1895. Artistic training at the *École des Arts Décoratifs*. First
exhibition in 1923.

BECKMANN MAX, 129. *Germany*
Born in Leipzig in 1884. Began exhibiting
in Berlin in 1906. He was persecuted, left
Frankfurt and went to Berlin as a refugee;
later went to Amsterdam in 1936. United
States in 1947 and died there in 1950.

BELLOWS GEORGE, 42. *United States*
(1882-1925). Studied the University of
Ohio; also in New York. Caricaturist,
painter and lithographer.

BENOIS ALEXANDRE, 29, 57. *France*
Born in St. Petersburg in 1870. Received
artistic training in Paris from 1871 to 1899.
Took an active part in *Mir Izkoustva* and
in the *Théâtre des Arts* in Moscow. Went
to Paris with Diaghilev where he settled.

BENTON THOMAS HART, 148. *United States*
Born in Missouri in 1889. Received his
artistic training in Chicago. Lived in Paris.
Produced illustrations and ceramics; also
mural decorations on a large scale.

BERGHE FRITS VAN DEN, 114. *Belgium*
Born in Ghent in 1883. Settled in Laethem-
Saint-Martin. Spiritual head of the second
Laethem group. United States in 1913 and
Holland during the war. Returned to Os-
tende in 1922 and to Ghent in 1925 where
he died in 1939.

BERGMAN ANNA-EVA, 184. *France*
Born in Stockholm in 1909. Artistic training Oslo, Vienna. Married Hartung.

BERKE HUBERT, 183. *Germany*
Born in 1908 in Buer, Westphalia. Studied
art and philosophy. Pupil of Klée. Is now
living in Cologne since 1934.

BERKEL SABRI, 185. *Turkey*
Turkish; born in Jugoslavia in 1907.

BERLEWI HENRI, 94. *Poland*
Born in 1884 in Warsaw where he studied
before going to Antwerp and Paris. Knew
Lissitzky in 1922. Created the *Mechano-
factur* in 1924. Lives in Paris.

BERMAN EUGÈNE, 170. *United States*
Born in St. Petersburg in 1899. Studied
in Germany, Switzerland and France where
he lived up to 1935, then settled in the
United States. Scenic designs.

BERNARD EMILE, 29. *France*
(Born in Lille in 1869 - died in Paris in
1941). Studied at the *École des Beaux-Arts*.
Worked in Brittany with Gauguin in 1886.
Travelled extensively in Italy and the East
from 1893 to 1914. Promoter of the magazine *La Rénovatiion Esthétique*.

BERTHOLLE JEAN, 150, 173, 174, 185.
France
Born in Dijon in 1909. Received artistic
training in Lyons. Took part in the *Témoignage* group. A friend of Bissière. Was
decorator at the factories in Gien.

BERTRAND HUGUETTE, 182, 198. *France*
Born in Ecouen in 1925. First exhibition
in 1946. Travelled to the United States and
exhibited there in 1956.

BERTRAND GASTON, 182. *Belgium*
Born in Wonck in 1910. Studied in Brussels. First exhibition in 1942. One of the
best representatives of the *Jeune Peinture
belge* group. Is now living in Brussels.

BIJELIC JOVAN, 57. *Jugoslavia*
Born in 1886 at Kolunicu (Bosnia). Studied
in Paris, Prague and Cracow.

BILL MAX, 168, 194. *Switzerland*
Born in Winterthur in 1908. Studied in
Zurich and the *Bauhaus*. Architect, painter
and publicist since 1929. In 1944 organized
Konkrete Kunst in Basel. Great success in
Sao-Paulo in 1951. Founder and director
of the *Hochschule für Gestaltung* in Ulm up
to 1956. Lives in Zurich and Ulm.

BIROLLI RENATO, 182. *Italy*
Born in 1906 in Verona where he studied.
Settled in Milan in 1928. After a visit to
Paris in 1936 he helped form the *Corrente*
group. Was persecuted by the Fascists.
Paris in 1947 and became acquainted with
Picasso and Pignon. One of the promotors
of *Fronte nuovo delle Arti*, then belonged to
the *Huit Peintres* group. Awarded Carnegie
Prize in 1955. Died in 1959.

BISSIER JULIUS, 183, 196. *Germany*
Born in 1893 in Freiburg-am-Brisgau.

Studied in Karlsruhe. A friend of Schlemmer and Baumeister. In 1939 led a withdrawn life in Hagnau.

BISSIÈRE ROGER, 150, 151, 174. *France*
Born in 1888 in Villeréal. Settled in Paris
in 1910. A friend of Braque. Professor at
the *Académie Ranson* from 1925 to 1938.
During the war he went to Lot as a refugee
and resumed his activities in the art field
after the Liberation.

BITRAN ALBERT, 198. *Turkey*
Born in Turkey in 1929. Settled in Paris
in 1949.

BJERKE-PETERSEN WILHELM, 132.
Denmark
Took an active part in the magazine *Konkretion* from 1935 to 1937 and in the Surrealist movement from 1934 to 1940.

BJORKLUND NILS, 184. *Sweden*
Born in Högsjö in 1912.

BLEYL FRITZ, 51. *Germany*
Born in 1880.

BLUME PETER, 143. *United States*
Born in Russia in 1906. Settled in the United States at a very early age.

BOCCIONI UMBERTO, 64, 65, 96. *Italy*
Born in 1882 in Reggio Calabria. Worked
in Rome with Balla and Severini. Signer
of the Futurist Manifesto. Paris from 1911
to 1912. Died from a fall while riding
horseback in Verona in 1916.

BOECKL HERBERT, 129. *Austria*
Born in Klagenfurt in 1894. Travelled to
Sicily, Germany and Paris. 1935 professor
at the Vienna Academy of which he was
rector several times. Murals in 1952.

BOGGIO ANTONIO, 34. *Venezuela*
Born in La Guaira in 1857. Studied in Paris.
Lived in Italy. 1919 he returned to Venezuela for exhibition. Died 1920 in Auvers-
sur-Oise.

BOHROD AARON, 143. *United States*
Born in the United States in 1907.

BOLIN GUSTAV, 175. *Sweden*
Born in Stockholm in 1920. Completed
his artistic training in Paris where he settled
after the war.

BOLOTOWSKY ILYA, 168. *United States*
Born in St. Petersburg in 1907. United
States in 1923 where he studied as also in
Europe. Abstract since 1933. A founder
of the *American Abstract Artists* in 1936.
Professor at the University of Wyoming.

BONHOMME LÉON, 36. *France*
Born in Paris in 1870. Pupil of Gustave
Moreau. A friend of Léon Bloy and Octave
Mirbeau. Died in Saint-Denis in 1924.

BONNARD PIERRE, 18, 30, 35. *France*
Born in Fontenay-aux-Roses in 1867. Attended the *Académie Julian* where the Nabis
group was formed under Sérusier. From
1912 to 1938 he lived either in Vernon, or
in Le Cannet in 1925. His permanent residence there in 1940 and died in 1947.

BONNET ANNE, 182. *Belgium*
Born in 1908 in Brussels where she studied.
In 1939 with Louis Van Lint and Bertrand
organized *La route libre*; later formed *La*

Jeune Peinture belge group. First exhibition in 1941. Interested in abstract painting in 1950.

BORDONI ENRICO, 187.   *Italy*
Born in Altare in 1906. Took an active part in the *Movimento d'Arte Concreta* which appeared in 1948. Lives in Milan.

BORDUAS PAUL-EMILE, 188.   *Canada*
Born in 1905. Published *Refus global* in 1948. Settled in New York in 1952. Went to Paris in 1955 where he died in 1960.

BORES FRANCISCO, 150, 151, 153. *Spain*
Born in 1898 in Madrid where he received his artistic training. In 1922 he belonged to the *Ultraïste* group and became known in 1925. Settled in Paris in the same year. First exhibition in 1927.

BOTELHO CARLOS, 185.   *Portugal*
Born in 1899 in Lisbon where he received his artistic training in an atmosphere of intense musicianship. Paris from 1931 to decorate the Portuguese Pavillon at the international exhibitions.

BOTT FRANCIS, 198.   *France*
Born in Frankfurt-on-Main in 1904. Travelled throughout Europe. Was a journalist. A friend of Kokoschka. Began to paint in 1936. Settled in Paris in 1937. Produced stained-glass windows.

BOUSSINGAULT JEAN-LOUIS, 107. *France*
Born in Paris in 1883. A friend of Segonzac and Luc-Albert Moreau whom he met at Julian's. Made his début in the art field in 1909. Produced designs for Poiret and the *Théâtre de Chaillot*. Died in 1943.

BOWEN DENIS, 185.   *Great Britain*
Born in 1921.

BRAQUE GEORGES, 36, 44, 49, 58, 59, 61,
    70, 79, 86.   *France*
Born in Argenteuil. Began as a house painter. Artistic training at the *Beaux-Arts* in Rouen; later *Académie Humbert* in Paris where he settled in 1900. A friend of Friesz and Picasso. First exhibition in 1908. Wounded and trepanned in 1915. Continued painting in 1917. Reached full development between 1930 and 1935.

BRAUNER VICTOR, 132.   *France*
Born in Rumania in 1903. Lived in Paris in 1933. First exhibition in 1934 and became associated with the Surrealist group. Returned to Paris in 1938 and sought refuge in the Alps during the war. Took part in the Surrealist exhibitions.

BREER ROBERT, 187.   *United States*
Born in Detroit in 1926. Artistic training in Stanford. Settled in Paris in 1949.

BREITNER GEORGE HENDRICK, 34.
                                Netherlands
Born in Rotterdam in 1857. Studied at The Hague where he met Van Gogh. Lived in Paris in 1884. Settled in Amsterdam in 1886. Became ill in 1904. Died in 1923.

BREUILLAUD ANDRÉ, 114.   *France*
Born in Lisy-sur-Ourcq in 1898. Studied at the *Beaux-Arts* and various art schools up to 1917. First exhibition in 1924. Professor in the art schools.

BRIANCHON MAURICE, 30, 114, 133.
                                     France
Born in Fresnay-sur-Sarthe in 1899. Stu-

dent at the *Arts Décoratifs* from 1919 to 1925 where he met Legueult. Opened a studio with him. Was awarded the Blumenthal Prize in 1925 and the Carnegie Prize in 1939. Professor at the *Arts Décoratifs* in 1937; later at the *Beaux-Arts*.

BRISEL BELLA, 185.   *Israel*
Born in 1929 in Jerusalem. Studied with Marcel Jancon in Tel-Aviv. Lives in Paris since 1950.

BRUSSELMANS JEAN, 58.   *Belgium*
Born in 1884 in Brussels where he received his artistic training. Début in 1914. In Dilbeek since 1924. Died in 1953.

BROOKS JAMES, 194.   *United States*
Born in 1906 in St. Louis. Studied in Dallas. New York 1927 to 1930. Worked with Tomlin in 1931. Produced murals for the W.P.A. Federal Art Project from 1938 to 1942. Since 1948 professor at the Pratt Institute, Brooklyn. First exhibition in 1950.

BRUCE PATRICK HENRY, 94. *United States*
Born in 1880 in Virginia. Studied in New York with Robert Henri. Paris in 1907 at the *Académie Matisse*. Took part in the Armory Show in 1913. He destroyed a large part of his works in 1933. Died in New York in 1937.

BRUNING PETER, 194.   *Germany*
Born in 1929, of Rhinish origin.

BRYEN CAMILLE, 174.   *France*
Born in 1907 in Nantes. In 1926 settled in Paris where he soon published his poems. Began exhibiting in 1934. Took part in several Surrealist exhibitions. After the Liberation in the following movements: *Non-Figuration psychique, Signifiants de l'Informel, Un art autre.*

BUCHHEISTER KARL, 183.   *Germany*
Born in 1890 in Hanover where he studied and later in Berlin. In Hanover together with Schwitters formed a group of abstract painters after the first World War. Member of *Cercle et Carré* and *Abstraction-Création*. Now living in Hanover as professor since 1945.

BUFFET BERNARD, 141, 168.   *France*
Born in Paris in 1928. Artistic training in evening courses and at the *Beaux-Arts*. In 1947 he obtained the *Prix de la Jeune Peinture* and in 1948 the *Prix de la Critique*.

BULCKE GUY, 182.   *Belgium*
Born in 1931.

BULTMANN FRITZ, 180.   *United States*
Born in New Orleans, U.S.A., in 1919, he studied in his native city, in Germany, New York and Provincetown. Exhibitions: New York 1952, Turin 1959, Munich 1960. He lives in the United States.

BURLE-MARX ROBERTO, 185.   *Brazil*
Born in 1909.

BURRI ALBERTO, 183.   *Italy*
Born in 1915 in Città di Castello. Studied medicine. Began to paint in 1944, prisoner of war in the United States. Settled in Rome in 1945; First exhibition in 1947.

BURSSENS JAN, 182.   *Belgium*
Born in 1925 in Malines. Studied in Ghent where he lives. Travelled through Europe.

BURTIN MARCEL, 174.   *France*
Born in Tunisia in 1902. Settled in Paris. Acquainted with Pignon.

BURY POL, 187.   *Belgium*
Born in Belgium in 1922. Studied in Mons. Since 1947 associated with the *Jeune Peinture Belge*. Lives in Maine-Saint-Paul.

BUSSE JACQUES, 181.   *France*
Born in Paris in 1922. Pupil of Friesz at the Grande Chaumière where the group *L'Échelle* was formed together with Calmettes, Cortot, Patrix, Dalmbert. He is a member of the *Salon de Mai* Committee.

CACERES JORGE, 141.   *Chile*
Head of the Surrealist group *Mandragora* in 1938 in Santiago.

CAILLARD CHRISTIAN, 114, 130. *France*
Born in 1899 in Paris where he attended the *École Centrale* before taking up painting in 1921. He cultivated the friendship of Dabit and Loutreuil. Travelled widely, especially to Morocco.

CAILLAUD ARISTIDE, 33.   *France*
Born in Moulens in 1902. Self-taught. Porkbutcher. Took up painting in 1943 while he was prisoner of war. A sense of mysticism is often evident in his work.

CALMETTES JEAN-MARIE, 181.   *France*
Born in 1918 in Seine-et-Oise. Artistic training at the *École des Arts Appliqués, Beaux-Arts, Arts Décoratifs*. Helped form the group *L'Échelle*. First exhibition 1943.

CAMACHO JORGE, 186.   *Cuba*
Born in 1934.

CAMOIN CHARLES, 44.   *France*
Born in Marseilles in 1879. Worked in the studio of Gustave Moreau. Frequented the circles of Marquet, Cézanne, Matisse and Renoir. Retired in Saint-Tropez.

CAMPIGLI MASSIMO, 148.   *Italy*
Born in Florence in 1895. Went to Paris in 1919 after the war; a journalist before devoting himself to painting. First exhibition in Rome in 1923.

CAÑAS CARLOS, 197.   *Argentina*
Born in Buenos Aires in 1928. Studied at the *École Supérieure des Beaux-Arts*. Part of various exhibitions since 1953 and associated with the *Groupe du Sud* since 1959. Europe on scholarship in 1961.

CANOGAR RAFAEL, 194.   *Spain*
Born in 1934.

CAPOGROSSI GIUSEPPE, 166, 196. *Italy*
Born in Rome in 1900. Studied law, then took up painting. Took part in the *Origine* group in Rome. Known in 1928. Works in Rome.

CARLES ARTHUR B., 168. *United States*
One of the pioneers of abstract art (1882-1952).

CARLETTI MARIO, 163.   *Italy*
Born in Turin in 1912; long trips to France and to America. He lives in Milan.

CARLSTEDT BIRGER JARL, 187. *Finland*
Born in Helsinki in 1907. Travelled widely in Europe. First exhibition in 1930. Lives in Helsinki.

CARLSUND Otto Gustaf, 168. *Sweden*
Born in St. Petersburg in 1897. Spent his youth in Sweden. Obtained his artistic training after the war in Dresden and Oslo; later in Paris with Léger. Made the acquaintance of Mondrian. President of the *Club des Artistes* in Stockholm in 1947, where he died the following year.

CARO Anita de, 181. *France*
Born in 1909 in New York where she studied with Hofmann. First exhibition Zurich where she lived from 1935 to 1938; after that in Paris where she married the engraver Roger Vieillard.

CARRÀ Carlo, 64, 68, 144. *Italy*
Born in Quargnento in 1881. Studied in Milan. A friend of Boccioni. Signer of the Futurist Manifesto which he renounced in 1915. With Chirico, Savinio and De Pisis took part in the movement called *Valori Plastici* and in 1922 belonged to the *Novecento* group. Critic.

CARREÑO Mario, 186. *Cuba*
Born in Havana in 1913.

CARVALLO Feliciano, 33, 35. *Venezuela*
Born in La Guaira in 1919. Self-taught.

CARVÂO Aluisio, 187. *Brazil*
Born in Para in 1918. Works at the Museum of Modern Art, Sao-Paulo. Exhibiting since 1953.

CARZOU, 165. *France*
Born in Alep in 1907. Came to France to study architecture before devoting himself to painting. Exhibiting since 1930. Scenic designs.

CASORATI Felice, 144. *Italy*
Born in Novara in 1886. Studied law. Painted in 1907. Lived in Naples, Verona and Turin.

CASSINARI Bruno, 164, 183. *Italy*
Born in Piacenza in 1912. Received his artistic training in Milan where he now lives. One of the *Corrente* group in 1938. Long residence in France. In 1946 A founder of the *Fronte Nuovo delle Arti.*

CAVALLON Giorgio, 169. *United States*
Born in Italy in 1904. Emigrated to the United States where he studied with Hofmann. Since 1936 he has been exhibiting with the *American Abstract Artists* group. Resided in Europe and now lives in New York.

CELIC Stojan, 185. *Jugoslavia*
Born in Bosanski Novi in 1925. Studied in Belgrade where he teaches.

CÉZANNE Paul, 8, 12, 29, 30, 35, 49, 58, 61, 63. *France*
Aix-en-Provence 1839-1906.

CHABAUD Auguste, 44. *France*
Born in Nîmes in 1882. Associated with the Fauves in Paris. Retired to the South in Graveson, dividing his time in painting, sculpture and literature. He died in 1955.

CHAGALL Marc, 103, 105, 119, 170. *France*
Born in Vitebsk. He studied in St. Petersburg. 1911 settled in Paris at La Ruche where he became acquainted with Modigliani, Cendrars and Apollinaire. 1914 returned to Russia as director at the *Beaux-*

Arts. 1922 returned to Paris. Resided in Palestine and Syria. During the war in the United States from where he returned in 1947. Illustrations, theatrical scenery and stained-glass windows.

CHAISSAC Gaston, 33. *France*
Born in Avallon in 1910. Shoemaker, painter, poet, letterwriter. 1936 was the pupil of Freundlich. First exhibition 1937. Lives in Sainte-Florence-de-l'Oie, Vendée.

CHAPELAIN-MIDY Roger, 114. *France*
Born in Paris in 1904. Studied at the *Beaux-Arts.* 1930 worked on decorative panels. He produced theatrical scenery and is professor at the *Beaux-Arts.*

CHARLOT Jean, 129. *United States*
Born in 1898. Studied in Paris. Working in Mexico since 1921.

CHASTEL Roger, 150, 175. *France*
Born in Paris in 1897. Artistic training at the *Académie Julian.* First exhibition in 1926. Lives in Saint-Germain-en-Laye. Received the Grand Prize at the First Biennial in Sao-Paulo in 1951.

CHELIMSKY Oscar, 186. *United States*
Born in New York in 1923. Studied with Hofmann. Settled in Paris in 1948. First exhibition in 1953.

CHILDS Bernard, 194. *United States*
Born in New York in 1910. After the war worked with Ozenfant. He went to Rome and then settled in Paris in 1952.

CHIRICO Giorgio de, 94, 95, 97, 144. *Italy*
Born in Thessaly in 1888. Studied in Athens, then in Munich. Italy in 1909. First characteristic productions in 1910. Settled in Paris in 1911 where he became acquainted with Apollinaire. Ferrara in 1915 where he met Carrà. There was a period of metaphysical painting. Founded *Valori Plastici* in Rome in 1919. Returned to Paris in 1924 where he was triumphantly received by the Surrealists. 1929 published *Hebdomeros.* Returned to the academic style in 1930.

CINGRIA Alexandre, 58. *Switzerland*
Born in Geneva in 1879. Studied in Paris and Italy. Murals, mosaics and stained-glass windows.

CLAVÉ Antoni, 193. *France*
Born in Barcelona in 1913. Went to France as refugee in 1938. Produced scenic designs and posters.

CONDOPOULOS Alekos, 185. *Greece*
Born in Athens in 1905 where he lived and worked.

CONSTANT, 193. *Netherlands*
Born in Amsterdam in 1920.

CONSUEGRA Hugo, 186. *Cuba*
Born in 1930.

COPLEY William, 141. *United States*
Born in New York in 1919. In 1948 opened a Surrealist gallery in Hollywood. First exhibition in Paris in 1953 where he settled.

CORINTH Lovis, 34, 129. *Germany*
Born in East Prussia in 1858. Studied in

Munich, Antwerp and Paris. 1900 settled in Berlin after spending ten years in Munich. Spent summers in Walchensee. 1918 up to his death in 1925 lived in Zandvoort, Holland.

CORNEILLE (Cornélis van Beverloo), 178, 193. *Netherlands*
Born in Liège in 1922 of Dutch parents. Studied in Amsterdam. Took part in establishing *Cobra* in 1948. Travelled in Africa and the Antilles. Works in Paris.

CORNELL Joseph, 141. *United States*
First exhibition of collages at the Surrealist gathering headed by Julien Lévy in 1932, New York. In recent years he has specialized in crystal cages.

CORPORA Antonio, 183. *Italy*
Born in Tunis in 1909 where he received his artistic training; later in Florence. First exhibition in Florence in 1930. Resided in Paris. He was in Tunis during the war. He settled in Rome in 1945 and took part in the *Fronte Nuovo delle Arti.* One of the creators of the *Huit Peintres* group.

CORREA Jaime Lopez, 186, 189. *Colombia*
Born in Chiquinquiera Boyaca in 1933. Is now working in Bogota.

CORTOT Jean, 181. *France*
Born in Alexandria in 1925. Studied in Paris. He studied with Friesz in 1942 and took part in forming the *L'Échelle* group. First exhibition in 1944. He received the *Prix de la Jeune Peinture* in 1948.

COTTAVOZ André, 181. *France*
Born in Saint-Marcelin in 1922.

COUTAUD Lucien, 110, 132. *France*
Born in Meynes in the Gard in 1903. Received his artistic training in Nîmes, then in Paris. In 1928 he began his first decorations for Dullin; later for Copeau, Claudel, etc. He also produced murals and tapestry sketches. He is a member and founder of the *Salon de Mai.*

COVERT John, 94. *United States*
Born in Pittsburgh in 1882. Received his artistic training in Munich. He was in Paris from 1912 to 1914. One of the first abstract painters. He gave up painting in 1923.

CRIPPA Roberto, 183. *Italy*
Born in Monza in 1921. Received his artistic training in Milan where he is now working. First exhibition in 1947.

CSONTVARY-KOSZTKA Théodore, 33. *Hungary*
(1853 - 1919). Was called the « inspired madman » by his contemporaries. Received his artistic training in Munich, and in Paris at the *Académie Julian.*

CUEVAS José Luis, 131. *Mexico*
Born in 1933.

CUIXART Modesto, 194. *Spain*
Born in 1925.

CURRY John Steuart, 148. *United States*
Born in Kansas in 1897. While earning his livelihood he studied at the Institute of Art in Chicago. Obtained a year's scholarship in Paris. Professor at the University of Wisconsin. Murals.

DACOSTA Antonio, 186. *Portugal*
Born in 1915. One of the heads of the Surrealist rebirth. Has been working in Paris for several years.

DACOSTA Milton, 186. *Brazil*
Born in Rio de Janeiro in 1915. Self-taught. Received scholarship in 1944. Took part in the *Salon de Mai*. Was awarded prize at the Biennial.

DALI Salvador, 107, 132, 170. *Spain*
Born in Figueras in 1904. Studied in Madrid. Known in 1925. He contacted the Surrealists and invited them to Cadaquès. He settled in the United States in 1940 where he obtained great success. Alternated between the United States and Cadaquès.

DAVIE Alan, 188. *Great Britain*
Born in Grangemouth in 1920. Studied in Edinburgh. Travelled through France and Italy. First exhibition in 1946. Lives in London.

DAVILA Alberto, 186. *Peru*
Born in Trujillo in 1912. Studied in Lima at the *École des Beaux-Arts* where he teaches.

DAVIS Stuart, 91, 94. *United States*
Born in Philadelphia in 1894. Studied in New York. Took part in the Armory Show. First exhibition in 1917. Paris from 1928 to 1929. Professor in New York at the Art Students League since 1931, later at the New School for Social Research. Lives in New York.

DAYEZ Georges, 174. *France*
Born in Paris in 1907. Studied at the *Beaux-Arts* and with Wlérick. Acquainted with Pignon. Worked in a printing-house for several years. Member of the committee of the *Salon de Mai*.

DEBRÉ Olivier, 198. *France*
Born in Paris in 1920. First took up architecture. Acquainted with Friesz, Picasso and Segonzac. First exhibition in 1949.

DECHELETTE Louis-Augustin, 33. *France*
Born in Cours in 1894, Rhône. House painter. First exhibition in 1942.

DEGAS Edgar, 5, 33, 42. *France*
(1834-1917).

DEGOTTEX Jean, 197. *France*
Born in Sathonay in 1918. Self-taught. He devoted himself to painting while on a trip to Tunisia. Since 1949 he is a non-figurative painter. First exhibition in 1955.

DELAHAUT Jo, 187. *Belgium*
Born in 1911 in Liège where he studied. Début in painting about 1940. Became an abstract painter. Formed the *Art abstrait* group in 1952. Friend of Herbin.

DELAUNAY Robert, 24, 58, 59, 75, 77, 79, 80, 94, 96, 172, 186. *France*
Born in Paris in 1885. He took up painting in 1905. A friend of Metzinger, Apollinaire and Macke. Took part in the *Blaue Reiter*. One man show in Berlin in 1913. Travelled through Portugal and worked with Diaghilev. Returned to Paris in 1921. He became an abstract painter about 1930. He died in Montpellier in 1941.

DELAUNAY Sonia Terk, 77. *France*
Born in Ukrania in 1885. Studied in St. Petersburg and in Germany. Settled in Paris in 1906. First exhibition in 1907. Married Robert Delaunay in 1910. She returned to Paris in 1921 and became interested in fashion and printed materials. Helped organize *Art Concret* in 1945. She then took up painting again.

DELVAUX Paul, 132. *Belgium*
Born in Antheit in 1897. Influenced by Chirico and Magritte, began to tend toward Surrealism about 1935. Travelled in Italy.

DEMUTH Charles, 63. *United States*
Born in Lancaster in 1883. Studied at the Pennsylvania Academy. Paris from 1904 to 1906. Later influenced by Cubistic heritage. Died in 1935.

DENIS Maria Zaldumbide de, 131. *Ecuador*
Born in 1905 in Quito where she received her artistic training, later in Paris. President of the Artists' Society of Quito.

DENIS Maurice, 29, 30. *France*
Born in Granville in 1870. Studied at the *Académie Julian* where he met Sérusier. He expounded the theory of the *Nabis*. 1896 was attracted by the *Nazaréens* and the Italian Primitives. In 1919 with Desvallières he set up studios dedicated to religious art. He works in Saint-Germain-en-Laye. Produced scenic decors. Wrote numerous critical texts. Died in 1943.

DERAIN André, 28, 36, 44, 46, 49. *France*
Born in Chatou in 1880. Studied with Carrière. Met Matisse. 1899 cultivated the friendship of Vlaminck and worked with him in Chatou. Quite active in the *Fauvisme* movement. Later interested in Cézanne and the Siennese Primitives. After the war he preferred the South and Italy. Scenic designs and illustrations. He died in 1954.

DERELLI Cevat, 129. *Turkey*
Born in Riza in 1900. Studied in Istanbul. Paris from 1924 to 1928. 1928 was one of the founders of a group of independent painters and sculptors. 1928 professor of the Academy of Fine Arts in Istanbul.

DESNOYER François, 138, 150, 151. *France*
Born in Montauban 1894. Studied with Bourdelle at the *Arts Décoratifs* where he was appointed professor in 1938. He began exhibiting in 1922. Retired in Sète.

DESPIERRE Jacques, 145, 150, 165. *France*
Born in Saint-Étienne in 1912. Son of the painter Céria. Studied in various art schools. Began exhibiting in 1935. Now professor at the *Arts Décoratifs*. A member and founder of the *Salon de Mai*.

DESVALLIÈRES Georges, 36. *France*
Born in Paris in 1861. Became the pupil of Gustave Moreau. Was attracted by religious art at an early age. Produced numerous decorations. Died in 1950.

DEWASNE Jean, 187. *France*
Born in 1921 near Lille. Studied architecture. An abstract painter in 1943. Founded and directed with Pillet the *Académie d'Art Abstrait* from 1950 to 1952.

DEYROLLE Jean 168, 187. *France*
Born in Nogent-sur-Marne in 1911. Travelled to Spain and Morocco. He admired Sérusier and Braque. Settled in Paris in 1942 and became acquainted with Domela. Lived in Denmark and Germany.

DIAS Cicero, 187. *Brazil*
Born in Pernambouc in 1908. Originally specialized in architecture. First exhibition in 1928. Now living in Paris since 1937.

DI CAVALCANTI Emiliano, 131. *Brazil*
Born in Rio in 1897. First exhibition in 1918. Travelled to Europe. Since 1929 he has been producing famous murals.

DIEHL Gösta, 185. *Finland*
Born in 1909.

DIETRICH Adolf, 33. *Switzerland*
Born in Berlingen in 1877. First exhibition in 1909. In 1926 he devoted himself exclusively to art. Died in 1957.

DILLER Burgoyne, 169. *United States*
Born in New York in 1906. A follower of Mondrian since 1934. Lives in New York.

DIX Otto, 115, 148. *Germany*
Born of peasant stock in Thuringia in 1891. Studied in Dresden. He took part in the *Neue Sachlichkeit* movement. Influenced by Dürer and Holbein. Since 1928 professor at the Academy of Dusseldorf.

DMITRIENKO Pierre, 181. *France*
Born in Paris in 1925. Training in architecture and painting. After the Liberation he worked with Arnal and Rezvani. Became known in 1948. He is now living in a village on the Oise, in Dieudonné.

DOBROVIC Petar, 57. *Jugoslavia*
(1890-1942).

DOESBURG Théo van, 22, 88, 150. *Netherlands*
Born in Utrecht in 1883. First exhibition in 1908. Met Mondrian in 1915 and with him promoted *De Stijl* in 1917. 1925 published the manifesto of the *Elémentarisme* movement in opposition to Mondrian. Paris in 1929 where he published *Art Concret*. Died in Davos in 1931.

DOMELA César, 186. *France*
Born in Amsterdam in 1900. He lived in Switzerland in 1922 and then in Germany where he was one of the *Novembergruppe*. Friend of Mondrian. Berlin from 1927 to 1933. Then definitely settled in Paris.

DOMINGUEZ Oscar, 132. *Spain*
Born in Tenerifa in 1906. He was a commercial artist. First exhibition in 1933 as a Surrealist. Settled in Paris in 1934 and took part in all Surrealist shows. Committed suicide in 1957.

DONGEN Kees van, 31, 36, 44, 49, 52. *France*
Born in Delshaven in 1877. Draughtsman in Rotterdam. Settled in Paris in 1897. First exhibition in 1904. Took part in *Fauvisme* and *Die Brücke*. Portrait painter after the First World War.

DORAZIO Piero, 183. *Italy*
Born in 1927 in Italy. Studied in Paris. Taken an active part in abstract art since 1947. Travelled to the United States. Working in Rome.

DOUCET Jacques, 198. *France*
Born in Boulogne-sur-Seine in 1924. Knew Max Jacob. First exhibition in 1948.

DOVE Arthur, 168. *United States*
Born in Canandaigua in 1880. Studied in the United States, France and Italy. First exhibition at the Stieglitz Gallery in 1910. A tendency toward abstract art in 1912. Died in Huntington in 1946.

DREIER Katherine, 21, 168. *United States*
Born in 1877 in New York where she studied. She later went to Paris, London and Munich. Returned to New York in 1913 and took part in the Armory Show. Founded the *Société Anonyme* in 1920 with Duchamp, Man Ray. Lived in China. Paris in 1925 where she met Mondrian. Promoted rotary exhibitions of abstract art. Died in Milford in 1952.

DRISSI Moulay Ahmed, 33. *Morocco*
Born in Marrakech in 1924. Self-taught. Has worked in France.

DRYSDALE Russell, 141. *Australia*
Born in 1912.

DUBUFFET Jean, 128, 188. *France*
Born in Le Havre in 1901. Worked at the *Académie Julian* for some time in 1918, painting late in life. First exhibition under Drouin in 1945. In 1948 he organized *L'Art brut*. A friend of Paulhan, Eluard, Fraigneau. Lived in New York.

DUCHAMP Marcel, 59, 62, 78, 94, 131, 168. *France*
Born near Rouen in 1887. Brother of the sculptor Duchamp-Villon and Jacques Villon. In 1909 he devote himself to painting. 1913 settled in New York. Met Picabia and with him became a promotor of *Dada*. Took an active part in all Surrealist exhibitions.

DUDANT Roger, 182. *Belgium*
Born in 1929.

DUFFAUT Prefete, 33. *Haiti*
Born in Jacmel in 1923. Is a boat-builder. Painted fresco in the church in Port-au-Prince.

DUFOUR Bernard, 181. *France*
Born in Paris in 1922. Completed hi studies in agricultural engineering after the war and at the same time worked in art schools. First exhibition in 1951.

DUFRESNE Charles, 34, 107, 165. *France*
Born in Millemont in 1876. Some training at the *Beaux-Arts*. Became known in 1905. 1910 a scholarship for two years in Algiers. After the war professor at the *Académie Scandinave*. Scenic designs, tapestries and murals. Died at La Seyne in 1938.

DUFY Raoul, 24, 37, 44, 51. *France*
Born in Le Havre in 1877 where he attended evening school. He was attracted by the *Fauvisme* movement for several years, but followed a more serious style after 1909. Scenery, ceramics, tapestries. Died in Forcalquier in 1953.

DUNOYER DE SEGONZAC André, 44, 87, 107. *France*
Born in Boussy-Saint-Antoine in 1884. Artistic training in art schools. Worked with Boussingault. During the war he worked in and was director of the Camouflage Department. Formed *La bande noire*. Engraver, illustrator and watercolourist.

EGUCHI Sogen, 197. *Japan*
Born in Japan in 1919. Exhibited at the Penmanship Institute. In 1952 he became a member of the School of Bokuzin-Kai.

ELLIOT Ronnie, 186. *United States*
Born in New York in 1916 where she studied. Known in 1935. Developed from Surrealism to an abstract artist. Lived in Paris. Works in New York.

ENCKELL Magnus, 57. *Finland*
(1870-1925). Studied in Helsingfors and Paris where he returned in 1908 as representative of the Finnish section at the Salon d'Automne. Frescoes and stained-glass windows.

ENDE Edgar, 141. *Germany*
Born in 1901.

ENGONOPOULOS Nicos, 141. *Greece*
Poet and Surrealist painter.

ENGSTRÖM Leander, 57. *Sweden*
Born in Ytterhogdal in 1886. Artistic training in Sweden, later at the *Académie Matisse*. Returned to Scandinavia in 1912. Lived in Italy. Died in 1927.

ENSOR James, 15, 24, 34, 35, 42. *Belgium*
Born in Ostend in 1860. Received artistic training in Brussels, then returned to Ostend in 1880 for permanent residence. The best part of his work was produced between 1888 and 1892. He died in 1949.

ERNST Max, 98, 105, 131, 132, 170, 188. *France*
Born in Bruhl near Cologne in 1891. Acquainted with Arp in 1914. After the war he formed the *Dadaïste* group of Cologne. 1921 settled in Paris and took an active part in the Surrealist movement. During the last war he went to the United States as a refugee, then to Mexico. Finally returned to France. Received the Venice Biennial Prize in 1954.

ESTÈVE Maurice, 156, 170, 172. *France*
Born in Culan in 1904. Attended evening school. Worked in Barcelona. First exhibition in 1930. Collaborated with Delaunay at the 1937 Exhibition.

EVANS Merlyn 146. *Great Britain*
Born in 1910 at Cardiff, one of the leading abstract artists in England. Professor of fine arts school. Exhibited at the Venice Biennial.

EVENEPOEL Henri, 58. *Belgium*
Born in Nice in 1872. Received artistic training in Brussels and Paris with Moreau. Painted in Algeria. Died in Paris in 1899.

FASSBENDER Josef, 183. *Germany*
Born in Cologne in 1903 where he received his artistic training and lives.

FATHWINDER, 183. *Germany*
Born in Mainz-Castel in 1906. Self-taught. First exhibition in 1931. His work was interrupted by the Nazis. After the war he lived and exhibited in Paris. Now living in Dusseldorf.

FAUTRIER Jean, 151. *France*
Born in Paris in 1898. Spent his childhood in London. First exhibition in 1921. Was sponsored by Paul Guillaume. His talents were recognized especially after the Liberation. He was awarded the Venice Biennial Prize in 1960.

FEININGER Lyonel, 35, 78, 80, 86, 170. *United States*
Born in New York in 1871. Studied in Berlin and Paris. Took part in the *Blaue Reiter*. Professor at the *Bauhaus*. Permanent residence in New York in 1937 and died there in 1956.

FEITO, 194. *Spain*
Born in 1929 in Madrid where he received his artistic training. First exhibition in 1954. Was awarded the prize for painting at the Venice Biennial in 1960.

FERAT Serge (Gastrebzoff), 61. *France*
Born in Moscow in 1881. Went to Paris in 1901 to paint. Acquainted with « Douanier » Rousseau, Picasso and Apollinaire. 1913 directed *Les Soirées de Paris*. Abandoned by his friends, he is now leading a withdrawn life.

FIAMINGHI Hermelindo, 187. *Brazil*
Born in Sao Paulo in 1920 where he studied. Known in 1955. Belongs to the *Art Concret* group.

FIGARI Pedro, 33. *Uruguay*
(1861-1938).

FILLA Emil, 63. *Poland*
Born in Chropyne in 1892. Studied in Prague. Holland from 1914 to 1919. He took an active part in the artistic life of Prague after the war. Died in 1953.

FINK Don, 194. *United States*
Born in Minnesota in 1923. Studied in Minneapolis and New York. Working in Paris at intervals since 1953.

FJELL Kai, 33. *Norway*
Born in Sköger in 1907. Studied with a friend of Munch. 1930 settled in Telemark.

FLEISCHMANN Adolf Richard, 82. *United States*
Born in Essling in 1892. Studied in Stuttgart. Switzerland from 1930 to 1933, Spain up to 1936 and in Italy. Then settled in France which he left in 1952 and went to the United States where he became a member of the American Abstract Artists.

FLEXOR Sanson, 187. *Brazil*
Born in Rumania in 1907. Went to Paris in 1924 where he studied. 1948 in Brazil where he set up a studio of abstract art in Sao Paulo.

FONTANA Lucio 183. *Italy*
Born in 1899 in Rosario Santa Fé. Lived in Argentina. 1934 took part in the *Abstraction Création* movement. 1948 created the *Spatial* movement in Milan with Dova and Crippa. Sculptor, ceramist.

FOUKOUZAWA Ichiro, 141. *Japan*
Before the war he created the *Bijutsiu-Bunka* movement which tends towards Surrealism.

FRANCIS Sam, 186. *United States*
Born in San Mateo in 1923. Studied medicine, Has been in Paris since 1950.

FREDDIE Wilhelm, 141. *Denmark*
Born in Copenhagen in 1909. An active

organizer of Surrealism in Scandinavia. Went to Sweden as refugee during the war. A founder of the *Imaginistes*.

FREUNDLICH OTTO, 186.   *France*
Born in Stolp in 1878. Began to paint at the age of 27. Paris in 1909 where he made the acquaintance of Picasso. Exhibited with the Cubistic painters. Member of *Abstraction-Création*. Set up a studio of abstract art. Deported and died in 1943.

FRIESZ OTHON, 44, 49.   *France*
Born in Le Havre in 1879 where he studied and became acquainted with Dufy. Took part in the *Fauvisme* movement which he gave up in 1908 and became interested in composition. Was professor in art schools. Died in 1949.

FUCHS ERNST, 143.   *Austria*
Born in 1930. Pupil of Gütersloh.

GALLEN-KALLELA AXEL, 51.   *Finland* (1865-1931).

GAUGUIN PAUL, 7, 8, 16, 24, 29, 30, 33, 35, 49, 51, 57, 58, 80.   *France* (1848-1903).

GEAR WILLIAM, 185.   *Great Britain*
Born in Scotland in 1915 where he studied. Paris from 1947-1950. Living in Buckinghamshire.

GENERALIC IVAN, 33, 148.   *Jugoslavia*
Born in Hlebine in 1914. Even though a shepherd, he was encouraged by the painter Hegedusic. Exhibited in 1931 with the *Terre* group. First exhibition in 1936. Now continuing his peasant life in Hlebine.

GHARBAOUI JILALI, 197.   *Morocco*
Born in Le Gharb in 1930. Received his artistic training in Paris and Rome. First exhibition in 1956.

GHIKA NICOLAS, 183.   *Greece*
Studied in Paris for several years. Professor at the Polytechnic School in Athens.

GIACOMETTI ALBERTO, 181. *Switzerland*
Born in Stampa in 1901. His father was an artist. Studied in Geneva and Paris with Bourdelle. Lives in Paris.

GILLET ROGER EDGARD, 198.   *France*
Born in Paris in 1924. Artistic training at the *École Boulle* and *Arts Décoratifs*. First exhibition in 1953. Member of the Committee of the *Salon de Mai*.

GISCHIA LÉON, 150, 170, 172, 173, 176.   *France*
Born in Dax in 1903. Devoted himself to painting in 1923. Lived in the United States. Worked with Léger and Le Corbusier, was present at the 1937 Exhibition. One of the founders of the *Salon de Mai*.

GLACKENS WILLIAM, 42. *United States* (1870-1938).

GLARNER FRITZ, 169, 170. *United State*
Born in Zurich in 1899. Studied in Italy and Paris. Member of *Abstraction-Création*. Settled in New York in 1936. A friend of Mondrian.

GLEIZES ALBERT, 59, 63.   *France*
Born in Paris in 1881. Received artistic training from his family. Was a theorist of Cubism and exerted great influence. Formed the art colony of Moly-Sabata near Avignon where he died in 1953.

GOGH VINCENT VAN, 8, 9, 16, 29, 34, 35, 42, 44, 51, 57, 77.   *Netherlands*
(Groot Zundert 1853 - Auvers-sur-Oise 1890).

GONDOUIN EMMANUEL, 108.   *France*
Born in Versailles in 1883. Attended evening school. A friend of Modigliani. First exhibition in 1921. Died in 1934.

GONTCHAROVA NATHALIA, 79, 94.   *France*
Born in Russia in 1881. Artistic training in Moscow where she exhibited in 1900. With Larionov she took part in the *Rayonnisme* movement. 1914 settled in Paris. Produced ballet scenery. Painted again in 1956.

GONZALEZ JULIO 85.   *Spain*

GORKY ARSHILE, 143, 170, 188, 193.   *United States*
Born in Turkish Armenia in 1904. Studied engineering in Tiflis. Settled in the United States in 1920. Professor for drawing in 1924. Known in 1930. Took part in the *Abstraction-Création* movement. First exhibition in 1932. Met Breton and Ernst during the war. His works partially destroyed by a fire in 1946. He committed suicide in 1948.

GOTTLIEB ADOLPH, 193.   *United States*
Born in New York in 1903. Received part of his artistic training in Europe. First exhibition in 1930. Lives in New York.

GÖTZ KARL OTTO, 193.   *Germany*
Born in Aix-la-Chapelle in 1914. Had contacts with the Bauhaus. Known after the war. Took part in *Cobra*. Published the magazine *Meta* from 1948 to 1953. Works in Frankfurt.

GRAU ENRIQUE, 186.   *Colombia*
Born in Carthagena in 1920. Studied in Bogota; later in New York from 1940 to 1943.

GRAVES MORRIS, 170.   *United States*
Born in Fox Valley in 1910. Travelled to Japan in 1930 and to Puerto Rico in 1940. One Man Show in 1942 at the Museum of Modern Art. Recently visited Europe.

GREIS OTTO, 194.   *Germany*
Born in Frankfurt-am-Main in 1913. Took up painting in 1933. Acquainted with Nay in 1945. He lived in Bad Soden and in the suburbs of Paris.

GRILLO SARAH, 187.   *Argentina*
Born in Buenos Aires in 1920. Self-taught.

GRIS JUAN (JOSÈ VICTORIANO GONZALÈS), 59, 61, 71, 151.   *Spain*
Born in Madrid in 1887 where he studied engineering. At the age of 19 he went to Paris, became acquainted with Picasso and in 1912 took part in the Cubistic movement. His health failed him in 1920 and he died in 1927.

GROCHOWIAK THOMAS, 196. *Germany*
Born in 1914. Became an abstract painter in 1958.

GROMAIRE MARCEL, 108, 122, 142, 172.   *France*
Born in Noyelles-sur-Sambre in 1892. Frequented the studios of Montparnasse in 1910. Lived in northern Europe. Known

after the war. During the Second World War became interested in tapestry.

GRONHOLM PAUL, 185.   *Finland*
Born in 1907.

GROPPER WILLIAM, 143. *United States*
Born in New York in 1897. Worked with Bellows and Henri. A caricaturist and lithographer: also murals.

GROSZ GEORGE, 108, 115, 148, 170.   *Germany*
Born in Berlin in 1893 where he studied. Produced humouristic drawings. He became known during the war. Was a member of the *Dada* group in Berlin in 1918, later to the *Neue Sachlichkeit*. 1932 emigrated to New York where he was appointed professor.

GRUBER FRANCIS, 112, 150, 165, 173.   *France*
Born in Paris in 1912. Studied at the *Académie Scandinave* with Friesz and Dufresne. Famous at the age of 18. First exhibition in 1935. Produced mural decorations in 1936. Professor at the *Académie Ranson* in 1942. One of the founders of the *Salon de Mai*. Was affected with tuberculosis and died in 1948.

GRUNEWALD ISAAC, 51, 57.   *Sweden*
Born in Stockholm in 1889 where he studied. Later went to Paris where he attended the *Académie Matisse* from 1908 to 1911. Professor at the Académie in 1932. Frescoes.

GUAYASAMIN OSWALDO, 131. *Ecuador*
Born in Quito in 1919 where he studied. Exhibitions since 1943. Murals.

GUBLER MAX, 129.   *Switzerland*
Born in 1898 in Zurich where he studied. Paris from 1930 to 1937. Later returned of work in Zurich.

GUDNASON ZVAVAR, 193.   *Iceland*
Born in Iceland in 1909. Studied in Copenhagen; later went to Paris to study with Léger. Worked in Copenhagen during the ast war. Lives in Reykjavik.

GUERRERO XAVIER, 129.   *Mexico*
Born in 1896.

GUEVARA-MORENO LUIS, 186.   *Venezuela*
Born in Valencia in 1926. Studied in Caracas; later in Paris. He passed through an abstract period. Director of the School of Fine Arts in Caracas.

GUIDO ALFREDO, 149.   *Argentina*
Born in 1892.

GUSTON PHILIP, 186.   *United States*
Born in Montreal in 1913. Studied in Los Angeles. First exhibition in 1945. Abstract since 1948. Works in New York.

GUTTUSO RENATO, 114.   *Italy*
Born in Palermo, 1912. He took part in the movement *Corrente*, one of the founders of *Fronte Nuovo delle Arti* and of the neorealistic movement. Lives in Rome.

HAARDT GEORGES VAN BRODNICKI, 196.   *Poland*
Born in 1907 in Poznan. Magistrate in Poland up to 1939. Left Poland and travelled to Italy and Turkey. Lived in Palestine. He settled in Paris in 1950.

HAMOUDI JAMIL, 198. *Irak*
Born in 1924 in Bagdad where he studied. Living in Paris since 1947. First exhibition in 1952.

HANTAI SIMON, 131. *France*
Born in Bia in 1922. Studied Budapest. Paris in 1949. Introduced at his first exhibition in 1953 by Breton.

HARTLEY MARSDEN, 94, 63, 124.
United States
Born in Lewiston in 1877. Studied in New York. Paris in 1912. Became associated with the Cubistic painters and the *Blaue Reiter*. Lived in Germany from 1915 to 1916. Gave up abstract painting in 1918. Died in Ellsworth in 1943.

HARTUNG HANS, 21, 169, 194. *France*
Born in Leipzig in 1904. Studied in Dresden where he lived up to 1932. Became an abstract painter in 1922. First exhibition in 1932. Balearic Islands from 1933 to 1934. Settled in Paris in 1935. Enlisted in 1939. Was wounded and had a leg amputated in 1944. Lives in Paris. Awarded the Venice Biennial Prize in 1960.

HASSAM CHILDE, 34. *United States*
Born in 1859. Began as a business man in Boston. Became interested in engraving. Worked in Paris at the *Académie Julian*. Died in 1935.

HAUSNER RUDOLF, 143. *Austria*
Born in 1923. One of the first promotors of Surrealism in Austria.

HAYDEN HENRI, 63. *France*
Born in 1885 in Warsaw. Undecided whether to take up engineering or painting. Settled in 1907. First exhibition in 1911. Took up the cause of Cubism.

HAYTER STANLEY WILLIAM, 185.
Great Britain
Born in London in 1901. Studied in Paris. 1927 set up *L'Atelier* 17 (Studio 17) for engraving. Took part in the Surrealist movement. New York from 1940 to 1950. Returned to Paris and opened his studio.

HEATH ADRIAN, 187. *Great Britain*
Born in Burma in 1920. He began to paint in England 1938. After the war renewed studies in art London. Lived in France. Abstract painter since 1948. Lives in London.

HECKEL ERICK, 51. *Germany*
Born in Döbeln in 1883. Studied architecture in Dresden. Took part in forming *Die Brücke* in 1905. Settled in Berlin in 1909. Taught in Karlsruhe from 1949 to 1954. Lives in Hemmenhofen am Bodensee.

HEGEDUSIC KRSTO, 148. *Jugoslavia*
Born in Petrinja in 1901. Studied in Zagreb and Paris. Professor in Zagreb. 1928 formed the *Zemlja* group. Encouraged the young Generalic.

HERBIN AUGUSTE, 150, 186. *France*
Born in Quiévy in 1882. Studied in Lille. Paris in 1903. Exhibited in 1917. An abstract painter since 1926. Founder of *Abstraction-Création* in 1931; 1949 published *L'art non-figurativ non objectif*. A director of the *Salon des Réalités Nouvelles*. Died in 1960.

HEREDIA LUIS ALBERTO, 33. *Ecuador*
Born in 1909. Self-taught.

HEROLD JACQUES, 132. *France*
Born in Piatra in 1910.

HERRERA GUEVARA LUIS, 33. *Chili*
(1891-1945) Self-taught.

HIDAI TENRAI, 197. *JAPAN*
(1872-1939). A precursor of the Modern School and a master of penmanship.

HILL ANTHONY, 187. *Great Britain*
Born in London in 1930. Began to study science: later painting. An abstract painter since 1950. Lives in London.

HILLAIREAU GEORGES, 181. *France*
Born in Saint-Ouen in 1884. Self-taught. Painted only occasionally. Began to devote himself exclusively to painting in 1940. First exhibition in 1941. Died in 1954.

HILTON ROGER, 185. *Great Britain*
Born in Northwood in 1911. Studied in London and Paris with Bissière. Works in London.

HIRSHFIELD MORRIS, 33. *United States*
Born in Poland in 1872. Settled in the United States in 1890 as a tailor. Began to paint in 1936. First exhibition in 1943. Died in 1946.

HLITO ALFREDO, 187. *Argentina*
Born in Argentina in 1923 where he studied. Abstract painter in 1944. A member and founder of *Arte Concreto*. First exhibition in 1952.

HODLER FERDINAND, 24, 32, 58.
Switzerland
Born in Berne in 1853. Studied in Geneva. Paris in 1891, 1892 contributed in the Salon de la Rose-Croix. Lived in Geneva until his death in 1918.

HOEHME GERHARD, 194. *Germany*
Born in 1920 in Greppin near Dessau. Worked in Halle up to 1951: later in Düsseldorf-Kaiserswerth.

HOFMANN HANS, 169, 170, 193.
United States
Born in Weissenburg in 1880. Studied in Germany and Paris. First exhibition in Berlin in 1910. His own art school in Munich in 1915. Was later professor in Italy, France and finally in the United States where he settled in 1930 and opened Hofmann art school in 1934.

HOLT ALF KROGH, 184. *Norway*
Born in 1919.

HOLTY CARL, 169. *United States*
Born in Freiburg in 1900. Was taken to the United States, studied in Chicago and Munich with Hofmann. Europe from 1925 to 1933. First exhibition in New York where he is now living. A friend of Mondrian.

HOPPER EDWARD, 148. *United States*
Born in Nyack, near New York in 1882. Artistic training with Henri. Went to Paris in 1906. Took part in the Armory Show. In 1920 he worked only with watercolour.

HOSIASSON PHILIPPE, 193. *France*
Born in Odessa in 1898. Numerous trips

to Europe. Lived in Italy after the war: later in Berlin. Settled in Paris in 1924. A founder of the *Surindépendants*. A non-figurative artist since 1947.

HULTBERG JOHN, 186. *United States*
Born in Berkeley, California in 1922.

HULTEN C. O., 141. *Sweden*
Born in 1916.

HUMBLOT ROBERT, 140, 149. *France*
Born in Fonteney-sous-Bois in 1907. Studied natural science before entering Beaux-Arts where he met Rohner and Jannot and together with them formed the *Forces Nouvelles* group in 1935. Escaped as war prisoner in 1941 and resumed his studies in the natural sciences.

HUNDERTWASSER FRITZ, 196. *Austria*
Born in 1928 in Vienna where he studied. Travelled through Africa and Europe. Atir exhibition in 1952. Works in Paris.

HURTADO ANGEL, 186. *Venezuela*
Born in 1927. Artistic training in Caracas: later in Paris where he produced experimental films. Professor at the School of Fine Arts in Caracas.

HYPPOLITE HECTOR, 33. *Haiti*
Born in Saint-Marc in 1894. Formed the *Artistes naïfs* group. Encouraged by Lam and Breton. Took part in the Surrealist exhibitions. Died Port-au-Prince 1948.

IDOUX CLAUDE, 187. *France*
Born in 1915 in Lyons where he studied. Belonged to the *Témoignage* group. With Lenormand became interested in frescoes. Various productions.

IMAI TOSHIMITSU, 194. *Japan*
Born in Kyoto in 1928. Lives in Paris.

INOUE YUICHI, 197. *Japan*
Born in Kyoto in 1916. Began as a schoolmaster. Attended courses in painting at the Shunyo-Kay Institute. Studied penmanship under Sokyu Ueda. In 1952 he formed the *Bokuzin-Kai* group which was outstanding in penmanship.

ISRAËLS ISAAC, 34. *Netherlands*
Born in Amsterdam in 1865. Self-taught. Painted factory scenes in Charleroi. In 1886 he worked in Amsterdam with Breitner. Associated with Liebermann in Scheveningen. Paris from 1903 to 1914: later in London and Switzerland. Visits to the Hague.

ISTRATI ALEXANDRE, 198. *Rumania*
Born in Dorohai in 1915. Studied art and law. 1947 he won a scholarship for Paris where he settled. First exhibition in 1952.

ITO TAKAYASU, 197. *Japan*
Born in Hyogo in 1934. First exhibition in 1959. In 1960 took part in *La meilleure oeuvre de l'année*, under the auspices of the Asahi Press. Now living in Tokyo.

JACOBSEN EGILL, 193. *Denmark*
Born in Copenhagen in 1910. One of the promoters of *Host* and *Spiralen*. First exhibition in Paris in 1961.

JAN ELVIRE, 181. *France*
Born in Russia in 1904.

JANNOT HENRI, 149. *France*
Born in Paris in 1905. Studied at the Beaux-

Arts from 1925 to 1932. Took part in forming *Forces Nouvelles*. A tendency toward mysticism is evident in his works.

JAWLENSKY ALEXEJ VON, 36, 54, 78, 80.
Russia
Born in Souslovo in 1864. Studied in Moscow and Munich. With Kubin and Kandinsky formed the Nouvelle Association des Artistes in Munich. Met Matisse. Lived in Switzerland during the war. Settled in Wiesbaden in 1921 where he died in 1942. Belonged to *Les quatre bleus* group.

JOHNS JASPER, 141.   *United States*
Born in 1930.

JOHNSON BUFFIE, 186.   *United States*
Born in 1912 in New York where she received her artistic training: later in Los Angeles. Frequent, long visits to Paris.

JONQUIERES EDUARDO, 186. *Argentina*
Born in 1918 in Buenos Aires where he studied art. Painter and poet.

JORN ASGER, 193.   *Denmark*
Born in Vejrun, Jutland in 1914. Worked in Paris in 1936 under Léger. In 1938 he published the magazine *Helhesten*. From 1938 to 1951 he belonged to the following groups: *Host*, *Spiralen* and *Cobra*. Frequent visits to Paris.

JOSEPHSON ERNST, 29.   *Sweden*
Born in Stockholm in 1851. His stay in Paris made him tend toward the Impressionists. 1882 returned to Paris and met Théo Van Gogh. 1886 a founder of the *Konstnörsfärbundet*. Retired in Brittany where he became mentally ill. Died 1906.

KALINOWSKI HORST EGON, 198. *Germany*
Born in Düsseldorf in 1924 where he studied. Settled in Paris in 1950 and attends the *Académie d'Art Abstrait*.

KALLOS PAUL, 198.   *Hungary*
Born in Hernadnemeti in 1928. Was in a concentration camp. Artistic training in Budapest. Settled in Paris in 1950. First exhibition in 1955.

KANDINSKY WASSILI, 16, 35, 36, 76, 77,
78, 79, 80, 84, 94, 150, 168, 186. *France*
Born in Moscow in 1866. 1896 went to Munich to study and associated with Jawlensky. First exhibition in 1901. Various visits to Paris and Tunisia. 1911 founded the *Blaue Reiter*. Returned to Russia during the war. Was professor in 1918, founded the *Institut de Culture Artistique*, 1921 professor and vice director at the Bauhaus. Settled in Paris in 1932 where he died in 1944.

KANE JOHN, 33.   *United States*
Born in Scotland in 1860. 1879 emigrated to the United States. Began to paint in 1900. Was awarded a Carnegie Prize in 1927. Died in Pittsburgh in 1934.

KANTOR TADEUSZ, 183.   *Poland*
Born in 1915. Studied in Crakow. Known in Warsaw in 1956. Founder of the Cricot experimental theatre in Crakow.

KAPTAN ARIS, 183.   *Turkey*
Born in 1906.

KELLY ELLSWORTH, 187.   *United States*
Born in Newburgh in 1923. Studied in

Brooklyn, Boston. Paris in 1948. First exhibition in 1951. Returned to the United States in 1954.

KEMP ROBERT, 185.   *Australia*
Born in Victoria in 1912.

KHNOPFF FERNAND, 32.   *Belgium*
Born in Termonde in 1858. Studied law: art with Mellery. 1879 studied under Moreau in Paris. Belonged to the *XX* group. Engraving, decorations, sculpture. Died in Brussels in 1921.

KINGMAN EDUARDO, 131, 186. *Ecuador*
Born in Loja in 1911. Studied in Quito.

KIRCHNER ERNST LUDWIG, 47, 51, 52,
57, 129, 183.   *Germany*
Born in Aschaffenburg in 1880. Promoter of *Die Brücke* in Dresden in 1905. Went to Berlin in 1911. His health failed him in 1917: settled in Switzerland near Davos where he committed suicide in 1938.

KISLING MOÏSE, 39, 105.   *France*
Born in Krakow in 1891. Artistic training under Pankiewicz. Settled in Montparnasse in 1910. Went to Céret with Picasso and Max Jacob. Wounded during the war. His success began in 1919. Went to the United States as a refugee from 1940 to 1946. Died in Sanaray in 1953.

KLÉE PAUL, 16, 79, 80, 118, 131. *Switzerland*
Born near Berne in 1879. Studied in Munich. Travelled to Italy and France. Belonged to the *Blaue Reiter*. Tunisia in 1914. Professor at the Bauhaus from 1921 to 1931. Returned to Switzerland in 1933 where he died in Muralto, Locarno in 1940.

KLIMT GUSTAV, 16, 29, 32, 58. *Austria*
Born in Vienna in 1862 where he studied. 1883 began painting murals. He gave up painting from 1892 to 1897. Was president of the Viennese Secession from which he withdrew in 1908 and formed the *Klimt Group*. Died in 1918.

KLINE FRANZ, 179, 194.   *United States*
Born in Wilkes Barre in 1910. Studied in Boston and London. First exhibition in 1950. Now professor in Brooklyn.

KOENIG JOHN FRANKLIN, 186.
United States
Born in Seattle in 1924. After the war attended school in Biarritz before returning in 1946. Studied in Washington. Settled in Paris where he founded an art gallery and published an art magazine.

KOKOSCHKA OSCAR, 16, 55, 58. *Austria*
Born in Pöchlarn in 1886. Studied in Vienna. Helped by Loos. Took part in *Der Sturm* in Berlin. Associate with Rilke. Professor in Dresden 1920 to 1924. Travelled extensively through Europe to 1933. Prague to 1938: in London to 1952 and finally in Villeneuve am Genfer See in Switzerland.

KOLOS-VARY SIGISMOND, 181. *France*
Born in Banffyhunyad in 1899. Studied in Budapest: Paris where he settled in 1926.

KOONING WILLEM DE, 143, 158, 170,
188, 193.   *United States*
Born in Rotterdam in 1904 where he attended night school and was also a house painter. Was given lessons by the *Stijl*.

Lived in Belgium. Settled in the United States in 1926. First exhibition in 1948. Lives in New York.

KOSICE GYULA, 187.   *Argentina*
Born in Hungary in 1924. Artistic training in Buenos Aires where he settled. One of the founders of *Madi* in 1946 together with Arden Quin. After that period was director of the magazine *Arte Madi*.

KOTIK JAN, 194.   *Czechoslovakia*
Born in 1916. Exhibition of all his works in Prague in 1957 and 1960.

KOUSNETSOV PAUL, 58   *Russia*
Born in Saratov in 1878. Artistic training in Moscow. Travelled to Paris. Was influenced by the Gauguin exhibition in 1906. Travelled through Central Asia between 1911 and 1914.

KRASNO RODOLFO, 197.   *Argentina*
Born in Chivilcoy, Argentina in 1916. Artistic training at the National School of Fine Arts in Buenos Aires. Was appointed professor. One man shows in 1953. One of the founders of the *Buenos Aires* group in 1958. Won a scholarship for Paris in 1959.

KREGAR STANE, 185.   *Jugoslavia*
Born in Lubliana in 1905. Studied in Prague.

KRILAND GÖSTA, 141.   *Sweden*
Born in 1917 at Forsbacka.

KROGH PER LASSON, 57.   *Norway*
Born in Asgardstrand in 1889. Son of the painter Christian Krogh. Brought up and received artistic training in Paris where he spent the greater part of his life. Pupil of Matisse.

KRUYDER HERMAN, 129.   *Holland*
Born in Lage Vuurse in 1881. Began as a house painter. Started artistic painting in 1910. Died in Amsterdam in 1955.

KUNIYOSHI YASUO, 143. *United States*
Born in Yokohama in 1893. Went to the United States in 1903. Received artistic training late in life in Los Angeles and New York where he was professor. Travelled through Europe from 1925 to 1928. Died in 1953.

KUPKA FRANÇOIS, 35, 74, 77.   *France*
Born in Opocno in 1871. Artistic training in Prague and Vienna. Settled in Paris in 1895. Produced illustrations. Became an abstract painter in 1910. Took part in *La section d'or*. Great success in Prague in 1946. Died in Puteaux in 1957.

KUTTER JOSEPH, 129.   *Luxembourg*
Born in Luxembourg in 1894. Artistic training in Munich. Returned in 1924. Painted in spite of his long illness which lasted from 1936 until his death in 1941.

LABISSE FÉLIX, 132.   *France*
Born in Douai in 1905. Artistic training in Brussels and Paris. Took part in the Surrealist movement. Produced numerous decorations, especially for J. L. Barrault.

LAFOUCRIÈRE PIERRE, 198.   *France*
Born in Louroux-de-Bouble (Allier), in 1927. Artistic training in Paris at the Ecole des Métiers d'Art.

LA FRESNAYE Roger de, 59, 63, 72, 96. *France*
Born in Le Mans in 1885. Studied in Paris under Julian and Ranson. Took part in *La section d'or.* Suffered from poison gas during the war. Slow death in Grasse 1925.

LAGAGE Pierre, 181. *France*
Born in Croix in 1911. Artistic training in Roubaix. First exhibition in 1932. Settled in Paris in 1937. Was prisoner of war. Gradually became an abstract artist.

LAGRANGE Jacques, 181. *France*
Born in Paris in 1917. Studied at the Arts Décoratifs and Beaux-Arts. Known after years spent as prisoner of war. Tapestry sketches.

LAM Wilfredo, 104, 132. *Cuba*
Born in Sagua in 1902. Studied in Havana, Madrid and Paris. A friend of Picasso and Dominguez. First exhibition in 1938. Cuba in 1941. Lived in the United States. Works in Paris.

LAN-BAR David, 183, 185. *Israel*
Born in Poland in 1911. Went to work in Paris shortly after the war.

LANSKOY André, 162, 188. *France*
Born in Moscow in 1902. Began to paint in Kiev. Settled in Paris in 1921. First exhibition in 1925. Became non-figurative in 1937. Tapestry sketches.

LANYON Peter, 185. *Great Britain*
Born in St. Ives in 1918. Studied in London under Ben Nicholson and Gabo. First exhibition in 1949. Is now teaching in St. Ives and Corsham.

LA PATELLIÈRE Amédée de, 108. *France*
Born in Bois-Benoît in 1890. Studied in Nantes. Went to Paris in 1912 and worked under Julian. Seriously wounded during the war. Settled in Saint-Paul-de-Vence from 1930 up to his death 1932.

LAPICQUE Charles, 150, 155, 170, 172, 173. *France*
Born in Theizé in 1898. Became an engineer. Took up painting in 1925 but continued his scientific studies. Produced decorations in 1937. Has been influenced by Venice. Publications.

LAPOUJADE Robert, 181. *France*
Born in Montauban in 1921. Self-taught. Settled in Paris in 1945. First exhibition in 1947. Published *Les mécanismes de fascination* in 1955. Professor in drawing.

LAPRADE Pierre, 44. *France*
Born in Narbonne in 1875. Worked with Bourdelle. Associated with the *Fauves* for a short time. Visited Italy several times. Decorations and illustrations. Died in 1931.

LARIONOV Michel, 79, 94. *France*
Born in Tiraspol in 1881; studied in Moscow where he took an active part in the art field in 1898. Promoted the *Rayonnisme* movement. A friend of Malevitch and Tatlin. Paris in 1914, sponsored by Apollinaire. Works for the Ballets Russes.

LASNE Jean, 149. *France*
Born in Bolbec in 1911. Went to Paris in 1930. Was at the Beaux-Arts for several months where he met Humblot, Jannot. Killed during the war in 1940.

LASTATER Gérard, 193. *Netherlands*
Born in Schaesberg in 1920. Artistic training in Maestricht and Amsterdam.

LAUBIÈS René, 197. *France*
Born in Cholonville, Cochinchine in 1922. First exhibition in 1953 in Paris where he is now working.

LAURENCIN Marie, 19, 33. *France*
Born in Paris in 1885. Attended evening school and the Académie Humbert. Associated with the Cubists through Apollinaire. Illustrations. Died in 1956.

LAURENS Henri, 93. *France*
Born in Paris, 1885. Began as a sculptor and designer, about 1911 turned to Cubism. Then made *collages*. 1916 belonged to the North-South group. Exhibition at the National Museum of Modern Art, Paris. Died 1954.

LAWSON Ernest, 42. *United States*
(1873-1939).

LEBENSTEIN Jan, 198. *Poland*
Born in Brzesc in 1930. Artistic training in Warsaw. First exhibition in 1956. Was awarded Paris Biennial Prize.

LE FAUCONNIER Henri, 59, 107. *France*
Born in Hesdin in 1881. Settled in Paris and worked under Julian. Associated with the Cubists in 1911. Professor at the Académie de La Palette. Holland during the war. Returned to France in 1920. Died in 1946.

LÉGER Fernand, 24, 59, 61, 77, 79, 88, 94, 109, 129, 150, 170. *France*
Born in Argentan in 1881. Received training in architecture: later at the Arts Décoratifs. Lived in La Ruche. Created a Cubism of his own. First exhibition in 1912. Discharged from the army in 1917 and became interested in machinery. Produced a film entitled *Le ballet mécanique.* Several visits to the United States, the last being 1940 to 1947. Murals' mosaics, stained-glass windows and ceramics. Died in 1955.

LEGUEULT Raymond, 114, 134. *France*
Born in Paris in 1898. Studied at the Arts Décoratifs where he was professor in 1925. Worked with Brianchon. Decorations. Now professor at the Beaux-Arts.

LEHMDEN Anton, 143. *Austria*
Born in 1929.

LE MOAL Jean, 150, 170, 173, 174. *France*
Born in Authon-du-Perche in 1909. Studied at the Arts Décoratifs under Ranson together with Bissière. Frequent visits to Brittany. First exhibition in 1938. Member and founder of the Salon de Mai. Decorations and stained-glass windows.

LENORMAND Albert, 187. *France*
Born in La Roche-Vineuse in 1915. Artistic training in Lyons and Paris. Belonged to the *Témoignage* group.

LEROY Eugene, 110. *France*
Born at Tourcoing in 1910. Studied at Wasquehal.

LESIEUR Pierre, 181. *France*

LEUPPI Léo, 168. *Switzerland*
Born in Zurich in 1893. Founder of *Die Allianz.* Lives in Zurich.

LEVINE Jack, 143. *United States*
Born in the United States in 1915.

LEVY Rudolf, 58. *Germany*
Born in Stettin in 1875. Artistic training in Munich and Paris. After the war he worked in Düsseldorf: later in Berlin.

LEWIS Percy Wyndham, 94. *Great Britain*
Born in Canada in 1882. Studied in London, Munich and Paris. Received Marinetti in London in 1913. Formed the *Vorticisme* movement, the manifesto was published in 1914. Died in 1957.

LHOTE André, 63, 83. *France*
Born in Bordeaux in 1885. Worked under a sculptor-decorator: self-taught in painting. First exhibition in 1910. Active critic and professor in 1918. Founded his academy in 1912. Publications.

LIMA Mauricio Nogueira, 187. *Brazil*
Born in Pernambuc in 1930. Studied architecture and painting. Belonged to the *Art Concret* group.

LIMOUSE Roger, 114. *France*
Born near Constantine in 1894. Worked in Tunisia. Settled in Paris in 1919. Studied under Julian. Professor in drawing. Travelled extensively. Awarded the Vikings Prize in 1953.

LINARES Ezequiel, 197. *Argentina*
Born in 1927. Studied in Buenos Aires. One man shows in 1956. Member of the *Groupe du Sud* in 1959. Scholarship to Europe in 1960.

LINT Louis van, 182. *Belgium*
Born in 1909 in Brussels where he studied. Founded the *Route libre* with Anne Bonnet and Bertrand. First exhibition in 1941. A promoter of *La Jeune Peinture belge.* Decorations.

LISSITZKY Eliezer, 86, 94. *U.S.S.R.*
Born near Smolensk in 1890. Studied engineering in Darmstadt. 1919 took part in the constructive movement with Rodchenko and Tatlin. Was professor in Moscow. Later went to Berlin, Switzerland and Hanover; was collaborator in publications. Returned to Moscow in 1928 where he died in 1941.

LOMBARD Jean, 181. *France*
Born in Dijon in 1895. Mainly self-taught in Lyons and Paris. Known in Paris in 1922. Founded the Académie du *Vert-Bois* in 1942 which trained young students.

LOUTREUIL Maurice, 108. *France*
Born in Montmirail in 1885. Self-taught. Travelled to Guinea. Headed the Pré Saint-Germain group which included Masson, Desnoyer, Caillard and Sabouraud. Died in Paris in 1925.

LUBARDA Petar, 129. *Jugoslavia*
Born in Ljubotenje in 1907. Artistic training in Belgrade and Paris. Exerted a great influence on the younger generation.

LUKS George, 42. *United States*
(1867-1933).

LUNDSTRÖM Vilhelm, 63. *Denmark*

LURÇAT Jean, 143. *France*
Born in Bruyères in 1892. Artistic training in Nancy under Prouvé: later in Paris

with Naudin. Travelled extensively after the war. In 1939 he gave a new impetus to the production of tapestry in Aubusson. Partial residence in Saint-Céré.

MABE MANABU, 194.   *Brazil*
Born in Japan in 1910. Emigrated to Brazil. Studied at the age of 23. Début in art in 1950.

MACDONALD-WRIGHT STANTON, 21, 94.   *United States*
Born in Charlottesville in 1890. Went to Paris in 1907 where he received his artistic training and met Russell with whom he began the *Synchronisme* movement in 1912. Exhibitions in Munich and Paris. Returned in 1916, first exhibition in New York in 1917. Lived in Japan in 1947 and 1952. Returned to abstract art in 1954. Lives in Santa Monica.

MACKE AUGUST, 16, 56, 77, 79, 80, 96. *Germany*
Born in Meschede in 1887. Studied in Düsseldorf. Travelled extensively. Lived in London and especially in Paris. 1910 associated with Marc and Kandinsky in Munich and with Delaunay in Paris. Belonged to the *Blaue Reiter*. Travelled to Tunisia with Klée in 1914. Killed during the war in 1914.

MAGNELLI ALBERTO, 144, 186.   *Italy*
Born in Florence in 1888. Self-taught. Took several trips to Paris where he associated with Apollinaire and Picasso. Favoured the Futurists. Became an abstract artist in Florence in 1915. Settled in Paris in 1933.

MAGRITTE RENÉ, 100, 132.   *Belgium*
Born in Lessines in 1898. Studied in Brussels. Travelled through Europe. Attracted by fantastic art in 1925. Associated with the Surrealists in 1927. Works in Brussels.

MÄKILÄ OTTO, 141.   *Finland*
(1904-1955).

MALCZEWSKI RAFAL, 148.   *Poland*
Born in Poland in 1892. Studied in Vienna and Krakow. Début in art in 1921.

MALDONADO TOMAS, 187.   *Argentina*
Born in 1922 in Buenos Aires where he studied. A founder of *Arte Concreto*. Friend of Bill and Vantongerloo. Abstract artist since 1944. Lived in Europe in 1948. Director of the magazine *Nueva Vision*. Professor in Ulm in 1955.

MALEVITCH CASIMIR, 79, 80, 88, 168.   *U.S.S.R.*
Born in Kiev in 1878. In Moscow belonged to the *Valet de carreau* group. Travelled to Paris in 1912. The first elements of the *Suprématisme* movement appeared in 1913. Manifesto published in 1915. Professor in Moscow; later in Leningrad. 1926 went to Germany for the publication of *Le monde sans objet*. Died in Leningrad in 1935.

MANESSIER ALFRED, 148, 150, 170, 172, 174, 182.   *France*
Born in La Somme in 1911. Studied in Amiens, later in Paris. Worked together with Bissière under Ranson where he became associated with Le Moal, Bertholle and Martin. Belonged to the *Témoignage* group. A member and founder of the Salon de Mai. Stained-glass windows, tapestries, murals and lithographs.

MANGUIN HENRI, 44.   *France*
Born in Paris in 1874. Studied under Moreau. Known in 1902. Took part in the *Fauvisme* movement. Died in Saint-Tropez in 1943.

MARC FRANZ, 53, 96.   *Germany*
Born in 1880 in Munich where he studied. Travelled and lived in Italy, Greece and Paris. Settled in Sindelsdorf in 1910. Associated with Macke and Kandinsky. Founded *Der Blaue Reiter* with them. Friendly with Delaunay. Was killed during the war in 1916.

MARCHAND ANDRÉ, 136, 150, 165, 172, 182.   *France*
Born in 1907 in Aix where he studied. Did odd jobs until he settled in Paris. Known in 1930. Lived in Provence and Biskra. Awarded the Paul Guillaume Prize in 1937. During the war he lived alternately in Saulieu and Paris. A member and founder of the Salon de Mai. Lived in Provence, Burgundy and, more rarely, in Paris.

MARCOUSSIS LOUIS, 59, 61.   *France*
Born in Warsaw in 1883. Studied in Krakow and Paris. Known in 1907. Took part in the Cubistic movement. Served during the war. United States in 1933. Died in Cusset in 1941.

MARFAING ANDRÉ, 198.   *France*
Born in Toulouse in 1925. Studied law. Took up painting in Paris in 1950. First contacts with abstract art in 1953.

MARIN JOHN, 58, 63, 120.   *United States*
Born in Rutherford in 1870. Studied in Philadelphia. Began working as an architect. Long residence in Paris. On returning to New York, he was sponsored by Stieglitz. Took part in the Armory Show. Travelled extensively in the United States. Died in Cope Split in 1953.

MARINOT MAURICE, 44.   *France*
Born in Troyes in 1882. Took part in the *Fauvisme* movement. In 1911 he devoted himself to working in glass.

MARLE FÉLIX DEL, 186.   *France*
Born in Pont-sur-Sambre in 1889. Studied in Brussels and Paris. Associated with Kupka and Mondrian. A founder of the *Salon des Réalités Nouvelles*. Died in 1952.

MARQUET ALBERT, 26, 44, 49.   *France*
Born in Bordeaux in 1875. Studied in Paris at the Arts Décoratifs and Beaux-Arts. Associated with Matisse. Known in 1901. Took part in the early stages of the *Fauvisme* movement, but soon gave it up. Travelled extensively. Died in Paris in 1947.

MARTIN KENNETH, 187.   *Great Britain*
Born in Sheffield in 1905. Studied in London where he was appointed professor. Publications together with Pasmore. Promoter and defender of abstract art.

MARTIN VICENTE, 185.   *Uruguay*
Born in 1911 in Montevideo where he studied especially under Torres Garcia. 1950 on he produced murals.

MARTINEZ RICARDO, 149.   *Mexico*
Born in Mexico in 1918.

MARTINS DA SILVIERA ELISA, 33.   *Brazil*
Born in Teregina in 1912. Self-taught. Began to paint in 1952.

MARYAN PINCHAS BURSTEIN, 198. *Poland*
Born in 1927 in Nouy-Sacz, Poland. Was in a deportation camp. Lived in Israel from 1947 to 1950. Settled in Paris. First exhibition in 1952.

MARZELLE JEAN, 181.   *France*
Born in Lauzun in 1916.

MASSON ANDRÉ, 99, 108, 131, 132, 170.   *France*
Born in Balagny in 1896. Self-taught. Became known in 1922. Took part in the Surrealist movement in 1924. Settled in Aix in 1947. Illustrations, murals and decorations.

MATHIEU GEORGES, 188.   *France*
Born in Boulogne-sur-Mer in 1921. Began to paint in 1942. Settled in Paris in 1947. Organized exhibitions of lyric abstract art. Travelled to Japan and Brazil.

MATISSE HENRI, 16, 24, 25, 27, 36, 44, 49, 51, 57, 58, 80, 94, 172, 181, 193. *France*
Born in Le Cateau in 1896. Studied in Paris under Moreau; later with Carrière. Creator of *Fauvisme* of which he published the principles in 1908. Lived in Morocco. In 1917 he settled in Nice. In 1930 he travelled to the United States and Oceania. Produced decoration in Merion for Barnes in 1938. Completed the *Chapelle de Vence* where he lived, in 1951. Died in 1954.

MATTA ECHAURREN ROBERTO, 132, 147, 186.   *Chile*
Born in Santiago in 1912. Studied architecture under Le Corbusier. In 1938 he took part in the Surrealist movement. Settled in the United States in 1939. A friend of Duchamp. Long residence in Rome. Lives in Paris.

MAURER ALFRED HENRY, 58. *United States*
(1868-1932).

MAZZON GALLIANO, 187.   *Italy*
Born in Camisano in 1896. Travelled to Brazil. Works in Milan.

MEISTERMANN GEORG, 184. *Germany*
Born in Solingen in 1911. Studied in Düsseldorf. Began as a painter-glass-blower. Developed into the field of non-figurative painting. Professor in Frankfurt, 1953.

MELLERY XAVIER, 32.   *Belgium*
(1845-1921).

MENDELSON MARC, 183.   *Belgium*
Born in London in 1915. Studied in Brussels where he lives. Founder of the *Jeune Peinture belge* group. Mural decorations.

MERIDA CARLOS, 129.   *Mexico*
Born in Guatemala in 1893. Went to Europe at 17 where he studied. Returned to the United States after the war. Later went to Mexico where he took up a permanent residence in 1921. Tended toward abstract painting since 1930. Murals decorations.

MESSAGIER JEAN, 181.   *France*
Born in Paris in 1920.

METELLI ORNEORE, 33. *Italy*
Born in 1872 in Terni where he was a shoemaker. Began to paint in 1922. Was also a musician. Died in 1938.

METZINGER JEAN, 59. *France*
Born in Nantes in 1883. Artistic training in Paris. Favoured Cubism. Took part in *La Section d'Or*. Together with Gleizes published *Du Cubisme* in 1912. Died in Paris in 1956.

MIHELIC FRANZ, 148. *Jugoslavia*
Born in 1907 at Skofialoca (Slavonia), Studied in Zagreb. Prize in 1954 at the Biennial in Venice.

MIKL JOSEPH, 187. *Austria*
Born in Vienna in 1929.

MILLARES MANUEL, 194. *Spain*
Born in 1926.

MILLER GODFREY, 185. *Australia*
Born in 1895.

MILIAN RAUL, 186. *Cuba*
Born in Cuba in 1914.

MINAUX ANDRÉ, 165. *France*
Born in Paris in 1923. Studied at the Arts Décoratifs. First exhibition in 1946.

MIRO JUAN, 90, 131, 132. *Spain*
Born in Montroig in 1893. Artistic training in Barcelona: later in Paris. Worked in these two cities. Associated with Picasso. Took part in the Surrealist exhibitions. Produced ceramics in 1944. Lithographs and murals.

MODERSOHN-BECKER PAULA, 50, 57. *Germany*
Born in Dresden in 1876. Artistic training in Berlin. Travelled to Paris. A friend of Rilke. Settled in Worpswede where she died in 1907.

MODIGLIANI AMEDEO, 79, 81, 96, 105. *Italy*
Born in Leghorn where he began to paint. Settled in Paris in 1906. Led a bohemian life. Took up sculpture, encouraged by Brancusi. He died in 1920.

MOESCHLIN WALTER, 141. *Switzerland*
Born in Basel in 1902. Travelled through Sumatra from 1920 to 1922. Headed the *Kunstler Gruppe* in Basel. Publications.

MOHOLY-NAGY LASZLO, 80, 86, 170, 187. *Hungary*
Born in Bacsbarsod in 1895. Began to draw during the war. Became an abstract artist in 1920. Professor Bauhaus 1922 to 1928. Lived in Amsterdam and London. Publications. United States in 1937. His own school in Chicago where he died in 1946.

MOISSET RAYMOND, 181. *France*
Born in Paris in 1906. Artistic training at the Arts Appliqués. Devoted himself to painting in 1934.

MOLL OSCAR, 58. *Germany*
Born in Brieg in 1875. Studied under Corinth; later Matisse in Paris. Professor at the Breslau Academy; later director from 1925 to 1932.

MONDRIAN PIET, 62, 63, 77, 88, 92, 150, 168, 169, 170, 186, 187. *Netherlands*
Born in Amersfoort in 1872. Studied in Amsterdam. A friend of Sluyters, Toorop. Paris 1912 to 1914. Holland up to 1919 where he created *De Stijl* together with Van Doesburg. 1920 published *Le Néo-Plasticisme* in Paris and *Neue Gestaltung* at the Bauhaus in 1925. Member of *Cercle et Carré* and *Abstraction-Création*. London as refugee in 1938 and New York in 1940 where he died in 1944.

MONET CLAUDE, 33, 34, 77. *France*
(Paris 1840 - Giverny 1926).

MONNET GIANNI, 187. *Italy*
Born in Turin in 1912. 1949 in the formation of the *Mouvement pour l'Art Concret* in Milan. Architect and art critic.

MORALIS YANNIS, 185, 191. *Greece*

MORANDI GIORGIO, 144, 165. *Italy*
Born in 1890 in Bologna where he studied. He never left his city. Began to paint and engrave in 1911. Took part in the *Pittura metafisica* movement in 1918. Associated with the *Valori Plastici*. Is now leading a withdrawn life.

MORDECAI ARDON, 168, 192. *Israel*
Born in Poland in 1897. Studied at the Bauhaus. 1933 settled in Jerusalem where he was professor, later director of the Bezabel School. Awarded the Unesco Prize at the Venice Biennial in 1954.

MOREAU GUSTAVE, 32, 36, 44. *France*
(1826-1898).

MOREAU LUC ALBERT, 44, 107.
Born in Paris in 1882. Studied under Julian. Associated with Segonzac and Boussingault. Influenced by Cubism. Wounded during the war. Took up painting again in 1920. From 1925 on he lived preferably in Saint-Tropez. Lithographs. Died in 1946.

MORENI MATTIA, 183. *Italy*
Born in Pavia in 1920. Studied in Turin. First exhibition in 1946. Works in Bologna.

MORITA SHIRYU, 197. *Japan*
Born in Japan in 1912. 1938 defended penmanship as a plastic art. 1952 member of the Bokuzin-Kai School. Director magazines *Bokubi* and *Bokuzin*.

MORLOTTI ENNIO, 183. *Italy*
Born in Lecco in 1910. Took part in *Corrente*, *Fronte Nuovo delle Arti* and in the *Huit* group. Is now working in Milan.

MORÓN RENÉ, 197. *Argentina*
Born in Sant Antonio Oests, Argentina in 1929. Studied in Buenos Aires. Many one man shows. Murals. Took part in the *Groupe du Sud* exhibition in 1960.

MORRICE JAMES WILSON, 58. *Canada*

MORRIS GEORGE L. K., 125, 168. *United States*
Born in New York in 1906. Studied at Yale; later in Paris under Léger. Travelled extensively in 1933. President of *American Abstract Artists* up to 1951.

MORTENSEN RICHARD, 187. *Denmark*
Born in 1910 in Copenhagen where he studied. Discovered the work of Kandinsky in Germany. An abstract artist since 1933. Lived in Paris 1937 and settled there permanently in 1947.

MORTIER ANTOINE, 194. *Belgium*
Born in 1908.

MOSER WILFRID, 198. *Switzerland*
Born in Zurich in 1914. Travelled extensively. Settled in Paris in 1946 at which time he became an abstract artist.

MOSES GRANDMA (ANNA MARY ROBERTSON), 33. *United States*
Born in Eagle Bridge in 1860 where she spent her entire life. Had ten children. Began to paint in 1930. Published her memoirs in 1952.

MOTHERWELL ROBERT, 127, 143, 170, 193. *United States*
Born in Aberdeen in 1915. Studied philosophy and the history of Art at Harvard, Grenoble and Colombia. Self-taught in painting. Studied engraving under Hayter. First exhibition in 1944. Professor in New York. Publications.

MOULY MARCEL, 174. *France*
Born in Paris in 1918.

MUCHE GEORG, 80. *Germany*
Born in Querfurt in 1895. Studied architecture and painting in Berlin and Munich. Professor at the Bauhaus 1920 to 1927. Taught in Berlin and Breslau.

MUELLER OTTO, 51. *Germany*
Born in Liebau in 1874. Studied in Breslau and Dresden. Berlin in 1908. Took part in *Die Brücke*. Worked with Kirchner. After the war professor in Breslau where he died in 1930.

MULLER BRUNO, 198. *Switzerland*
Born in Basel in 1929. Works in Paris.

MUNCH EDVARD, 29, 34, 35, 48, 51, 52, 57. *Norway*
Born in Löten in 1863. Studied in Oslo. 1890 to 1908 worked in France, Italy and Germany. On returning to Oslo he produced mural decorations from 1909 to 1911 and from 1921-1922. Retired to Ekely near Oslo where he died in 1944.

MUNTER GABRIELLE, 79. *Germany*
Born in Berlin in 1877. Studied in Munich under Kandinsky in 1902. In 1909 helped found the *Neue Künstlervereinigung München*, 1911 the *Blaue Reiter*; settled in Murnau in 1931.

MURTIC EDO, 183. *Jugoslavia*
Born in Velika Pizanica in 1921.

NAKAMURA BOKUSHI, 197. *Japan*
Born in Japan in 1916 where he is now working. Took part in the numerous exhibitions of abstract penmanship.

NALLARD LOUIS, 198. *France*
Born in Algiers in 1918 where he received his artistic training. First exhibition in 1945. Settled in Paris in 1947.

NAPPER JOHN, 185. *Great Britain*
Born in London in 1926. Works in Paris.

NASH PAUL, 143. *Great Britain*
Born in London in 1889 where he studied. 1933 a founder of *Unit One*. Headed the Association of Industrial Artists for a short time. Died in Boscombe in 1946.

NATIVI GUALTIERO, 187. *Italy*
Born in Pistoia in 1921. Studied in Florence. A founder of *Arte d'Oggi*.

NAY Ernest Wilhelm, 139, 183.
Germany
Born in 1902 in Berlin, studied under Hofer. Friendly with Munch. Abstract artist since 1950. Works in Cologne.

NEGREIROS Almada, 187. *Portugal*
Born in 1893.

NEJAD Mehmed, 198. *Turkey*
Born in 1923 in Istanbul where he studied. Settled in Paris in 1945. First exhibition in 1950.

NEMES Endre, 184. *Sweden*
Born in 1909. Founder of the *Minotaure* group. From 1947 to 1955 he was director of the Valand School.

NICHOLSON Ben, 126, 168. *Great Britain*
Born in Denham in 1894. Studied in London. Travelled extensively. Lived in Paris. 1933 member of *Abstraction-Création* and *Axis*. Associated with Mondrian. Produced mural decorations. Worked in Saint Ives with a group of young painters.

NICOLAO Theresa, 186. *Brazil*
Born in 1928 in Rio de Janeiro where she studied. Paris under Szenes from 1948 to 1950. Worked with Portinari on a mural in New York.

NIETO Ernesto, 186. *Peru*
Born Arequipa in 1920. Studied in Lima.

NIEVA Francisco, 194. *Spain*
Born in Valdepenas in 1924. Artistic training in Madrid. At first produced decorations. Devoted himself to painting in 1950

NIKIFOR, 33. *Poland*
Born in Lemkowszeryzna in 1893. Self-taught. Began exhibiting in 1930. Now living in Krynica.

NOLAN Sidney, 141. *Australia*
Born in 1917 in Melbourne where he received his artistic training. In 1950 he travelled to Italy and Greece. He now prefers to live in London.

NOLDE Emil (Hansen), 16, 51, 52, 57, 59. *Germany*
Born in 1867. Studied in Munich, Dachau and Paris. 1904 settled in Berlin. Took part in *Die Brücke*. Associated with the *Blaue Reiter*. The Pacific in 1913. Lived after the war, in Berlin and Seebull where he died in 1956.

NONELL Y MONTURIOL Isidor, 42. *Spain*
Born in 1873 in Barcelona where he studied. Lived in Paris. Died in 1911.

OBIN Philomé, 33. *Haiti*
Born in 1892 in Cape Haiti where he lived. Self-taught. Was hairdresser and decorator. Part of the group headed by Hypolite.

OBREGON Alejandro, 186. *Colombia*
Born in Barcelona in 1920 of a Colombian family. Studied in Spain, Boston, Bogota. Murals in Colombia.

OCAMPO Miguel, 187. *Argentina*
Born in 1922 in Buenos Aires where he studied. Began to paint in 1944. Travelled to Europe in 1948. Works in Paris.

OELZE Richard, 132. *Germany*
Born in Magdeburg in 1900. Studied at the Bauhaus 1921 to 1926. Lived in Dresden, Ascona and Berlin. 1932 to 1936 Paris where he took part in the Surrealist exhibitions. 1945 worked in Worpswede.

OKAMOTO Taro, 141. *Japan*
Born in Tokyo in 1911. Paris 1929 to 1940. Took part in the abstract art exhibitions and those of Surrealism. One man shows in Tokyo in 1941.

OLSEN Gudmund, 141, 184. *Denmark*
Born in 1913 in Copenhagen where he studied. Lived in Paris for several years.

OLSON Erik, 93, 184. *Sweden*
A promoter of the Surrealist group in Halmstadt in 1934. Became known in Paris. Murals.

OMCIKOUS Pierre, 185. *Jugoslavia*
Born in Rijeka in 1926. Studied in Belgrade. Known in 1949. Settled in Paris in 1952.

ONGENAE Josef, 187. *Holland*
Born in Antwerp in 1921. Self-taught. Travelled to the United States, Congo and Asia. Murals in Amsterdam where he now works.

ONSLOW-FORD Gordon, 141. *Great Britain*
Born in 1916. Took up painting with Matta in France; later in New York.

OPPI Ubaldo, 144. *Italy*
Born in Bologna in 1889. Studied in Vienna, Paris from 1919 to 1921.

ORELLANA H., 197. *Peru*
Born in Viscap in 1935. Studied in Mexico. Associated with Tamayo. Travelled the United States and lived in Italy where his first exhibition took place. Paris since 1957.

OROZCO José Clemente, 24, 95, 129, 130, 131. *Mexico*
Born in Ciudad Cuzman in 1883. Studied in Mexico. Caricaturist in 1913 at time of the revolution. Associated with Rivera and Siqueiros. 1923 he began mural decorations. Lived in the United States and Europe 1930 to 1934. Died in Mexico in 1949.

OROZCO-ROMERO Carlos, 129.
Born in Mexico in 1898. *Mexico*

OSAWA Gakin, 197. *Japan*
Born in Japan in 1890. Poet and novelist. 1933 took up penmanship under Tenrai Hidai. His work was destroyed in the bombardments which took place in Tokyo. Worked again after the war. Died in 1953.

OSTERLIN Anders, 141. *Sweden*
Belonged to the Malmö group. Exhibited with the *Imaginistes* in Göteborg in 1952.

OTERO Alejandro, 187. *Venezuela*
Born in El Manteco in 1921. Studied in Caracas; Paris from 1945 to 1951. Professor in Caracas. Murals. Works in Paris.

OUDOT Roland, 114, 135. *France*
Born in Paris in 1897. Studied at the Arts Décoratifs where he was professor. Known in 1919. Decorations.

OZENFANT Amédée, 88, 170. *France*
Born in Saint-Quentin in 1886. Studied in Paris at the Académie de la Palette. Known in 1908. Travelled to Italy and Russia. Director of the magazine *L'Elan*; together with Le Corbusier of *L'Esprit Nouveau* from 1920 to 1925. Promoter of the *Purisme* movement. His own art school. Travelled to London and the United States.

PAALEN Wolfgang, 132. *Mexico*
Born in Vienna in 1907. Studied in France, Germany and Italy. Travelled to America. 1936 took part in the Surrealist exhibitions. Mexico in 1939. Created the magazine *Dyn*. Visits Paris.

PACHECO Maria Luisa, 186. *Bolivia*
Born in La Paz in 1919 where she studied; later in Madrid. Professor at La Paz since 1951.

PADAMSEE Akbar, 183. *India*
Born in Bombay in 1928. where he studied and then went to Paris.

PALAZUELO Pablo, 198. *Spain*
Born in Madrid in 1916. Began to paint in 1940. Settled in Paris in 1948. First exhibition in 1955 Maeght Gallery.

PANCETTI José, 33. *Brazil*
Born in 1900.

PAPS (Le peintre) (The painter), 33. *Germany*
Born in Naumburg in 1881. An occulist. Began to paint at the age of 70.

PASCIN Julius (Pincas), 105, 116. *United States*
Born in Bulgaria in 1885. Studied in Munich. Settled in Paris in 1905. United States from 1914 to 1920 where he became an American citizen. Returned to Paris and travelled continually. Committed suicide in 1930.

PASMORE Victor, 187. *Great Britain*
Born in Chelsham in 1908. Employed up to 1937. Attended evening courses in drawing. Began as abstract artist, then gave up abstract art and returned to it in 1947. Exhibition in London 1954. Taught at the University of Durham.

PAULA Inime de, 186. *Brazil*
Born in Minas Gerais, in 1918. Europe 1957 to 1959. Lives in Rio de Janeiro.

PECHSTEIN Max, 16, 51, 52. *Germany*
Born in Zwickau in 1881. Studied in Dresden. Associated with Heckel. Belonged to *Die Brücke*. Travelled to Paris. Lived in Italy, The South Seas. Returned to Switzerland and Italy; later to France after the war. Mosaics, stained-glass windows.

PEDERSEN Carl Henning, 141. *Denmark*
Born in 1913. One of the heads of the separation from *Konkretion* in favour of the new groups *Host* and *Spiralen*.

PELAEZ Amélia, 185. *Cuba*
Born in Yaguajay in 1897.

PELAYO Orlando, 198. *Spain*
Born in Gijon in 1920. Lives in Paris for some time.

PELIZZA DA VOLPEDO Giuseppe, 58. *Italy*
Born in Tortona in 1868. Artistic training in Bergamo and Milan. Took an active

part in the *Divisionnisme* movement in 1898. Died in Milan in 1907.

PELLAN ALFRED, 196. *Canada*
Born in Quebec in 1908. Studied with Ranson in Paris. Worked from 1926 to 1940.

PERSIO LOIO, 186. *Brazil*
Born in Brazil in 1928. Studied law and painting. First exhibition in 1956.

PETORRUTI EMILIO, 186. *Argentina*
Born in La Plata in 1895. Began painting at the age of 14. Director of the Museum of La Plata from 1930 to 1947. Settled in Paris in 1953. Awarded the Guggenheim Prize in 1956.

PENROSE ROLAND, 141. *Great Britain*
Born in 1900. Promotor of the British Surrealist movement.

PERMEKE CONSTANT, 60, 115. *Belgium*
Born in Antwerp in 1886. Studied in Bruges and Ghent. 1906 settled in Laethem-Saint-Martin. Wounded during the war and evacuated to England. Tended toward Expressionism. On his return, he settled in Jabbeke. Lived in Brittany in 1951. Died in Ostende in 1952.

PIAUBERT JEAN, 182, 187. *France*
Born in Le Pian in 1900. Studied in Bordeaux. Paris in 1922 and worked with Poiret. First exhibition in 1932. Became abstract in 1946. Lithographs.

PICABIA FRANCIS, 59, 62, 73, 77, 101, 131. *France*
Born in Paris in 1879 where he studied. Travelled to Spain, and United States in 1913 and 1915. Created the magazine 291 with Duchamp. 1916 in Barcelona published the magazine «391» which he continued in Paris. Associated with *Dada*. Took part in the Surrealist movement. Lived in Cannes. Returned to Paris in 1945 and became abstract once again. Died in 1953.

PICASSO PABLO, 16, 35, 36, 38, 43, 58, 59, 61, 69, 77, 79, 88, 131, 132, 150, 181. *Spain*
Born in Malaga in 1881. Studied with his father and in Barcelona. Settled permanently in 1904 in Paris. Creator of Cubism in 1907. Rome in 1917. Lived in Spain in 1934. *Guernica* in 1937. After the war he worked in Vallauris, later in Cannes. Engravings and ceramics.

PICELJ IVAN, 187. *Jugoslavia*
Born in Okucani in 1924. Studied in Zagreb, where he is now living. 1951 formed the *Éxact* 51 group with the painter Srnec and the architects Bernardi, Bregovac, Radic, etc.

PICKETT JOSEPH, 33. *United States*
Born in New Hope in 1848. Travelled with a circus for which he provided the decorations. Became a grocer and continued to paint. Died in New Hope in 1918.

PIGNON ÉDOUARD, 82, 150, 170, 172, 174, 182. *France*
Born in Marles-les Mines in 1905. Began as a miner; later was a labourer in Paris and also a printer while he attended evening school. Began to paint in 1930. A friend of Picasso. A member and founder of the *Salon de Mai* Often worked in the South.

PILLET EDGARD, 187. *France*
Born in La Gironde in 1912. Studied in Bordeaux. Several years in Algeria. Settled in Paris in 1945. Secretary general of *Art d'Aujourd'hui* from 1949 to 1954. First exhibition in 1951. Director of the studio of Abstract Art with Dewasne from 1950 to 1952. United States in 1955. Mural decorations and films.

PIPPIN HORACE, 33. *United States*
Born in West Chester in 1888. Did the odd jobs which were possible for a negro. Wounded in France during the war. Painted from 1930 up to his death in 1947.

PLANSON ANDRÉ, 114. *France*
Born in La Ferté in 1898. Studied under Ranson. Blumenthal Prize in 1932.

PLATSCHECK HANS, 183. *Germany*
Born in Berlin in 1923. South America from 1939 to 1953. Munich since 1955.

POLEO HECTOR, 149. *Venezuela*
Born in 1918 in Caracas where he studied; later in Mexico. First exhibition in 1937. Several times to the United States and France where he now lives.

POLIAKOFF SERGE, 177, 188. *France*
Born in 1906 in Moscow. Lived in Constantinople, Sofia and Berlin. 1924 he settled in Paris where he obtained his artistic training; London from 1935 to 1937. Friend of Kandinsky and Freundlich. Abstract before the war.

POLLOCK JACKSON, 157, 170, 188. *United States*
Born in Wyoming in 1912. Studied in Los Angeles and New York. 1938 to 1942 worked for the W. A. Federal Art Project. Abstract about 1940. First exhibition in 1944. Settled in Springs in 1946. Killed in an automobile accident in 1956.

PORTINARI CANDIDO, 131. *Brazil*
Born in Brodowsky in Brazil in 1903. Studied in Rio; later in Paris. Mural decorations.

POSADA JOSÉ GUADALUPE, 33. *Mexico*
(1851-1913).

POSTRUZNIK OTON, 148. *Jugoslavia*
Born in 1900 at Maribor (Slavonia). Professor in Zagreb.

POTWOROWSKI PETER, 185. *Poland*
Born in Warsaw in 1898. Russia from 1915 to 1918; France 1924 to 1933; Sweden and England 1939 to 1958. Settled in Posen in 1958.

POUGET MARCEL, 198. *France*
Born in Oran in 1923. Works in Paris.

POUGNY JEAN (PUNI), 154, 181. *France*
Born near St. Petersburg in 1894. Travelled to Paris in 1912. Took part in the exhibitions of the *Suprématistes* and *Constructivistes*. Settled in Berlin in 1921; later in Paris where he returned to figurative art.

PRAMPOLINI ENRICO, 64, 150. *Italy*
Born in Modena in 1896. Studied in Rome. Futurist at a very early age. Lived in Paris from 1925 to 1937 where he produced scenic designs. Took part in *Abstraction-Création*. Died in Rome in 1956.

PRASSINOS MARIO, 181. *France*
Born in Constantinople in 1916. Artistic training in Paris. Became known in 1937. Illustrations; also decors.

PRENDERGAST MAURICE, 4. *United States*
Born in Boston in 1861. Studied in Paris at the Beaux-Arts and under Julian. Travelled to Italy. Took part in the *Huit* group. Lived in Boston. In 1916 settled in New York where he died in 1924.

PRETE DANILO DI, 185. *Brazil*
Born in Pise in 1911. Self-taught. Settled in Brazil in 1946.

PREVIATI GAETANO, 58. *Italy*
Born in Ferrara in 1851. Artistic training in Florence. In 1891 he took part in the exhibition of the Italian Divisionists at the Milan Triennial. Died in Lavagno in 1920.

PROBST JOSEPH, 187. *Luxembourg*
Born in Vianden in 1911. Artistic training in Luxembourg, Brussels and Vienna. Abstract since 1948. Murals.

PROTIC MIODRAG, 185, 195. *Jugoslavia*
Born in Vrnjackoj Banji, Serbia, in 1922. Self-taught. Publications.

PURRMANN HANS, 58. *Germany*
Born in 1880. Studied in Karlsruhe, Munich. Paris 1906 to 1914 where he worked with Matisse.

PUY JEAN, 44. *France*
Born in Roanne in 1876. Studied architecture in Lyons, then took up painting. Worked in Paris with Carrière and associated with Matisse. Took part in *Fauvisme* for a short time.

QUENTIN BERNARD, 188. *France*
Born in Flamicourt in 1923. Artistic training at the Arts Décoratifs. Travelled through Europe. Became abstract in 1947.

RAMIREZ EDUARDO, 187. *Colombia*
Born in Pamplona in 1923. Artistic training in Bogota where he became professor of ceramics. Sculpture in 1952.

RAUSCHENBERG ROBERT, 141. *United States*
Born in 1925.

RAVEL DANIEL, 181. *France*
Born in Aix in 1915. Artistic training in Grenoble and Paris. Became known in 1945. First exhibition in 1956.

RAY MAN, 131, 132, 168. *United States*
Born in Philadelphia in 1890. First exhibition in 1912. With Duchamp formed the *Dada* group in New York in 1917, later the *Société Anonyme* in 1920. Settled in Paris in 1921. Interested especially in photography and the cinema. Active part in Surrealism. Hollywood from 1940 to 1951. Returned to Paris later.

RAYMOND MARIE, 187. *France*
Born in Colle-sur-Loup in 1911. Artistic training in Nice and Paris. First exhibition in 1934. Settled in Paris in 1945.

RAZA S. H., 185. *India*
Born in 1922 in Bafarid. Studied in Bombay and in Paris. First exhibition in 1947. Worked in Paris since 1950.

REBEYROLLE PAUL, 174. *France*
Born in Eymoutiers in 1926. Settled in

Paris in 1945. Lives in La Ruche. *Prix de la Jeune Peinture* in 1950 and Prix Fénélon in 1951.

REDON ODILON, 10, 32, 77. *France*
Born in Bordeaux in 1840. Artistic training at the Beaux-Arts and under Bresdin. First exhibition of lithographs and charcoal drawings in 1881; exhibition of paintings and pastels in 1894. Died in 1916.

REGGIANI MAURO, 187. *Italy*
Born in Modena in 1897. Artistic training in Florence. Signed the First manifesto of Italian abstract art in Milan in 1934. First exhibition in 1936. Works in Milan.

RENDON MANUEL, 186. *Ecuador*
Born in Paris in 1894, son of the Ambassador of Ecuador to Paris. First exhibition in 1925. Returned to Ecuador in 1937. Worked alone for five years in Cuenca. Lived in Paris. Works near Guayaquil.

RENOIR AUGUSTE, 33. *France*
(Limoges 1841-Cagnes 1919).

RETH ALFRED, 63. *France*
Born in Budapest in 1884. Settled in Paris in 1905 where he studied. Took part in Cubism. Member of *Abstraction-Création*.

REVERON ARMANDO, 34. *Venezuela*
Born in 1889 in Caracas where he studied. Later went to Madrid and Paris. Settled in Macuto in 1921 in a house which he built himself and worked alone, near the sea. Died in Caracas in 1954.

REWOLD AXEL, 57. *Norway*
Born in Alesund in 1887. Studied in Oslo; Paris under Matisse from 1908 to 1911. Travelled to Italy, Tunisia, Egypt. Professor in Oslo in 1925. Murals.

REYNOLDS ALAN, 143. *Great Britain*
Born in 1926. First exhibition in 1952.

REZVANI SERGE, 198. *Iran*
Born in Teheran in 1928. Went to France where he studied. First exhibition in 1945. Abstract since 1947.

RIBEIRO DA FONSECA MENES, 185.
Born in 1926. *Portugal*

RIOPELLE JEAN-PAUL, 188, 193. *Canada*
Born in 1924 in Montreal where he received his artistic training. Settled in Paris in 1946. First exhibition in 1947.

RIPPL-RONAI JOSEPH, 16, 30. *Hungary*
Born in Kaposvar in 1861. Studied in Munich, later in Paris. Associated with the *Nabis*. 1902 worked in Budapest and Kaposvar. Died in Budapest in 1930.

RISSANEN JULIO, 57. *Finland*
Born in 1873. Studied in Helsingfors and St. Petersburg. A founder of the *Septem* group. Travelled to Paris several times. Frescoes and stained-glass windows. Died in 1950.

RITSCHL OTTO, 187. *Germany*
Born in Erfurt in 1885. Self-taught. Began as a writer. Began to paint in 1919. Went to Paris in 1928. Slowly developed as abstract artist. Works in Wiesbaden.

RIVERA DIEGO, 24, 129, 130, 131. *Mexico*
Born in Guanajuato in 1886. Studied in Mexico. In 1907 went to Paris to study.

Associated with the Cubists. Friend of Modigliani. Travelled to Germany and Russia. Returned to Mexico in 1921. Undertook a cycle of mural decorations on a large scale. Lived in the United States and the U.S.S.R. Died in Mexico in 1957.

ROBERTS WILLIAM, 120. *Great Britain*
Born in London in 1895. Took part in the *Vorticisme* movement. After the war tended toward Expressionism.

ROBIN GABRIEL, 173. *France*
Born in Nantes in 1902. Settled in Paris at an early age. Self-taught. Was obliged to earn his livelihood and was therefore never able to devote himself exclusively to painting. Lives in Aulnay-sous-Bois.

ROGER SUZANNE, 150, 151. *France*
Born in 1898 in Paris where she received her artistic training. Lived in Italy. A friend of Juan Gris. Became known after 1920. Married Beaudin.

ROHLFS CHRISTIAN, 57. *Germany*
Born in Niendorf in 1849. Studied in Weimar where he was professor. 1902 he discovered the works of Van Gogh at the Museum of Hagen where he returned in 1912. Died in 1938.

ROHNER GEORGES, 115, 149. *France*
Born in Paris in 1913. Studied Beaux-Arts from 1929 to 1933. 1935, after returning from the Antilles, formed the *Forces Nouvelles* group with his friends Humblot and Jannot. First exhibition in 1937. Was prisoner of war. Later resumed his activities. Tapestry sketches.

ROLFSEN ALF, 57. *Norway*
Born in Oslo in 1895. Received artistic training in Copenhagen from 1913 to 1916. Lived in Paris, Italy and Greece. Designs.

ROLLIER CHARLES, 184. *Switzerland*
Born in 1912 in Milan where he received his artistic training. Of Swiss origin, became known in Basel in 1934. Settled in Paris in 1938. Mirmande during the war with Bolin and Garbell. Worked in Geneva and Paris.

ROMATHIER GEORGES, 198. *France*
Born in Lyons in 1927.

ROMITI SERGIO, 184. *Italy*
Born in 1928.

ROSAI OTTONE, 64. *Italy*
Born in Florence in 1895. Influenced by Soffici.

ROSSI GINO, 57. *Italy*
Born in Venice in 1884. Went to Paris in 1907, 1912 and 1918. Worked in Venice; later in Treviso. Confined to a hospital in 1925 and 1929. Died in 1947.

ROSSINÉ (WLADIMIR BARANOFF), 77.
France
Born in Kherson, Russia in 1888. Received artistic training in St. Petersburg. Exhibited in 1902. Travelled to Europe. Settled in Paris in 1910. Returned to Russia in 1914. Returned to Paris in 1930. Shot by the Germans in 1942.

ROTHKO MARK, 194. *United States*
Born in Dvinsk in 1903. United States in 1913. Studied in New York under Weber. First exhibition in 1933. Abstract since 1945. Works in New York.

ROUAULT GEORGES, 36, 41, 42, 43, 49, 113. *France*
Born in Paris in 1871. Worked in the shop of a glassblower. Studied under Moreau. A founder of the Salon d'Automne. Became associated with the *Fauvisme* movement. First exhibition in 1910. 1914 produced numerous illustrations for Vollard; Ceramics, decorations and stained-glass windows. Died in 1958 after a long illness.

ROUSSEAU HENRI (LE DOUANIER), 17, 33. *France*
Born in Laval in 1844. Was employed at the custom house. Pensioned off in 1885 and began to paint and exhibit at the *Indépendants*. Discovered in 1906 by Apollinaire and Picasso. Died in 1910.

ROUSSEL KER-XAVIER, 30. *France*
Born in Lorry-les-Metz in 1867. At school he associated with Vuillard. Studied under Julian. Belonged to the *Nabis*. About 1905 he was influenced by the Provence. Several decorations. Died in 1944.

ROUVRE YVES, 181. *France*
Born in Paris in 1910.

ROY PIERRE, 132. *France*
Born in Nantes in 1880. Went to Paris in 1904. Studied at the Beaux-Arts and Arts Décoratifs. Associated with Salmon, Max Jacob. Took part in the Surrealist exhibitions. Produced decorations. Died in 1950.

RUDE OLAF, 57. *Denmark*
Born in 1886. Influenced by Cubism in 1910.

RUSSEL JOHN, 34. *Australia*
A friend of Monet, Rodin and Van Gogh. Lived in Belle-Isle for several years.

RUSSEL MORGAN, 94. *United States*
Born in New York in 1886. Studied under Matisse. 1912 created the Sunchromist movement with Macdonald Wright. Lived a withdrawn life in France for a long time. Returned to the United States in 1946. General exhibition of his works in New York in 1950. Died in Broomall in 1953.

RUSSOLO LUIGI, 64. *Italy*
Born near Venice in 1885. Associated with Boccioni in 1909. Signed the Futurist Manifesto. Also fond of music. Died in Cerro Laveno in 1947.

SAGE KAY, 141. *United States*
Born in Albany in 1906. Spent her childhood in Europe, especially in Italy. Exhibited in Milan in 1936; in Paris in 1937. Became associated with the Surrealists. Married Tanguy. 1939 returned to the United States. A painter and poet.

SAITO YOSHISHIGÉ, 194. *Japan*
Born in Tokyo in 1905. Works in Chiba-Ken.

SALLINEN TYKO, 57. *Finland*
Born in 1879. Studied in Helsingfors and Paris in 1909. Died in 1955.

SANDELS GÖSTA, 57. *Sweden*
Born in Göteborg in 1887. Artistic training in Stockholm. Frequent visits to France and Spain where he died in 1919.

SARTHOU MAURICE, 181. *France*
Born in Bayonne in 1911. Studied in Bordeaux. Working in Paris since 1950.

SAURA ANTONIO, 194.   *Spain*
Born in Huesca in 1930. First exhibition
in 1950. Works in Madrid and Paris.

SAVINIO ALBERTO, 106.   *Italy*
Born in Athens in 1891, died in Rome in
1952. Writer, painter, composer of music.

SCANAVINO EMILIO, 183.   *Italy*
Born in Genoa in 1922. Works in Milan.

SCHATZ BEZABEL, 198.   *Israel*
Born in Jerusalem in 1912. Artistic training
in Paris and New York. Works in Israel.

SCHIELE EGON, 58.   *Austria*
Born in Tulln in 1890. Artistic training
in Vienna. Influenced by Klimt, Hodler
and the art of the Far East. Died in 1918.

SCHLEMMER OSKAR, 80, 148. *Germany*
Born in 1888 in Stuttgart where he re-
ceived his artistic training together with
Baumeister. Lived in Paris in 1914.
Professor at the Bauhaus from 1921 to
1929. Then taught in Breslau and Berlin.

SCHMIDT-ROTTLUFF KARL, 51, 57.
                                       Germany
Born near Chemnitz in 1884. Studied
architecture in Dresden where he met
Heckel and Kirchner. Belonged to *Die
Brücke*. Worked with Nolde. Travelled
to Italy and France. 1946 professor in
Berlin.

SCHNEIDER GÉRARD, 171, 194, 195. *France*
Born in Sainte-Croix, Switzerland in 1896.
Settled in Paris in 1916. Studied at the
Arts Décoratifs. Switzerland from 1920 to
1924. Earned his living as restorer of paintings. Became abstract in 1944. A member
of the Committee of the Salon de Mai for
several years.

SCHÖNBERG ARNOLD, 148.   *Germany*
Born in Vienna in 1874. Professor at the
Conservatory of Berlin, later in Vienna,
then again in Berlin from 1925 to 1933.
United States in 1934 where he died in
1951. Painted from 1907 to 1912. Belonged to the *Blaue Reiter*.

SCHRIMPF GEORG, 148.   *Germany*
Born in Munich in 1889. Self-taught. Did
odd jobs. First exhibition in 1915. Went
to Munich in 1918. Lived in Italy.

SCHWITTERS KURT, 121, 131. *Germany*
Born in Hanover in 1887. Artistic training
in Dresden. Returned to Hanover. From
1923 to 1932 he published the magazine
Merz and began his *Merzbau*, which he
continued near Oslo, later in Ambleside,
England where he died in 1948. Publications.

SCIPIONE (BONICHI), 129.   *Italy*
Born in Le Marche in 1904. Died in a sa-
natorium in 1937.

SCOTT WILLIAM, 183.   *Great Britain*
Born in Greenock in 1913. Studied in
Belfast. France before the war. First ex-
hibition in 1942. Works in London.

SEGALL LASAR, 131.   *Brazil*
Born in Vilna in 1891. Studied in Berlin
Dresden and Holland. First exhibition in
1910. Dresden 1916 to 1923. Settled in
Brazil. Travelled to Germany, Paris. Pro-
moter of *Spam* in Sao Paulo. Died in 1957.

SEILER HANS, 185.   *Switzerland*
Born in Neuchâtel in 1907. Settled in Paris.

SEKIYA YOSHIMICHI, 197.   *Japan*
Born in Japan in 1920. Studied in Gifu.
From 1949 to 1951 exhibited with the
penmanship Institute and the Academy.
1952 member of the Bokuzin-Kai School.

SELIGMANN KURT, 132, 170.
                                  Switzerland
Born in 1900. Works in the U.S.A.

SEPEHRI SOHRAB, 197.   *Iran*
Born in Teheran in 1928. Lived in Paris.
Is now living in Teheran.

SERAPHINE LOUIS 33.   *France*
Born in Assy in 1864. A shepherdess, then
housekeeper in Senlis where she died in
1934. First exhibition in 1927.

SERPA IVAN, 187.   *Brazil*
Born in 1923 in Rio de Janeiro where he
studied. First exhibition in 1951. Professor
in Rio. Scholarship to Europe in 1957.

SERPAN IAROSLAV, 198.   *France*
Born in Prague in 1922. Settled in Paris
in 1929. Began to paint in 1940. At first
attracted by Surrealism. Publications.

SERUSIER PAUL, 30, 33.   *France*
Born in Paris in 1863. Formed a group of
friends at the Académie Julian under the
name of *Nabis*. Studied under Gauguin in
1888. Associated with the monks in Beuron in 1895. Italy in 1904. Professor at
Ranson. After the war in Château-neuf-
du-Faou. Died in 1927.

SERVAES ALBERT, 42.   *Belgium*
Born in 1883 in Ghent where he received
his artistic training. In 1904 he settled in
Laethem-Saint-Martin.

SEURAT GEORGES, 11, 24, 29, 35, 51, 58.
(Paris 1859-1891).   *France*

SEVERELLI CESARE, 183.   *Italy*
Born in Milan in 1922. Works in Paris.

SEVERINI GINO, 58, 64, 66, 77.   *Italy*
Born in Cortona in 1883. Rome in 1901.
Associated with Balla and Boccioni. Paris
in 1906. Took part in the Futurist movement. 1913 married the daughter of Paul
Fort. After the war he had a tendency to
Classicism. Italy from 1933 to 1947 where
he published his memoirs. He then returned to Paris.

SHAHN BEN, 143.   *United States*
Born in Lithuania in 1898. Settled in the
United States in 1906. Began in the science
field before taking part in the campaigns
regarding the Sacco-Vanzetti case and
becoming the assistant of Rivéra.

SHEELER CHARLES, 94.   *United States*
Born in Philadelphia in 1883 where he
received his artistic training. Took part in
the Armory Show. Photographer. Awarded the Harris Prize in 1945.

SHINODA TOKO, 197.   *Japan*
Born in Japan in 1912. Took part in the
various penmanship exhibitions.

SHINN EVERETT, 42.   *United States*
(1876-1953).

SICKERT WALTER, 29, 34. *Great Britain*
Born in Munich in 1868 of an Anglo-
Danish family. Studied in London with

Whistler. Paris from 1900 to 1905 and at
different intervals. Died in Paris in 1942.

SIGNAC PAUL, 49, 77.   *France*
Born in Paris in 1863. 1884 a founder of
the Indépendants of which he was president
for 26 years. A friend of Seurat. 1899
published *De Delacroix au Néo-Impressionis-
me*. He was very fond of the sea. Worked
in Saint-Tropez. Died in 1935.

SIGURDSSON HJÖRLEIFUR, 184. *Iceland*
Born in Reykjavik in 1925.

SIMA JOSEPH, 194.   *France*
Born in Jaromer in 1896. Studied in Prague. Paris in 1922. Took part in the Surrealist exhibitions. Painted again after 1947.

SINGIER GUSTAVE, 160, 170, 175, 182. *France*
Born in Warneton in 1909. Paris in 1919.
Studied at the École Boulle. Became
known in 1935. Member and founder of
he Salon de Mai.

SIPILÄ SULHO, 33.   *Finland*
(1895-1949). Self-taught; modern trends
are evident in his work.

SIQUEIROS DAVID ALFARO, 24, 129,
  130.   *Mexico*
Born in Chihuahua in 1898. Studied at
the San Carlos Academy. France and Belgium from 1919 to 1922. Founder of a
Centre of Modern Realistic Art. Travelled
to the U.S.S.R. Murals.

SIRONI MARIO, 64, 148.   *Italy*
Born in Sardinia in 1885. Pursued scientific studies at the university in Rome. Associated with Balla and Boccioni. Accepted Futurism in 1915. Took an active
part in the *Novecento*. Frescoes and mosaics.

SKULASON THORVALDUR, 187, 193.
                                     Iceland
Born in Bordeyri in 1906. Studied in
Oslo. Travelled to Europe. Paris from
1931 to 1933 and from 1938 to 1948. Denmark during the war. Became abstract in
1938. Lives in Reykjavik.

SLEVOGT MAX, 34.   *Germany*
Born in Landshut in 1868. Studied in Munich. Lived in Paris and Italy. Worked
in Munich, Frankfurt and Berlin. Illustrations and decorations. Died in 1932.

SLOAN JOHN, 42.   *United States*
Born in Pennsylvania in 1871 where he
studied. Journalist and illustrator. Taught
in New York. Died in 1951.

SLUYTERS JAN, 42, 63, 129. *Netherlands*
Born in Bois-le-Duc in 1881. Studied in
Amsterdam. Travelled to Italy and Spain.
Paris 1906, in Staphorst from 1915-1916.
Later in Amsterdam until his death in 1957.

SMET GUSTAVE DE, 114.   *Belgium*
Born in 1877 in Ghent where he studied.
Settled in Laethem-Saint-Martin with Van
den Berghe, Permeke and his brother Léon
de Smet and formed the second Laethem
group. Holland from 1914 to 1918. Member of the *Sélection* group. Died in Deurle
in 1943.

SMITH MATTHEW, 57.   *Great Britain*
Born in Halifax in 1879. Studied in Slade;
later under Matisse. Paris up to 1914. Became known in 1915 with the *London
Group*. Visits to Provence.

SOFFICI ARDENGO, 64, 148. *Italy*
Born in Rignano sull'Arno in 1879. Studied in Florence and in Paris where he associated with Picasso and Apollinaire. On his return to Florence he divided his time between literature and painting. 1920 he retired to the countryside near Florence. Mural decorations.

SOLANA JOSÉ GUTIERREZ, 42. *Spain*
Born in 1886 in Madrid where he studied. Travelled to Paris. Worked all his life in Madrid where he died in 1945. Engravings and literary publications.

SOLDATI ATANASIO, 187. *Italy*
Born in Parma in 1896. First exhibition in 1922. Influenced by Klée and Kandinsky. Became entirely abstract after the Second World War. Worked in Milan. Died in Parma in 1953.

SONDENBORG K.R.M., 193. *Germany*
Born in 1923. Was in a concentration camp. Studied in Hamburg. Travelled to Italy. 1953 worked in Paris with Hayter. Lives in Hamburg.

SÖRENSEN HENRIK INGVAR, 57. *Norway*
Born in Varmeland in 1882 of Norwegian parents. Studied in Oslo, Copenhagen and Paris under Matisse. Travelled extensively through Europe and Africa. Spent his summers in Norway. Several frescoes.

SOTO JESUS, 187. *Venezuela*
Born in Ciudad Bolivar in 1923. Studied in Caracas. Worked in Paris in 1950.

SOULAGES PIERRE, 152, 194. *France*
Born in 1919 in Rodez where he worked alone. Paris in 1946. Became known there. First exhibition in 1949. Produced décors.

SOUTINE CHAIM, 105, 117. *France*
Born in Smilovitch in 1894. Studied in Vilno. Paris in 1911. Associated with Chagall, Lipchitz and Cendrars at La Ruche. Céret in 1919, to Cagnes in 1925 and to Chatel-Guyon in 1929 where he frequently returned. Died in 1943.

SPALA VACLAV, 57. *Czechoslovakia*
Born in Zlunice in 1885. Artistic training in Prague where he died in 1946.

SPAZZAPAN LUIGI, 183. *Italy*
Born in Gradisca, 1889. Died in Turin, 1958.

SPIROPOULOS JANNIS, 185. *Greece*
Born in Pilos, Greece in 1912. Awarded the UNESCO Prize at Venice Biennial in 1960. Lives in Patisia near Athens.

STAËL NICOLAS DE, 167, 188. *France*
Born in Leningrad in 1914. Studied in Brussels and Holland. Paris in 1932. Travelled to Spain and Italy. First exhibition in 1945. Committed suicide in 1955.

STANISLAWSKI JEAN, 194. *Poland*
1860-1907.

STAMOS THEODOROS, 194. *United States*
Born in 1922 in New York where he studied. Began as a sculptor. First exhibition in painting in 1943.

STEER PHILIP, 34. *Great Britain*
Born in Birkenhead in 1860. Studied in Gloucester; later Paris. Founder of the New English Art Club. Taught in London from 1893 to 1930. Died in 1942.

STEINLEN THÉOPHILE, 35, 42. *France*
(Lausanne 1859 - Paris 1923).

STELLA JOSEPH, 168. *United States*
Born in Italy in 1877. Died in 1946.

STILL CLYFFORD, 194. *United States*
Born in Grandin in 1904. Artistic training in Washington where he taught from 1933 to 1941; later at the California School in 1949 and 1950. Finally went to New York. First exhibition in San Francisco in 1941.

STROCEN STEFAN, 197. *Argentina*
Born in Buenos Aires in 1930 where he studied. Professor in drawing. One man shows in 1955. A founder of the *Buenos Aires* group in 1958. Scholarship to Paris in 1959.

STRZEMINSKI WLADISLAS, 94. *Poland*
Born in Minsk in 1893. A promoter in group who published the magazine *Blok* in 1924. Died in Lodz in 1952.

STRYSKY HINDRICH, 132. *Czechoslovakia*
Born in 1899.

SUGAI KUMI, 194. *Japan*
Born in Kobe in 1919. Studied in Osaka. Kobe up to 1951. Paris in 1952.

SUTHERLAND GRAHAM, 143, 149.
Great Britain
Born in London in 1903. Trained as engraver. Taught in Chelsea. Began to paint in 1935. Decorations in 1944. Awarded Venice Biennial Prize in 1952.

SWANBERG MAX WALTER, 141. *Sweden*
Born in Malmoe in 1912. Took an active part in Surrealism. In 1955 he exhibited in Paris at the *Etoile scellée*.

SZENES ARPAD, 181. *France*
Born in Budapest in 1900. Studied under Léger and Bissière. Paris in 1925. Married Vieira da Silva. Brazil 1932 to 1947.

SZYSZLO FERNANDO DE PERU, 186. *Peru*
Born in 1925 in Lima where he received his artistic training. Produced murals.

TABUCHI YASSE, 198. *Japan*
Born in Japan in 1921. Artistic training in Tokyo. Settled in Paris in 1951.

TAEUBER ARP SOPHIE, 96, 150. *France*
Born in Davos in 1889. Studied in Switzerland and Munich. Professor in Zurich 1916 to 1929. Took part in *Dada* with Arp whom she married in 1921. Murals and stained-glass windows in Strasbourg. Meudon from 1927 to 1940. Belonged to *Abstraction-Création* and *Die Allianz*. Grasse from 1941 to 1943. Died in 1943.

TAILLEUX FRANCIS, 150, 165. *France*
Born in Paris in 1913. Spent his childhood in Dieppe. Went to Paris in 1930 where he worked under Friesz and Dufresne. Visited London. Decorations.

TAL COAT PIERRE, 149, 165, 172, 182.
France
Born in Clohars-Carnoët in 1905. Became interested in art. Lived in Paris. In 1926 he settled near Pouldu. Paris in 1931. Belonged to *Forces Nouvelles*. Worked alone. 1940 Aix-en-Provence.

TAMAYO RUFINO, 24, 131, 159. *Mexico*
Born in Oaxaca in 1899. Studied in Mexico. Produced his first mural decorations

in 1933. Professor in Mexico. 1943 he went to New York for several years. Lives in Paris.

TAMIJI KITAGAWA, 33. *Japan*
Self-taught.

TANGUY YVES, 102, 132, 170. *France*
Born in Paris in 1900. Began as a sailor. Took up painting and frequented the Surrealist circles in 1925. Took part in all their exhibitions. In 1939 he settled in the United States where he died in 1955.

TANNING DOROTHEA, 141. *United States*
Born in Galesburg in 1891. Studied in New York. 1936 tended toward Surrealism. Married Max Ernst in 1946. Lives in Paris.

TAPIES ANTONIO, 188, 194. *Spain*
Born in Barcelona in 1923. A founder of the magazine and group *Dau al Set* in 1948. Lived in Paris in 1950; New York in 1953. Works in Barcelona.

TCHELITCHEW PAVEL, 170. *United States*
Born in Moscow in 1898. Studied in Berlin, later in Paris. Emigrated to the United States shortly before the war.

TCHURLIONIS M. K., 77. *Lithuania*
Born about 1875. Produced abstract paintings in 1904. Died in 1911. Exhibition the same year in Moscow.

TEJIMA YUKEI, 197. *Japan*
Born in Kochi in 1901. Artistic training in Tokyo under Hidai.

TERECHKOVITCH COSTIA, 114, 137.
France
Born in 1902 near Moscow where he studied; later in Paris in 1920. Known in 1925.

THIELER FRED, 184. *Germany*
Born in Königsberg in 1916. First studied medicine; took up painting after the war. Paris 1951 to 1952. Works in Munich.

THOMSON MICHEL, 173. *France*
Born in Fontenay-aux-Roses in 1921.

TINGUELY JEAN, 187. *Switzerland*
Born in 1925 in Basel where he studied. 1944 devoted himself to the research of motion in space. Works in Paris and Basel.

TOBEY MARK, 21, 170, 194. *United States*
Born in Centerville in 1890. Self-taught. First exhibition in 1917. Seattle in 1923. 1927 travelled to Europe and the Near East. England from 1931 to 1938, then travelled to Mexico and Asia. In 1939 he returned to Seattle where he lives.

TOMLIN BRADLEY WALKER, 194.
United States
Born in New York State in 1899. Went to Europe after the war. Taught in New York from 1932 to 1941. First exhibition in 1924. Died in 1953.

TOOROP CHARLEY (ANNIE PONTIFEX), 42. *Netherlands*
Born in Katwijk-sur-Mer in 1891. Daughter of Jean Toorop. Associated with Mondrian. 1921 founded an art colony in Bergen where she died in 1955.

TOOROP JEAN, 42. *Netherlands*
Born on the island of Java in 1858. Holland in 1869. Took up painting in 1880.

Symbolist in 1890. Religious paintings in 1905. Invalided in 1918 and died at The Hague in 1927.

TORRES AGUERO Léopold, 186. *Argentina*
Born in 1924 in Buenos Aires where he studied. First exhibition in 1949. Murals.

TORRES GARCIA Joaquin, 88, 168. *Uruguay*
Born in Montevideo in 1874. Studied in Barcelona. Paris in 1910. New York from 1920-1922. Paris from 1924 to 1932. Formed *Cercle et Carré*. Returned to Montevideo where he set up an art school. Died there in 1949. Murals and publications.

TOULOUSE-LAUTREC Henri de, 16, 24, 34, 35, 36, 42. *France*
(Albi 1864-1901).

TOZZI Mario, 148. *Italy*
Born in Fossombrone in 1895. Artistic training in Bologna. Settled in Paris in 1919. Associated with *Novecento*.

TOYEN, 132. *Czechoslovakia*
Born in Prague in 1902. In 1922 he belonged to the *Devetsil* group. Surrealist in 1933. Settled in Paris in 1946.

TRIER Hann, 183. *Germany*
Born in 1915 in Düsseldorf where he studied. Travelled to France, Holland and Colombia. Lives in Cologne.

TROKES Heinz, 143. *Germany*
Born in Hamborn in 1913. Artistic training at the Bauhaus. Has been working in the Balearic Islands since 1952.

TRYGGVADOTTIR Nina, 184. *Iceland*
Born in Seydisfjordur in 1913. Artistic training in Copenhagen, Paris and New York where she had her first exhibition in 1945. Settled in Paris in 1952.

TSINGOS Thanos, 198. *Greece*
Born in Eleysis in 1914. Studied architecture. Settled in Paris after the war and started to paint. First exhibition in 1952.

TSUJI Futoshi, 197. *Japan*
Born in Gifu in 1925. Member of the modern penmen group.

TURCATO Giulio, 183. *Italy*
Born in Mantua in 1912. Works in Rome.

TYTGAT Edgar, 33. *Belgium*
Born in 1879 in Brussels where he studied. Known in 1913. London during the war. On returning he settled in Woluwé-St. Lambert where he died in 1957. Woodcuts and lithographs.

TWORKOV Jack, 194. *United States*
Born in Poland in 1900. Went to the United States in 1913. Studied in New York. Teaching since 1948.

UBAC Raoul, 170, 174. *France*
Born in Malmédy in 1910. University in Paris in 1929 and gave up his studies for painting. Took part in the Surrealist exhibitions in 1934. Photographer. 1942 devoted himself to painting and to slate work.

UMEHARA Ryuzaburo, 129. *Japan*
Born in Kyoto in 1888. France from 1908 to 1913. Associated with Renoir. On returning to Japan, he formed the *Nika-Kai* group. 1920 travelled to France and Italy.

1926 founded the *Kouga-Kai*. Returned to Europe after the war. Works in Tokyo.

URTEAGA Mario, 33. *Peru*
Born in Cajamarca in 1875. First exhibition in 1934. Honoured by the Institute of Contemporary Art in Lima in 1955.

UTRILLO Maurice, 20, 36, 42, 96. *France*
Born in Paris in 1883. Took up painting in 1902 under the influence of his mother, Suzanne Valadon. His so-called Montmagny period lasted up to 1906; his White period up to 1914. From 1914 to 1921 he was confined several times to private hospitals. His exhibition in 1919 obtained great success. He married Pauwels' widow in 1935. He died in Dax in 1955.

VALADON Suzanne, 30, 32, 36, 42. *France*
Born in Bessines in 1867. Was a trapeze artist; later, the model of Puvis de Chavannes and Renoir. Encouraged by Degas, she took up painting. Married Paul Moussis in 1896, then Utter in 1909. She died in 1938.

VALTAT Louis, 44. *France*
Born in Dieppe in 1869; Artistic training in Paris at the Académie Julian and under Moreau. Took part in the *Fauvisme* movement. His sight failed him in 1948. Died in 1952.

VANDENBRANDEN Guy, 187. *Belgium*
Born in 1926.

VANDERCAM Serge, 182. *Belgium*
Born in 1924.

VANTONGERLOO Georges, 88, 150. *Belgium*
Born in Antwerp in 1886. Imprisoned in Holland during the war; associated with Van Doesburg. Belonged to *De Stijl*. Menton from 1919 to 1927, later in Paris. With Herbin he founded *Abstraction-Création*.

VASARELY Victor, 175, 187. *France*
Born in Pecs, Hungary in 1908. Artistic training in Budapest, at the *Mühely*. Associated with Moholy Nagy. Settled in Paris in 1930. First exhibition in 1930.

VAZIRI Mohsèn, 197. *Iran*
Born in Teheran in 1924. Lives in Teheran.

VEDOVA Emilio, 183. *Italy*
Born in Venice in 1919. Self-taught. Became known in 1940. Took an active part in the *Nuovo Fronte delle Arti* in 1946. Works in Venice.

VELASQUEZ José Antonio, 33. *Honduras*
Born in Caridad in 1906. A hairdresser. Began to paint in 1933.

VELDE Bram van, 175. *Netherlands*
Born in Zonderwonde in 1895. Did odd jobs. Paris in 1924. Lived in the Balearic Islands. Settled in Paris in 1936.

VELDE Geer van, 13, 175, 184. *Netherlands*
Born in Lisse in 1898. Brother of Bram. Settled in Paris in 1925. Became known in 1926. First exhibition in 1938. Lived in Cagnes from 1939 to 1945.

VENARD Claude, 149. *France*
Born in Paris in 1913. Artistic training at the Beaux-Arts. Became known in 1938.

VENIER Bruno, 185. *Argentina*
Born in Venice in 1914. When young settled in Argentina.

VERKADE Jean, 23, 30. *Netherlands*
Born in Zaamden about 1869. Went to Paris in 1891. Introduced by de Haan to Gauguin with whom he worked in Pont Aven. Was converted in Vannes in 1892. Soon afterwards, he entered the Benedictine Monastery in Beuron. Produced frescoes in several churches in Austria and Czechoslovakia. Died shortly after the war.

VESPEIRA, 141, 185. *Portugal*
Born in 1925. Known in 1948. Began as a Surrealist, later became abstract.

VEZELAY Paul, 187. *Great Britain*
Born in England in 1893. Studied in London. First exhibition in 1921. Paris from 1923 to 1939. Took part in *Abstraction-Création*. Lives in London.

VICENTE Estévan, 194. *United States*
Born in Spain in 1906 where he worked up to 1935. Then settled in New York. Became known in 1928.

VIEIRA DA SILVA Maria Elena, 173, 175, 181. *France*
Born in Lisbon in 1908. From 1927 on she studied in Paris under Bourdelle, Friesz, Léger and Hayter. Married Arpad Szenès in 1930. Lived in Brazil during the war. First exhibition in 1933.

VIGAS Oswaldo, 186, 196, *Venezuela*
Born in Valencia in 1926. Completed studies as physician, but preferred to devote himself to painting. Working in Paris since 1954. Produced murals. Exhibitions in France, United States and Venezuela.

VILLACIS Anibal, 186. *Ecuador*
Born in Ambato in 1927. Studied in Madrid. Travelled thru South America.

VILLAMIZAR Ramirez, 187. *Colombia*
Working in Paris.

VILLEGAS Armando, 186. *Colombia*
Born in Peru in 1926. Has been working in Bogota for several years.

VILLON Jacques, 30, 35, 59, 63, 123, 143, 172. *France*
Born in Damville in 1875. Brother of Marcel Duchamp and of the sculptor Duchamp-Villon. Studied under Cormon. Produced humourous drawings. First exhibition in 1905. In 1911 meetings of the *Section d'Or* were held in his studio in Puteaux. After the war he was an engraver. Travelled to the United States. Awarded the Venice Biennial Prize in 1956.

VIVIN Louis, 33. *France*
Born in Hadol in 1861. Post Office employee. Devoted himself exclusively to painting when he was pensioned in 1922. Died in 1936.

VLAMINCK Maurice de, 36, 40, 44, 45, 49. *France*
Born in Paris in 1876. At first, lived in Chatou. Earned his living as bicycle racer and violinist. A friend of Derain. Took part in the *Fauvisme* movement. In 1925 he settled in Rueil-la-Gadelière where he died in 1958.

VORDEMBERGE-GILDERWART
FRIEDRICH, 187. *Netherlands*
Born in Osnabrück in 1899. Studied
architecture in Hanover. In 1924 he became
a member of *Sturm* and *De Stijl*. Visited
Paris several times. Took part in *Ab-*
straction-Création. Settled in Amsterdam in
1937. Professor in Ulm in 1955.

VUILLARD ÉDOUARD, 23, 30. *France*
Born in Cuiseaux in 1868. At the Académie Julian he formed *Les Nabis*. First exhibition in 1891. A member of the *Institut*.
Died in La Baule in 1940.

VULLIAMY GÉRARD, 174. *France*
Born in Paris in 1909. Studied decoration.
Studied under Lhote. Took part in *Ab-*
straction-Création. First exhibition in 1933.
Associated with the Surrealists for a short
time. Rejoined *Die Allianz*.

WADSWORTH EDWARD, 94.
Great Britain
Born in Yorkshire in 1889. Studied in
Munich. Took part in *Vorticisme* and the
magazine *Blast*. After the war he tended
toward a poetic realism. Died in 1949.

WALCH CHARLES, 150, 151. *France*
Born in Thann in 1898. Studied in Paris
at the Arts Décoratifs. Known in 1925.
First exhibition in 1938. Died in 1948.

WAROQUIER HENRY DE, 108. *France*
Born in Paris in 1881. At first studied
architecture. Self-taught with regard to
artistic training. Travelled extensively
through Italy and Spain.

WEBER MAX, 58. *United States*
Born in Bialystok in 1884. Went to the
United States in 1894. Studied in Paris
under Matisse. Returned to New York
where he had his first exhibition the following year. Was abstract in 1915; became
figurative expressionist.

WEIE EDWARD, 57. *Denmark*
(1897-1943). Worked in Paris in 1912.

WEILER MAX, 185. *Austria*
Born in Absam in the Tyrol region in
1910. Worked in Innsbruck.

WERNER THEODOR, 183. *Germany*
Born near Tübingen in 1886. Artistic
training in Stuttgart. Frequent trips to
Paris where he worked from 1930 to 1935.
Active after 1945. Lives in Munich.

WICKENBURG ALFRED, 129, 185, 190.
Austria
Born in Bad Gleichenberg in 1885. Studied in Munich and Paris (Académie Julian).
Completed his studies in Rome and Florence. Murals and Stained Glass Windows 1961. Lives in Graz (Austria).

WIEGERS JAN, 129. *Netherlands*
Born in Kommerzyl in 1893. Artistic
training in Groningen and The Hague.
Worked in Switzerland with Kirchner.
Taught in Amsterdam.

WILLUMSEN JENS, 29, 57. *Denmark*
Born in Copenhagen in 1863. During his
stay in France from 1888 to 1889 and from
1890 to 1894 he associated with Gauguin
and Sérusier. Acquainted with Redon.
Died in France in 1958.

WINTER FRITZ, 183. *Germany*
Born in Altenbögge in 1905. Studied at
the Bauhaus. Associated with Gabo. Travelled to Switzerland and France. Prisoner
in Russia. On his return, he retired in
Diessen-am-Ammersee.

WOLS (OTTO ALFRED SCHULZE BATTMAN),
188. *Germany*
Born in Berlin in 1913. Received part of
his artistic training at the Bauhaus. Paris
in 1932. Associated with Miro and Ernst.
Photographer in Spain and later in Paris.
Supported by Sartre during the war. Exhibition in 1945. Died in Paris in 1951.

WOOD CHRISTOPHER, 89, 148. *Great Britain*
Born 1901 at Knowsley, England. 1921
studied in Paris at the Académie Julian.
First exhibition 1927 in London. Died 1930.

WOOD GRANT, 148. *United States*
Born in Iowa in 1892. Studied in Minneapolis and Chicago in evening school. Settled and taught in Iowa. Trips to Europe
from 1920 to 1928. Founded the Stone art
colony. Died in 1942.

WOUTERS RIK, 58, 96. *Belgium*
Born in 1882 in Malines where he studied.
Settled in Brussels in 1905. Became known
soon afterwards. Went to Paris in 1912.
Development of his painting and sculpture.
Confined to a hospital in the Netherland,
died in Amsterdam in 1916.

YOUNGERMAN JACK, 186. *United States*
Born in the United States in 1925. Studied in Paris in 1947. First exhibition in
1951. Returned to the United States.

ZACK LÉON, 194. *France*
Born in Nijni-Novgorod in 1892. Studied
at the university in Moscow. After the war
he lived in Italy and Berlin. In 1923 he
settled in Paris. First exhibition in 1926.

ZAÑARTU ENRIQUE, 186. *Chile*
Born in Paris of Chilean parents in 1921.
Began to paint in Santiago in 1938. New
York in 1944. Student and later professor
at the studio of Hayter. Cuba from 1947
to 1949. Later settled in Paris. First exhibition in 1950. Illustrations.

ZAO WOU-KI, 196. *China*
Born in Peking in 1920. Studied in Han-
chow where he taught from 1941 to 1947.
Settled in Paris in 1948. First exhibition
in 1950.

ZARITZKY JOSEPH, 194. *Israels,*
Born in Borispol in 1891. Studied in Kiev.
Israel in 1923. Lived in Paris. A founder
of the *New Horizons* group.

ZIMMERMAN MAC, 143. *Germany*
Born in Stettin in 1912. Went to Hamburg
in 1934, to Berlin in 1938. Taught in
Dessau in 1946, later in Munich and in
1959 in Berlin.

BIBLIOGRAPHY

I. DICTIONARIES

Vollmer H.   Allgemeines Lexikon der bildenden Künstler des 20. Jahrhunderts. Leipzig, Seemann, 1953.

Dictionnaire de la peinture moderne. Paris, Hazan, 1954.

Seuphor M.   Dictionnaire de la peinture abstraite. Paris, Hazan, 1957.

II. POST-IMPRESSIONISM AND SYMBOLISM

Chassé Ch.   Le mouvement symboliste dans l'art du XIXe siècle. Paris, Floury, 1947.

Rewald J.   Post-Impressionism, from van Gogh to Gauguin. New York, 1956.

Humbert A.   Les Nabis et leur époque. Geneva, 1954.

III. FAUVISM AND EXPRESSIONISM

Duthuit G.   Les Fauves. Geneva, Trois Collines, 1949.

Myers B. S.   The German Expressionists. London, 1957.

Selz P.   German Expressionist Painting. Berkeley, 1957.

Leymarie J.   Le Fauvisme. Geneva, Skira, 1959.

IV. NAIVE ART

Jakovsky A.   Les peintres naïfs. Paris, 1956.

Bihalji-Merin O.   Les peintres naïfs. Paris, Delpire, 1961.

V. CUBISM

Barr A. H.   Cubism and Abstract Art. New York, Museum of Modern Art, 1936.

Severini G.   Balance du Cubisme. « Ver y estimar », 1950.

Habasque G.   Le Cubisme. Geneva, Skira, 1959.

VI. NEO-PLASTICISM

Jaffe H. L. C.   De Stijl 1917-1931. Amsterdam, 1956.

VII. DADAISM AND SURREALISM

Barr A. H.   Fantastic Art, Dada, Surrealism. New York, 1936.

Breton A.   Le Surréalisme et la peinture. New York, 1945.

Verkauf W.   Dada, Monography of a Movement. New York, 1957.

Jean M.   Histoire de la peinture surréaliste. Paris, Seuil, 1959.

VIII. PAINTERS OF POETIC REALITY

Assailly G. d'   Avec les peintres de la réalité poétique. Paris, 1949.

IX. ABSTRACT ART

Seuphor M.   L'Art abstrait, ses origines, ses premiers maîtres. Paris, Maeght, 1949.

Alvard J. and Gindertael R. V.: Témoignages pour l'art abstrait. Paris, Art d'aujourd'hui, 1951.

Tapie M.   Un art autre. Paris, Giraud, 1952.

Brion M.   Art abstrait. Paris, Albin Michel, 1956.

Ragon M.   L'Aventure de l'art abstrait. Paris, Laffont, 1956.

Bouret J.   L'Art abstrait. Paris, Club Français du Livre, 1957.

Cavellini A.   Arte astratta. Milan, Conchiglia, 1958.

X. GERMANY

Händler G.   Deutsche Malerei der Gegenwart. Berlin, 1956.

Schulze-Wellinghausen A. und Schroeder A.: Deutsche Kunst nach Baumeister. Recklinghausen, 1958.

XI. UNITED STATES

Motherwell R. and Reinhardt A.: Modern Artists in America. New York, Wittenborn, 1952.

Sweeney J. J.   Younger American Painters. New York, 1954.

Blesh R.   Modern Art U.S.A. New York, 1956.

Baur I. H.   New Art in America. New York Graphic Society, 1957.

XII. GREAT BRITAIN

Read H.   Contemporary British Art. Harmondsworth, 1951.

XIII. ITALY

Apollonio U.   Pittura moderna italiana. Venice, Neri Pozza, 1950.
Marchiori G.   Panorama dell'arte italiana. Turin, 1951.
Modesti R.   Pittura italiana contemporanea. Milan, Vallardi, 1958.

XIV. GENERAL WORKS ON CONTEMPORARY PAINTING

Huyghe R. and Bazin G.: Histoire de l'art contemporain. Paris, Amour de l'art, Alcan, 1934-1935.
Pevsner N.   Pioneers of the Modern Movement, from William Morris to Walter Gropius. London, 1936.
Diehl G.   Les problèmes de la peinture. Paris, Confluences, 1945.
Francastel P.   Nouveau dessin, nouvelle peinture. Paris, Médicis, 1946.
Dorival B.   Les étapes de la peinture française contemporaine, 3 tomes. Paris, N. R. F. 1943-1946.
Venturi L.   La peinture contemporaine. Milan, Hoepli, 1947.
Huyghe R.   Les Contemporains. Paris, Tisné, 1949.
Leepa A.   The Challenge of Modern Art. New York, Yoseloff, 1949.
Bazin G. and Diehl G.: Histoire de la peinture moderne. New York, Paris, London, Hypérion, 1950.
Histoire de la Peinture moderne, 3 volumes. Geneva, Paris, Skira, 1949-1951.
Rousseau M.   Introduction à la connaissance de l'art présent. Paris, Le Musée Vivant, 1953.
Lebel R.   Premier bilan de l'art actuel. Paris, Le Soleil Noir, 1953.

Francastel P.   Art et technique aux XIXᵉ et XXᵉ siècles. Paris, Editions de Minuit, 1956.
Degand L.   Langage et signification de la peinture. Paris, Architecture d'Aujourd'hui, 1956.
Dorival B.   Les peintres du vingtième siècle, 2 volumes. Paris, Tisné, 1956-1957.
McCurdy C.   Modern Art, A Pictorial Anthology. New York, Macmillan, 1958.
Waldemar G. and Cogniat R.: Encyclopédie de l'Art international contemporain. Paris, Prisme des Arts, 1958.
Courthion P.   Art Indépendant. Paris, Albin Michel, 1958.
Diehl G. and Colombo A.: Treasury of World Painting. New York, Tudor, 1959.
Ragon M.   La peinture actuelle. Paris, Fayard, 1959.
Grohmann W.   Art Since 1945. London, Thames and Hudson, 1959.
Documenta II, Malerei: Kunst nach 1945. Cologne, DuMont Schauberg, 1959.
Nacenta R.   L'École de Paris, son histoire, son époque. Paris, Seghers, 1960.
Muller J.-E.   La peinture moderne de Manet à Mondrian. Paris, Hazan, 1960.
Guichar-Meili J.   La peinture d'aujourd'hui. Paris, Seuil, 1960.
Langui E.   50 ans d'art moderne. Köln, DuMont Schauberg, 1960.
Ponente N.   Peinture moderne, tendances contemporaines. Geneva, Paris, Skira, 1960.
Cassou J.   Panorama des arts plastiques contemporains. Paris, N. R. F., 1960.
Read H.   Histoire de la Peinture Moderne. Paris, Somogy, 1960.
Taillandier Y.   Voyage de l'oeil. Paris, Calman-Lévy, 1961.
Restany P.   Lyrisme et abstraction. Paris, 1961.

CONTENTS